SOME INFERENCES CONCERNING
THE INTERNATIONAL ASPECTS OF
ECONOMIC FLUCTUATIONS

A thesis submitted to the Faculty of the Columbian College of
The George Washington University in partial satisfaction of the
requirements for the degree of Master of Arts.

Thesis directed by Dr. John Donaldson
and Dr. Arthur E. Burns

February 1947

# SOME INFERENCES CONCERNING THE INTERNATIONAL ASPECTS OF ECONOMIC FLUCTUATIONS

ROBERTO DE OLIVEIRA CAMPOS

Foreword by Ernesto Lozardo

FGV
EDITORA

ISBN — 85-225-0468-7

Copyright © 2004 by Roberto de Oliveira Campos

EDITORA FGV
Praia de Botafogo, 190 — 14º andar
22250-900 — Rio de Janeiro, RJ — Brazil
Phone.: 0800-21-7777 — 21-2559-5543
Fax: 21-2559-5532
e-mail: editora@fgv.br
web site: www.editora.fgv.br

Printed in Brazil

All rights reserved. No part of this book may be used or reproduced in any manner whatsoever without written permission, except in the case of brief quotations embodied in critical articles or reviews.

First edition: 2004

*Cover*: Ricardo Bouillet and Sergio de Carvalho Filgueiras

Cataloging-in-publication record prepared by
Mario Henrique Simonsen Library

Campos, Roberto, 1917-2001
   Some inferences concerning the international aspects of economic fluctuations / by Roberto de Oliveira Campos. — Rio de Janeiro : Editora FGV, 2004.
   260p.

   Includes bibliographical references.

   1. Economic cycles. 2. Capital flow. I. Fundação Getulio Vargas. II. Title.

CDD — 338.54

# TABLE OF CONTENTS

LIST OF TABLES .................................................................................. xi

FOREWORD ........................................................................................ xiii

INTRODUCTION: FRAGMENTS OF AN
INTERNATIONAL CYCLE THEORY ................................................ 1

I - THE THEORETICAL CONTRIBUTION ....................................... 5

    A - The Imperialistic Theory of Crises
    B - Sombart's "Expansionskonjunktur"
    C - Schumpter's Theory of Economic Development
    D - Walther Heinrich and the Universalistic School
    E - Neisser and the Theory of General Over-Production

II - THE EMPIRICAL CONTRIBUTION ........................................... 17

    A - Mitchell and the Contribution of the Business Annals
    B - Economic Evolution and the Duration of Cycles
    C - The Principle of Retardation of Industrial Growth

III - THE "CLOSED SYSTEM" THEORIES OF CYCLES ................ 29

## PART ONE

## PROPAGATION AND IMPULSE PROBLEMS IN THE ANALYSIS OF INTERNATIONAL CYCLES

I - CONCEPTS AND DEFINITIONS .................................................. 39

II - THE ORIGIN OF INTERNATIONAL FLUCTUATIONS ............ 43

    A - The Hypothesis of International "Konjunkturfaktoren"
    B - The Hypothesis of International Attrition

III - THE PROCESS OF PROPAGATION OF CYCLES ..................... 48

    A - Psychological and Economic Transmission
    B - Direction of Transmission

C - The Area of Cyclical Fluctuations
  1. Autonomous and induced changes
  2. Regional and functional relationships

IV- PROPAGATION AND IMPULSE PROBLEMS ........................................... 53

  A - The Type of Shock
  B - The Swinging Mechanism
    1 - Economic typology as a starting point for the study of transmissions
    2 - Classification of economic structures
      a. Wagemann's classification
      b. Colin Clark's classification

V - INTERNATIONAL STRUCTURAL RELATIONSHIPS AND
    PROPAGATION OF TYPES ........................................................................ 63

  A - Complementary and Similarity Relationships
  B - The "Degree of Openness"

# PART TWO

## THREE VEHICLES OF PROPAGATION OF CYCLES: MONETARY INTERDEPENDENCE, CAPITAL MOVEMENTS AND INTERNATIONAL TRADE

INTRODUCTION ............................................................................................... 71

### SECTION I

MONETARY SYSTEMS AND THE INTERNATIONAL
PROPAGATION OF BUSINESS FLUCTUATIONS ........................................ 73

I - THE CONTROVERSY ON THE GOLD STANDARD ............................. 75

  A - Hawtrey's Theory and the Cyclical Conductivity of the Gold Standard
  B - The Gold Exchange Standard

II - IRVING FISHER AND THE PRICE-LEVEL MECHANISM .................... 81

III - THE MONETARY NATIONALISM AND ITS
       THEORETICAL BASIS ................................................................. 83

   A - The Keynesian Influence
   B - The Hayekian Position

IV - THE GOLD STANDARD AND THE FREELY
      FLUCTUATING EXCHANGES .............................................. 89

V - THE MONETARY EXPERIENCE IN THE INTER-WAR PERIOD ......... 93

## SECTION II

## CAPITAL MOVEMENTS AND THE PROPAGATION OF CYCLES

**DEFINITION AND CONCEPTS** ................................................................. 97

I - THE THEORY OF CAPITAL TRANSFER FROM THE VIEWPOINT
    OF BUSINESS CYCLE ANALYSIS ......................................... 99

   A - Development in the Theory of Capital Transfer. Price, Demand,
       Income Aspects of Foreign Lending. The Savings-Investment Theory
       a. The cause or effect controversy
       b. The course of terms of trade
       c. The income effects of the capital transfer and the modern cyclical
          analysis
          1. The early Keynesian analysis
          2. The modern Keynesian analysis
          3. Practical implications of the savings-investment analysis
   B - The Over-Investment Theory and the Propagation of Cycles

II - EMPIRICAL AND STRUCTURAL FACTORS ........................................ 115

   A - Localization of Credit and Cyclical Behavior
       1. Imperfect mobility of capital
       2. Sectional mobility
       3. Cyclical mobility

III - THE INTERNATIONAL INVESTMENT EXPERIENCE ...................... 119
   Summary

# SECTION III

# INTERNATIONAL TRADE AND THE CYCLICAL BEHAVIOR

I - THE THEORY OF INTERNATIONAL TRADE AND
BUSINESS CYCLE ANALYSIS ............................................................. 125

    A - The Mechanism of Equilibrium and Adjustment. The Classical and Demand Schools. The Contribution of the Savings-Investment Analysis
    B - The Foreign-Trade Multiplier
        1. Basic concepts of the multiplier analysis
           a. Autonomous and consequential imports
           b. The marginal propensity to import
           c. The income-propagation period
        2. Limitations of the multiplier approach
        3. The principle of acceleration and the foreign-trade multiplier
        4. The multiplier and the balance of payments
        5. An evaluation of the contribution of the multiplier analysis for the study of cyclical propagation

II - EMPIRICAL AND STRUCTURAL FACTORS IN
THE SPREAD OF CYCLES ..................................................................... 143

    A - Localization of Trade and the Cyclical behavior
        1. The natural factors
        2. The artificial factors
           a. Tariff and the cyclical behavior
           b. The Regional insulation approach
    B - The "Law of Falling Export Quota". The Trade Slump of the Thirties and the Long-Term Trend of International Trade.

III - THE PARADOXES OF WORLD TRADE ............................................... 155

    A - The First Paradox. Contrasting Price Behavior in Industry and Agriculture
        1. The price scissors
        2. Price instability and the cyclical behavior
        3. Capital movements and the terms of trade
    B - The Second Paradox of World Trade

    Summary

# PART THREE

# PARALLELISM AND DIVERGENCIES OF CYCLICAL BEHAVIOR

## SECTION I

## REGULAR CYCLICAL VARIATIONS

I - THE INTERNATIONAL BEHAVIOR OF PRICES ................................... 171

    A - The Kondratieff Wave and the Movement of Wholesale Prices
    B - Monetary Policies and Recent Price Developments
    C - Sectional Prices
        1. Amplitude
        2. Procession of prices

    Summary

II - OUTPUT AND EMPLOYMENT ............................................................. 183

    A - The Sphere of Raw Materials of Agricultural Origin
    B - The Sphere of Raw Materials of Non-Agricultural Origin
    C - The Industrial Sphere

    Summary

## SECTION II

## IRREGULAR CYCLICAL VARIATIONS

I - THE BALANCE OF TRADE ..................................................................... 191

    A - Direction of Fluctuations
    B - Amplitude of Fluctuations
    C - Timing of Fluctuations

    Summary

II - THE CYCLICAL PATTERN OF CAPITAL MOVEMENTS ..................... 201

III - GOLD MOVEMENTS ............................................................... 209

IV - EXCHANGE RATES ................................................................ 215

V - THE BALANCE OF PAYMENTS ............................................... 217

SOME GENERAL INFERENCES ................................................... 221

APPENDIX ..................................................................................... 229

BIBLIOGRAPHY ............................................................................ 235

# LIST OF TABLES

1. Co-Variation of Cyclical Movements ................................................................ 20

2. Duration of Cycles ........................................................................................... 21

3. Volume of Production and National Income
Expressed as Percentages from 1929, for Selected Countries .......................... 22

4. Economic Types, Classified According to Intensity of Development ........... 57

5. Percentage Distribution of Occupied Population ........................................... 60

6. Trade of Certain Countries with their Economic Blocks ............................... 149

7. Net Barter Terms of Trade for 4 Industrial and for 4 Agricultural Areas .... 158

8. Composition of Exports from United Kingdom,
Germany and the United States ....................................................................... 162

9. Movement of Wholesale Prices ....................................................................... 174

10. Variability of Prices of Primary Products, 1936-1938 ................................. 177

11. Price Movements of Producers' and Consumers' Goods ........................... 179

12. Capital Movements and the Business Cycle ................................................ 206

13. Gold Movements in the French Balance of Payments ............................... 210

# FOREWORD

In the early 70s, on the suggestion of Mr. Roberto de Oliveira Campos, I participated in a training period at the World Bank, in Washington, D.C. During that period, I became acquainted with Professor Albert Hart, who told me that Mr. Campos had presented his thesis for the degree of Master of Arts in economics at the George Washington University. The information aroused my interest, since I had been hitherto unaware of the existence of this thesis, written by our illustrious Brazilian Minister and Ambassador. As soon as I found it, I made a copy and read it some years later in 1975, during my study program in economics at Columbia University. It was then that I discovered the greatness of Roberto Campos's intelligence in his ability to articulate the complexities of the economic issues needed to build a better world. Three decades later, during a conversation with the economist, writer and journalist Gilberto Paim, he told me that Roberto Campos had lost track of his thesis and regretted it a great deal, since it had expressed his theoretical understanding on the determinants of international economic growth and development.

This memorable academic writing by Roberto Campos, entitled *Some Inferences Concerning the International Aspects of Economic Fluctuations*, concluded in 1947, when he was 30 years old, and praised by renowned American economists, had gone missing for almost three decades. It is truly a seminal work, which has allowed Brazilian students of economics to follow the evolutionary process and the originality of the developmentist thought of one of the twentieth century's most illustrious Brazilians.

During two years, after his working day at the Brazilian Embassy in Washington D.C., Mr. Campos would go to the Library of the United States Congress to study and conceive the basis of his theoretical reference, an essential issue to the formulation of economic development policies, which would be implemented in Brazil in two distinct phases: The first between 1956 and 1959, when he was the President of BNDE, and then later, between 1964 and 1967, when he was the country's Planning Minister.

Among the men who preceded and succeeded him at this important post not many were able to leave behind such insightful theoretical documents that could stand the test of time, while critically and constructively dealing with the determinants of international economic development.

During the preparation for his MA in economics, Roberto de Oliveira Campos was under the guidance of Professors John Donaldson and Arthur E. Burns, both of George Washington University, located in the capital of the United States. Roberto Campos centered his analyses on one of the most important issues of the time, which remains valid up to the present: how to ensure, in one hand, the stability of international economic growth, while, in the other, providing for a balanced road to prosperity for the different countries that offer and demand capital. Economic growth and development issues have become increasingly relevant and crucial to the deepening of trade relations in an ever more financially and commercially integrated and internationalized world. Regretfully, however, during the last three decades, the theme of economic development has become merely a footnote in the basic economics textbooks.

The brightness of this academic project of the then young Brazilian economist lies as much in his criticism of the economic development theories of his time, as it does in his vision on the future of international capitalism. As he formulated his premises and criticism, validating, refuting or indicating alternative paths to the different development theories and theories of international economic cycles which were then current, mainly within the sphere of the World Bank and the IMF, Roberto Campos was building his analytic methodology of the determinants of economic development, which he would use throughout his life as a critical observer and builder of a new economic and social reality in Brazil.

In the development of his academic work, Roberto Campos mastered resourcefully the whole theoretical apparatus of economic development, and was extremely helpful in the formulation of the most singular price stabilization plan Brazil has ever had, the PAEG (1964-1966), aimed at boosting growth, reducing sector and regional imbalances and social inequalities, getting balanced federal budget, ensuring employment expansion, and restoring a balance of payments equilibrium. During this same period, Laws # 4595/64 and 4728/65 were created which gave rise to the modern and sophisticated structure of capital and monetary markets and to the Central Bank of Brazil, as well as to inflation adjustment in federal public debt securities, responsibility regarding tax expenditure, and a more adequate foreign exchange policy which was consistent with the Brazilian reality.

The new economy, created by Ministers Roberto Campos and Octavio Gouveia de Bulhões, resulted in one of the most prosperous phases of the history of the Brazilian economy, culminating in the so-called "Brazilian economic miracle" of 1968 to 1974, the fruit of the presence of solid economic foundations built between 1964 and 1967.

## Content of the Thesis

When structuring his master's degree thesis, Roberto Campos formulated his knowledge based on the determinants of sustainable economic growth, and presented a critical view of the different conceptions regarding the theories of international economic fluctuations. In this sense, three great thinkers and economists of that time guided his analytic structure: F. A. Hayek, Joseph Schumpeter and J. M. Keynes. The economist Hayek gave him the bases of liberal thought, in which personal and market liberties represent the pillars of the prosperity of capitalism; Schumpeter consolidated his development theory, with methodological instruments such as the theories of profit, credit, capital, innovation, and economic cycles; Keynesian economic thought provided him with the macroeconomic theoretical apparatus regarding the role of government in the revitalization of a weakened and poorly competitive economy.

The thesis initially presents a concise introduction on the different theories concerning economic and development cycles, and three sections covering the causes and effects of the economic fluctuations of both trade and international economic growth. In the introduction, a synthesis is made of the most significant theories on development and international economic fluctuations, from Marxists to structuralists, instrumentalists, liberals and monetarists. In the first section, Mr. Campos conducts several analyses on the causes of the propagation and impulses of international economic cycles. The second section presents the core of his academic study, in which he analyzes the three means of the propagation of international economic fluctuations: (a) The interdependence of monetary policies between nations; (b) The free capital movement between nations; and (c) The growth of international trade. The following subsections deal with the means of the propagation of economic cycles, essentially the independence of monetary policy, the free movement of international capital and its effects on international trade, as well as the disputes relating to the effects of the gold standard on monetary policy. He stresses the possible instability of monetary policy, prices and growth in countries where capital is scarce under a fixed exchange rate regime and where central banks are dependent on the financing needs of governmental authorities. Mr. Campos demonstrates his remarkable ability foreseeing the difficulties that the international economy would face by following the guidelines of the International Monetary Fund, which proclaimed the creation of a new order in the international monetary system steady enough to enable the expansion of trade and investments, and flexible enough to prevent deflationary adjustments in the cycle of world economic activities. The bases of this possibility would be obtained through a fixed exchange rate regime and capital mobility among nations. However, contrary to this formula, the last four decades of the twentieth century were full of international instabilities, mostly caused by the existence of the fixed exchange rate and by nonconvertible currencies pegged to the dollar.

In the last section, Mr. Campos brings up some theoretical inconsistencies on the existence of cyclical behavioral patterns of balances of payments and international trade based on the existence of flexible foreign exchange and monetary policies to be adopted as a rule in a world full of institutional imperfections and market structural differences between developed (industrialized) and underdeveloped (agricultural) nations. Then after an extensive process of consideration of the cyclical fluctuations of trade and international economic growth, he states that his work resulted in "more fatigue than satisfaction to the proceeds of our inquiry" for the conspicuous lack of conclusions regarding the possibility of obtaining normative instruments of economic policy that would influence the direction of international trade, growth, and employment. With this synthesis, Mr. Campos concludes his lucid writings by stating that "the theorist is neither a preacher nor a prophet", but should he be one or the other, it would be advisable that "he should render a sermon easier than a prophecy." When addressing the future of the theory of international economic cycles, he said: "Some years from now we shall look back upon business cycles merely as magnificent episodes of the nineteenth century which gradually disappear as the economic instinct loses ground to political and social motivations." It is extraordinary to observe Roberto Campos's keen mind in foreseeing the end of theories such as Kondratieff's price waves, international economic cycles, and planned economies.

## Pragmatic Contributions of the Thesis

Even if he could not establish solid ground in the theory of economic cycles so that monetary and foreign exchange policies could even up economic fluctuations, Mr. Campos did not fail to state his thoughts regarding the role of those policies in an unpredictable world. As for monetary interdependence between nations, the most important factors of dispute regarding international economic stability consisted of a certain international monetary standard, and a fixed exchange rate regime. He questioned the enforceability of monetary standard with regard to the different stages of institutional development between nations, such as the lack of both a sound financial system and a large capital market — the latter providing an indispensable source for the formation of savings, investments, and long-term capital stock. Regarding this understanding for the need of a sound and diversified financial system targeted to the production and utilization of the workforce, Mr. Campos presented the controversies related to the most appropriate foreign exchange regime as one of the conditions underlying the stability of international economic fluctuations, stressing his preference for the flexible exchange rate — proposed by Hayek — as opposed to the stable exchange rate of J. M. Keynes, based on the U.S. dollar pegged to gold. Contrasting his conceptual understanding with Keynesian thought, he states that "the importance of exchange rate stability is greater for capital movements than for international trade", but he emphasizes Hayek's position by stating that "flexible exchange is needed to protect trade balance". This thought dominates the whole content of Mr. Campos's analyses. This is due to the fact that, "in economies with scarce savings, there is greater inflow of international capital in periods of international prosperity, when the interest rates are low, and the levels of employment and production are high; the reverse takes place in periods of recession or economic depression". Therefore, the stable exchange rate regime could not be responsible for increasing capital flow in the international market, leveraging economic growth and making it possible to stabilize international economic fluctuations.

Hayek's hypotheses permeate the whole critical content, stressing that world economic growth is not a mere foreign exchange issue nor a monetary standard issue, but it concerns the efficiency of monetary systems, the flexibility of capital movement, and the international rules that are intended to uphold free trade between nations. Globalization is a word that appeared in 1990, but when Mr. Campos expressed his criticism of the stability of international economy he was thinking about that dimension, and his warnings remain untouchable.

The subjects and controversies on exchange rate regimes and an international monetary system, discussed in his study, are both timely issues, but it is important to point out that Roberto Campos concentrated his reflections on conceptual problems, on theoretical dilemmas and on practical issues, in an effort to build an international monetary system that would be able to mitigate the international economic fluctuations underlying the basic conditions for long-lasting prosperity. He made numerous suggestions of methodological and theoretical nature, presented many answers, raised relevant hypotheses, stressing that "it should prove possible for a better equipped investigator to create the final synthesis between the theory of international trade and the recent theory of employment; within this synthesis the successive reformulations of the classical theory of international trade would rank as particular cases of a more general theory, embracing, on the one extreme, the pure price-specie flow theorem appropriate for a Ricardian full-employment world and, on the other, the pure foreign trade multiplier mechanism of the more descriptive world of under-employment equilibrium".

Mr. Campos points out the restriction to domestic credit supply in less-developed countries as one of the major development bottlenecks, since, without enough savings to lever economic growth, development becomes a theoretical fiction. As a result, he highlights the importance of policies aimed at adding flexibility to international capital flows in order to meet the investment demands of countries with capital shortages, taking into account the organization of a financial system, which is diversified and efficient in funding and allocating family savings. Along this same line, he emphasizes the importance of the "exchange regime as part of growth macroeconomic policy, by making exports viable and protecting the balance of payments". The option for the flexible exchange rate regime becomes clear, in a time when the fixed exchange rate was a world rule to guide international sustainable growth. Although these aspects seem obvious nowadays, in 1947 they were certainly not the center of media debate they are now.[1]

Roberto Campos made a few critical and conclusive remarks regarding the subject matter of his study: "A truly international cycle theory would have to take into account not only the co-existence of different economic structures subject to simultaneous or lagging cyclical fluctuations, but also the relationship between the latter and the general course of economic evolution. The problem is both spatial and temporal: how different economic structures react to cyclical influences and how the cyclical behavior in turn is affected by the stage of economic development." He suggests the need to include a wide variety of social changes and no economic factors into a more general theory of economic fluctuations. Without this orientation, "the theory of development and economic fluctuations remains more philosophical and descriptive than interpretative".

## Conclusion and Acknowledgements

The liberal thought of Roberto Campos was already present in his master's degree thesis, but he was able to build upon his interpretation with an eager sense of pragmatic realism, and with respect to the determinants of economic growth with stability in a country which lacked capital, technology, and human resources, where the capital goods sectors presented a low productivity rate. Mr. Campos realized that the basis of development lies in the economic exploitation of a country's comparative advantages. This is his starting point towards the prosperity of a country in need of capital and technology. Once the country's comparative advantages are identified, it is justifiable to use directional economic policies as vectors to correct inequalities in an underdeveloped country. Those policies or strategies must guide the orientation of development, promote the formation of savings and investments, add flexibility to international capital inflow, integrate the economy into the international market, enable continuous productivity gains in all economic sectors, and through monetary and foreign exchange policies ensure the stability of prices, employment, and growth.

Those are Roberto Campos's basic conclusions in his MA paper on economics, which attest to the theoretical synthesis ability of a lucid and constructive thinker, who has left us a major analytic legacy on international economic policy. After reading this remarkable study it becomes clearer the reasons Mr. Campos stressed some many times during his life that "Brazilian developmentists know very little about economic development".

---

[1] Despite rising inflation, Brazil kept the fixed exchange rate regime between 1938 and 1953, distorting the stability of foreign accounts in the balance of payments.

During 1999, the *Bolsa de Mercadorias & Futuros* (Brazilian Mercantile & Futures Exchange, BM&F) reprinted and edited limited copies of Mr. Campos MA thesis. In November of that year, the BM&F organized restrict social event to return him the lost academic work. He was deeply moved.

On that occasion, Mr. Campos told his guests about the repercussions of his master's degree thesis and how he intended to publish it in a broader edition, after a few conceptual refinements. Even though these conceptual refinements were never made, in honorable memory of this inestimable economist we are now able to publish the thesis in a broader edition. When he addressed his guests at the BM&F event, Mr. Campos told of how, after finishing the paper, he had sent copies to the Harvard University Professors Gottfried Von Haberler and Joseph Schumpeter. After reading Mr. Campos's thesis, Mr. Von Habeler sent him a letter expressing his admiration for the refined economic culture of the young economist; Schumpeter's reaction was equally admiring, and he invited Mr. Campos to finish the required credits for his doctoral program in economics at Harvard University, since his master's dissertation had already been completed.

I must express my thanks to Dr. Carlos Ivan Simonsen Leal and Dr. Manoel Fernando Thompson Motta, the President and the Vice President of the *Escola de Administração de Empresas* of the *Fundação Getulio Vargas* without whose interest, support and enthusiasm this publication would no have been possible. I also thanks the BM&F Board of Executives and its staffs: Mr. Manoel Felix Cintra Neto, Chairman of the Board of Governors; Mr. Marco Aurélio Teixeira, Technical and Planning Director; and its editing team for their dedication and hard work in recovering and digitizing the time-worn copy of the original thesis. The publication is just one small attempt to pay fitting tribute to one of the last humanist economists in recent Brazilian history.

*Ernesto Lozardo* [2]
São Paulo, October, 2003.

---

[2] Professor of economics at *EAESP-Fundação Getulio Vargas*. I thank Professor Alkimar R. Moura for his helpful comments.

# INTRODUCTION
## FRAGMENTS OF AN INTERNATIONAL CYCLE THEORY

In scarcely any other field of the economic science has the enthusiasm for theorization been so strangely restrained as in the study of international cyclical behavior. To make matters worse, we have not even the consolation of ascribing this unusual theoretical anaemia to a healthy respect for inductive fact-finding. As we shall presently see, a priori theorizing in the rarefied atmosphere of "Closed System" (i.e., "one-market") equilibrium analysis is quite common in business cycle literature. But in the transition from a closed system, with given data, to the international field, few writers have managed to escape the double lure of Scylla and Charybdis. In fact, either international changes are conceived as merely magnified forms of closed economy changes (with a few extra idiosyncrasies) or, swinging to the opposite extreme, cycles have been considered as unrelated historical or geographical phenomena, whose common law of behavior is non-existent or non-attainable.

Viewed from a broad perspective, the explanation of international cyclical behavior is merely a chapter of a yet to be developed general theory of economic evolution. In fact, a truly international cyclical theory would have to take into account not only the co-existence of different economic structures subject to simultaneous or lagging cyclical fluctuations, but also the relationship between the latter and the general course of economic evolution. The problem is both spatial and temporal: How different economic structures react to cyclical influences and how the cyclical behavior in turn is affected by the stage of economic development. The fact that such a theory would have of necessity to include a broad variety of social changes and extra-economic factors decreases the share, but does not eliminate, the responsibility of the economist towards integrating the theory of a particular change (cyclical fluctuations) into a general theory of economic change.[1]

Anglo-Saxon literature—which, since Hume, has been imparted the blessings and evils of what Veblen termed the "matter-of-fact-approach"—is conspicuously lacking in any such an attempt. One cannot even fail to be perplexed at the paradox that, while its contribution towards broadening the basis of the theory of economic change is powerful and unsurpassed, the general tone of investigation has remained more empirical than philosophical, descriptive rather than interpretative.

---

[1] This conflict between the static theories of general and particular equilibrium, which attempt to organize the relationships of economic magnitudes within the "theoretical boxes" of unchanged data, and the dynamic study of changes in the data themselves, is well pointed out by Kuznetz: "We have in consequence two somewhat incommensurable parts in the general science of economics, one dealing in terms of absolute, independent, static systems, the other dealing with changing and developing phenomena which have apparently no uniformity or sequence in their appearance that could be welded with the discussion of the static system into a unified system of economics". S. Kuznetz, *Secular Movements in Production and Prices* (Houghton Mifflin, 1930), p. 324.

In the Continental literature more frequent examples of courageous generalizations are to be found. Their significance derives less from the correctness of the theorems on cyclical behavior than from the attempt to establish a relationship between the cyclical phenomena and general social dynamics. In some cases, the factual background has proved too slim to support the theoretical superstructure; the " theory-before-the-facts" approach tends to become an exercise in semantics. The effort remains nevertheless significant as a counter-remedy against the danger of an atomistic view of the economic processes, which characterizes most of the recent business cycle literature, with its impressive but uncoordinated array of inductive and statistical material.[2]

We shall subsequently review first the theoretical and then the empirical contribution towards the understanding of the problem of international fluctuations.

---

[2] Wesley C. Mitchell, who cannot be charged with excess love for theorization, expressed this idea very pointedly: " We stand to learn more about economic oscillations at large and about business cycles in particular, if we approach the problem of trends as theorists, than if we confine ourselves to strictly empirical work. The trends which promise the most important addition to our knowledge are those which correspond to rational hypotheses, although they may not "fit the data" so well as empirical constructions which are difficult to interpret. For it may prove possible to integrate the rational hypotheses which yield instructive trends with the theory of business cycles." *Business Cycles. The Problem and its Setting* ( National Bureau of Economic Research, 1927), p. 230.

# I - THE THEORETICAL CONTRIBUTION

## A. The Imperialistic Theory of Crises

The first and even now fully significant contribution is the Neo-Marxian theory of imperialistic crises, developed originally by Rosa Luxembourg, on foundations built less by Marx but rather by Rodbertus. Its theoretical importance derives less from the correctness of the theorem involved—which is open to serious question—out from the nexus established between periodical trade crises and the general Marxian interpretation of capitalistic development. The imperialistic theory is the first really international theory, in the sense that it links the cyclical episode to the co-existence in space of structurally contrasting economics at different stages of development, while the conventional cycle theory deals mostly with abstract economic magnitudes, separated, from any particular historical or geographical environment.

There are two distinct branches of the Imperialist theory; the older emphasizes the role of colonial spheres in delaying the paralysis of capitalistic accumulation that would result from the glut of the internal market, and the newer version emphasizes the colonial role in retarding the fall in the rate of profit entailed by the process of capitalistic accumulation.

Rosa Luxembourg and Steinberg can be taken as representatives of the first version and Hilferding or Dobbs as the chief expounders of the "rate-of-profit" version. Both explanations claim a direct Marxian ascendance, although Marx's own views on crises are far from a complete or even a consistent theory of cycles.

The main tenets of the under-consumption version of the Imperialistic theory are well known. It is held that capital accumulation in a closed system has the seed of its own destruction because it renders it impossible for the capitalist to realize the surplus value. By capital accumulation, the output of consumer's goods increase faster than the population, while the exploitative tendency of the capitalistic system and the technological displacement of laborers keep down the purchasing power of the masses. The increased output cannot be wholly absorbed by the capitalists both because of natural limits of demand and because they need to save and reinvest to prevent the stoppage of capital accumulation. Thus, that part of the total output which represents the surplus value and supplies the basis for accumulation will eventually remain unsold and threaten capitalism with a breakdown, which can only be averted by the sale of surplus commodities to non-capitalistic countries—the famous "third person" introduced by Rosa Luxembourg. To Marx's vision of the world as a homogeneous capitalistic group consisting only of capitalists and of workers, Rosa Luxembourg contrasts the historical process of territorial expansion of capitalistic powers over colonial areas, absorbers of their marketable surpluses.

The under-consumption version is open to objection on several counts. It has in common with the entire Marxian approach the weakness of being predicated on the labor theory of value; it depends moreover on the validity of the assumption of the "erweiterte Reproduktion" scheme, according to which savings are always invested in the same compartment of production (consumer's or producer's goods spheres); it also overlooks the fact that, to a certain extent, capitalistic expansion creates its own demands. These limitations would tend to weaken the Neo-Marxian dogma of unavoidability of a capitalistic breakdown, although they do not disprove the possibility or even the probability that under-consumption crises may cause maladjustments between the structure of production and the structure of demand.

The <u>colonial solution</u> adduced by the Imperialistic theory is not, moreover, such a logically simple historical interpretation as it seems. The problem of disposal of the surplus product cannot be handled merely through foreign trade, since this would involve an exchange of one type of commodity for another, what would merely shift rather than eliminate the under-consumption problem. Capital exports to undeveloped areas, or the exchange of commodities against titles, thus appear to be an indispensable logical element of the Imperialistic theory, as recognized by Rosa Luxembourg and Sternberg themselves.[3] But this brings us to the second version of the Neo-Marxian doctrine, in which colonial expansion is seen as a tonic for a weakening rate of profit rather than as a remedy for under-consumption.

Hilferding and Maurice Dobbs can be taken as representative of this viewpoint.[4] The argument runs as follows: profits are the mainspring of capitalist (i.e., private capital) society, but the very process of accumulation, by entailing changes in the organic composition of capital (i.e., an increase in the proportion of constant relativity to variable capital) would tend to put a downward pressure on the rate of profit, since the possibility of compensatory increases in the rate of exploitation is small. Now, the export of capital to colonial areas would delay the capitalist crisis,

---

[3] Hans Neisser, *Some International Aspects of Business Cycles*, (Philadelphia: 1936) Appendix.

[4] Maurice Dobbs, among others, calls attention to cyclical factors independent from the organic composition of capital which may also affect the rate of profit, such as the shortage of labor and materials (and attending high production costs) characteristic of the boom. In this case, colonial outlets would affect favorably the rate of profit by permitting both an extension of the area and an intensification of the rate of exploitation. The point is carefully discussed by Svend Laursen, in *International Propagation of Business Cycles* (unpublished Ph.D. dissertation, Harvard University, 1941).

both by increasing the extent of variable capital and by making possible an intensified rate of exploitation.[5]

It is not our purpose to engage in a refutation of the theoretical tenets of the Imperialistic interpretation—a task that would require a deep plunge into Marxian economics—but merely to point out the substance of internationalism that it contains and that is badly lacking in subsequent business cycle analyses. We may, however, pause a moment for an observation which thrown a non-Marxian light on some important Imperialistic episodes. In fact, neither the class struggle, the glut of internal markets, nor the effort to strengthen a weakening rate of profit could satisfactory explain such colonial adventures as the colonization of New England or the French conquest of North African. Religious impulses or political maneuvering are as important sources of motivation of territorial adventure as are the efforts to preserve a doomed capitalistic order.[6]

The particular significance of the Imperialistic theory, from our viewpoint, has already been mentioned; it gives to the phenomenon of the crisis and of the cycles—even though the Marxian discussion refers primarily to trend and long run spans than to the conventional industrial cycle—an <u>international scope</u>, by encompassing contrasting and not merely homogeneous economic structures, and a <u>temporal perspective</u>, by linking the recurrent crisis to the general dynamics of capitalistic evolution.

## B. Sombart's "Expansionskonjunktur"[7]

Although Sombart's disquisition on the capitalist conjuncture is by far less than his study of other aspects of capitalist evolution, it deserves mention for its breadth of vision and for the study of the influences of changes in economic motivation. Sombart draws a distinct line between the pre-capitalist or early capitalistic

---

[5] A curious parallel can be drawn between the theory of imperialism and the modern stagnation theory. The former lays more emphasis on social and institutional antinomies of capitalism, while the second calls attention to the progressive exhaustion of psychological incentives. Both, however, ascribe to territorial adventures a "safety valve" function. For the economic theory of imperialism, colonial areas play the role of "safety valve" against under-consumption. The stagnation thesis sees in horizontal or territorial expansion (usually accompanied by a vertical or demographic expansion) a "safety valve" against under-investment. Joseph Schumpter, *Capitalism, Socialism and Democracy* (Harper and Brothers, 1942), p.52.

[6] Neither does actual experience show great burst of exports of either goods or capital, from those countries which Luxembourg calls those of "High Capitalism", at those points in time which her theory requires.

[7] Werner Sombart, *Der modern Kapitalismus* (Leipzig, 1928), vol. III, part II.

crises, and the "Expansionskonjunktur" of capitalism. While the pre-capitalist crisis are mainly <u>market</u> crises (Absatzkrisen), the rise of modern capitalism ushered in the age of production crises, or capital crises, stricto sensu, characterized by a disproportionate increase in the output of inorganic products; the failure of agriculture and the industries that produce organic materials to share in the expansion process destroys the balance of the business world.

The reason for this divergence in cyclical behavior is double. One psychological or subjective, brought about by the emergence of the entrepreneur, and the other objective, i.e., the emancipation from the limitations imposed by organic nature. The emergence of the metal age expanded the capitalistic horizon.

Capital, labor and market are the three pre-requisites of capitalist evolution. The development of credit, the concentration of savings and the incentives to the accumulative instinct, provided a continuous flow of capital. Real capital was obtained by technological improvements in the utilization of resources, exploitation of new areas and depletion of natural resource.

The problem of the supply of labor was solved by capitalism through the dissolution of peasantry and handicraft organizations, seasonal migration, imposition of the machine-discipline, and increase in labor productivity. Technological displacement by labor saving devices and periodical contractions of employment contributed to create the Marxian "reserve army" whenever profits were threatened by the increase in labor costs. The movements of migratory masses in response to capitalist demand for labor and materials is given special emphasis by Sombart.

The problem of the market was solved by a continuous expansion of the intra-capitalist market—which Sombart calls the endogenous demand—and also of the exogenous demand, i.e., the demand for industrial products on the part of the unproductive classes of the handicraft group and of the peripheral areas of capitalism (raw material areas). The latter demand is historically the older and relatively static; the endogenous demand, on the other hand, is the by-product of the changing motivation, wants and techniques of capitalist evolution itself.

The appearance of the "Expansionskonjunktur" is directly linked to the prodigious rise in the production metals, facilitated by the development of credit and the increase in the supply of monetary gold; it is, at the same time, a monetary and a real phenomenon.

Industrial evolution can largely be described as a continuous drive towards greater independence from organic production (subject to a deterministic law of growth). This is revealed in the prodigious development of synthetic production, through which output ceases to be bound to natural factors and is made directly responsive to changes in economic motivation. The periodical unbalance between organic and inorganic production is therefore an inherent feature of modern capitalism.

The interest presented by Sombart's work, from our specific viewpoint, is his emphasis on the influence of economic motivation, and its change in space and time, upon the cyclical behavior.

The contrast between the "Expansionskonjunktur" and the "Bedarfsdeckungprinzip" has not merely the value of an historical interpretation; it is of very real importance to understand the difference in cyclical reactions of countries at different stages of development.

Although Sombart's theory is by far a less compact and "technical" body of thought than most of the mechanistic theories, it has also a much broader scope; it aims less at describing the mechanics of individual cycles than at laying the groundwork for a sociology of the business cycle. And for this no "self-generating model" can provide a substitute.

## C. Schumpeter's Theory of Economic Development

The two most important contributions of Schumpeter are contained in his earlier book, *Theory of Economic Development*, and in the recent two volume work on *Business Cycles*.[8] The central merit of Schumpeter's work is to visualize the business cycle not as a somewhat peculiar episode of economic life but as an integral part of a broader process of economic evolution.

Many of the so-called "external factors"—such as innovations, technological changes, discovery of new territories—which had largely remained (except perhaps in Spiothoff's and Cassel's work) outside the scope of cyclical analysis, are now called to play a distinct role in the business cycle. Thus, cyclical changes are regarded essentially as technological changes, and cyclical unemployment not phenomenon distinct from technological unemployment, but co-terminous with it.

The three dynamic factors of economic change in the capitalist conspectus are the entrepreneur, the banking system, and particularly, innovations, which constitute the major factor of change. The recurrence of cycles is explained by the clustering of innovations in discontinuous periods, which generates an upward fluctuation manifested in credit expansion, rising interest rates, shifts in favor of producer's goods, etc. As the innovation impulse spreads and slackens (the innovators being followed by imitators), a readjustment or absorption period ensues during which the economy contracts and returns to a new equilibrium position. Alongside the primary innovation wave there is a secondary wave (errors in forecasting, speculative tendencies), which tends to move the system further away from equilibrium. Although accepting the four-phase scheme—prosperity, reces-

---

[8] J. Schumpeter, *Theory of Economic Development*, Eng. transl., Harvard University Press, 1934) and *Business Cycles*, 2 vols. (New York: McGraw Hill Book Co., 1939).

sion, depression and revival—Schumpeter suggests that the measurement of cycle be made not from peak to peak, or from trough to trough, but from the beginning of prosperity (departure from the equilibrium position) to the end of revival (return to the neighborhood of equilibrium).

In the recent volume on *Business Cycles*, Schumpeter further elaborates his well-known three-cycle scheme and presents an impressive array of historical and statistical material, which in his view permits e clear outline of the contours of the superimposed Kitchin, Juglar and Kondratieff cycles for the Unites States, Great Britain, and Germany, from the end of the 18th Century up to the present. The first Kondratieff is associated with the emergence of the iron industry, of the steam power and cotton industry (1787–1842), the second with the railroadization era (1842–1897), and the third with the development of electrical industries and motor transportation (1898–1911).

From the viewpoint of an international theory of cycles, Schumpeter's contribution is of substantial importance. By linking business cycles to the general framework of capitalistic evolution, Schumpeter was able to escape the atomistic approach of the closed-system, or "one-market", business cycle theories which have almost wholly prevailed in England and the United States. Aspects emphasized by particular theories, such as the role of credit creation (monetary theories), of changes in the structure of production (over-investment theories), of errors of optimism and pessimism (psychological theories), can all be fitted into a broader scheme of cyclical behavior; the first two play an important part in the explanation of the primary wave generated by innovations, the second in the explanation of the secondary wave.

Another important services rendered by Schumpeter is the comparative analysis, qualitative and quantitative, of the cyclical behavior in the three major western industrial countries. A great deal of light is thus thrown on the import of institutional and structural differentiation upon economic fluctuations.[9]

The controversy provoked by Schumpeter's work has centered principally around the adequacy of the historical evidence bearing on the three-cycle scheme and on the validity of the innovation hypothesis, which assumes a self-generating mechanism of cycles. The main question raised is: why are innovations "bunched" or discontinuous in time, or to use Professor Angell's expression, why "are innovations innovated?" The explanation given by Schumpeter to this typical " innovation pause" runs in institutional terms; the discontinuity of the rhythm in innovation would derive from the discontinuity of the supply of new combination and

---

[9] The internationalization of the "closed system" theories would of course require also the analysis of the cyclical repercussions upon the "peripheral areas" of capitalism. Schumpeter's study, quite consistently with his view of cycles as "capitalist" episodes, is confined to the area of "Hochcapitalismus".

especially of technological inventions.[10] After the cyclical process is set in motion, the economic system must digest the innovation changes; during the process of digestion disequilibria are created which increase the psychological and monetary resistances to new productive combinations and place obstacles to the innovating instincts. The liquidation in the downswing, on the other hand, clears the ground, decreases organization resistance and creates favorable conditions for a new wave of new productive combinations.[11]

Misgivings have also been expressed by some authors as to the statistical validity of the three-cycle scheme. It is argued that the Kondratieff wave shows well only in monetary series (prices, interest rates) which are largely dominated by the peaks of the Napoleonic wars, of the 1870's and of the first World War, and does not show the same degree of clarity in series relating to production, trade or employment. Again, the existence of Kitchin cycles, except perhaps insofar as the United States are concerned, rests on a slim statistical basis. In fairness to Schumpeter, it must be said that his presentation of the three-cycle scheme is more carefully qualified than his critics imply and that the basic theory is in itself independent of the three-scheme descriptive device.

To enter into a detailed discussion of Schumpeter's theory is, however, well beyond the scope of the present observations. We are interested merely in bringing the salient points in Schumpeter's analysis, that constitute a significant departure from the "closed system" approach, towards a more nearly international approach to the cyclical experience. In this sense, his analysis of the process of evolution through time, in the setting of capitalistic institutional, retains its full significance.[12]

---

[10] This explanation, however, as noted by Kuznetz, might be satisfactory for the great technological changes (electricity, steam power), but would not explain the discontinuity in the supply of the less portentous innovations responsible for the Juglar or Kitchin cycles. *Cf.* his destructive criticism of Schumpeter's book, in the American Economic Review (June, 1940).

[11] This answer, as noted by Angell, in part begs the question; i.e., the casual role might well be reversed; innovations would be the effect rather than the causes of changes in business conditions.

[12] Moreover, Schumpeter's concepts, regardless of their specific assumptions and conclusions, have the great, advantage of shifting emphasis from the over-worked Anglo-American habit (perhaps unconsciously) of remaining in the framework of short-term periodicity of a mechanical type to fuller consideration of long-sweep changes. Since economic theory, after all, is at heart an attempt to explain economic reality, empirical observation strongly suggests that by now we can scarcely cling to neatly adopted three or four year periods, but must broaden our view and consider economic fluctuations in the fuller sense, even at the expense of losing of the traditional distinction between "long-run" equilibria which are really "short-run", and, on the other hand "historical periods". Here is better opportunity to seek the dynamic realities, and, accordingly, to free ourselves from the cramped connotation of the very word "cycle", and study "crises" or "konjunkturs" or, perhaps best "fluctuations". For even economic terminology may sometimes shackle economic analysis, and should not, especially in a field such as this one, where obviously fresh ground must be broken.

## D. Walther Heinrich and the Universalistic School

A bold attempt to formulate a dynamic theory of economic fluctuations can be found in Heinrich's "Grundlagen einer universalistischen Krisenlehre", which is a good sample of the most sanguine vein of the Austrian universalistic schools. At the outset Heinrich blurs the traditional line of demarcation between economic and extra-economic factors and questions, and the usefulness of the distinction between structural and cyclical changes, on the ground that they are equally dynamic and inseparable manifestation of economic evolution. In his scheme, which is extremely suggestive but too general to have any other significance than as a point of departure, the study of economic changes would encompass the impact of a wide variety of social factors, whose admission in the economic domain would throw overboard all hopes for quantitative treatment in economic theory. Contrary to what would be expected from the metaphysical tone of the universalistic school, Heinrich denies the validity of any casual approach and would restrict the aim of cycle theory to the establishment of a "Hierarchiè der Krisengrunden". Cyclical functions are thus regarded as the outward manifestations of a deep process of economic unfolding (Ungliedorung) which expresses itself through recurrent mutations of economic objectives (Zielwandlungen) or changes in the structure of means ( Aenderungen im Gebäud dor Mittels). The mutations in economic objectives are due to the impact of wars, of changes in fashions and tastes, or in institutional conditions, which constitute the process of economic innovation. Mutations in the structure of means may occur either through displacements or movements in economic organs (Teilganzen), or through maladjustments between units of economic activity (household, firm, national and world economy).

Crises of the "change in means" type may originate in manifold ways, e.g., (a) by organizational changes either of non-monetary nature (errors of planning, changes in allocation of resources, commercial and fiscal policies) or of a monetary nature (changes in the supply of the monetary medium and credit inflation, or contraction; (b) by changes in the conditions of production, the principal factor being in this case shifts in technical productivity and their repercussion on prices; (c) by changes in the productive structure (over and under-investment, speculation, etc.)

The world economy and the national economy are the two principal economic organisms, in which all the crises have their concrete manifestation. Since the national economy must reflect the movements of the world economic order, disturbances may occur whose origin lies outside the field of national control. The only possible defense against world crises lies in increasing the structural elasticity and the amount of economic self-sufficiency.

Three different modes of world crises can be distinguished. The first is the classical capitalistic "Expansionskonjunktur", characterized by recurrent over-capitalization crises, a mechanistic concept inherited from Marx. The international spread of the "Expansionskonjunktur" has been greatly facilitated by the development of an international capital market and by the interdependence between agrarian and industrial countries. A second type of crisis has its origin in production and organization changes induced by wars. The third and more general type of crisis derives from changes in economic motivation and economic methods, especially those caused by political and cultural factors (nationalism, imperialism, etc.).

A complete neutralization of cycles cannot be attained as long as there are continuous changes in economic aims. But a certain measure of stabilization of the konjunktur can be reached by internal and national insulation policies and organization reforms.

The universalistic theory of crisis is thus at the same time more modest and yet greatly ambitious than the "atomistic" business cycle theories; the abandonment of the search for causes, or general explanations in favor of the investigation of an "Hierarchie der Krisengründe" restrict considerably its theoretical range; on the other hand, the attempt to interpret economic fluctuations in terms of a broad set of social and political factors is a clearly desirable, but at this stage unmanageable, dilation of the theoretical horizon.[13] Heinrich's book is a good illustration of the dilemma of Scylla and Charybdis that faces business cycle theorizing; as the study broadens in extension by encompassing structural changes and extra-economic factors, it loses in precision, as well as in some respects, comprehension. The atomistic view implied in the monetary theories, on one side, and the disproportionality theories on the other, is replaced by an eclectisicism that comes dangerously close to the "everything depends on everything else" solution.

## E. Neisser and the Theory of General Over-Production

A comparative analysis of international cyclical relations was undertaken by Professor Neisser in his book *Some International Aspects of the Business Cycle*, published in 1936. He stresses the importance of capital flows, in addition to commodity trade, and distinguishes none too clearly between the transfer of commodities that derives merely from the geographical location and direction of investment, and that which is the result of the international division of labor. Neisser

---

[13] The generality and vagueness of the universalistic approach is well illustrated in the definition of crises: "Wirtschafttskrisen sind beftige Entsprechungsstörungen, dies aus Aenderungen der Ziele oder der Teilganzen oder der Weltwirtschaftlichen Stufenstellung der Volkswirtschaft herrühren und sich auf deren Stufen auswirken". W. Heinrich, *Grundlagen einer universalistischen Krisenlehre*, (Jena: Gustav Fischer, 1928), p. 346.

expands the field of the "closed system" analysis by taking into account the impact of the differentiation of economic structures upon the cyclical behavior. Under-saving and over-saving are seen not as two antipodal mechanism of crisis generation, but as subspecies of partial over-production, under-saving implying over-production in the capital goods sphere and over-saving in the consumption goods sphere. Once partial over-production exceeds the limits of particular industries to encompass a "whole sphere", there occurs a maladjustment between the structure of production and that of demand; the ensuing unbalance between costs and receipts may be caused by either under-saving or over-saving, over-production being then generalized by monetary deflation.

There is no uniform mechanism of cycle generation, the same crisis having different manifestations in different countries. Thus the American depression of 1929 had all the characteristics of an over-saving crisis German crisis was a typical case of under-saving while in Great Britain the determining factor was the deterioration of the foreign trade position; subsequently to the over-valuation of the pound.

A triple mechanism of propagation of cycles from principal centers to peripheral areas is described; debt collection or capital withdrawal by the financial center, decline in its demand for foreign products and finally intensification of competition in foreign markets and competitive price-deflation due to shrinkage of international demand.

The origin of industrial crises by losses and over-production in agricultural countries is rejected on the grounds that the decline in agricultural prices would release purchasing power in industrial countries, which might then be directed to other spheres of production without necessarily entailing a fall in aggregate demand[14]. No evidence of serious agricultural over-production was found in the decade preceding the great depression.

Recovery policies, by monetary expansion, can successfully be applied in the case of an "autonomous" but not of an "imposed" deflation. The international division of labor also makes it difficult to overcome over-production by investment, especially in the case of non-industrial countries which have to import instruments of production precisely when they suffer from international illiquidity. Autonomous recovery is only possible for self-sufficient or nearly self-sufficient countries.

---

[14] For diametrically opposite view, *cf.* Mento Bouniatian: "D'une façon generale, la diminution du pouvoir nominal d'achat des agricultaurs n'est pas compense par l'augmentation de ce pouvoir dans les autres classes de la population et la demande totale des produits industriels tombe, en changeant en même temps de nature. Il peut en resulter une superproduction partielle dans d'autres branches de l'economie nationale, en tout cas, leniveau general des prix s'abaisse et provoque un rallentissement de la vie economique". *Les Crises Economiques* (Paris: 1922), p. 139.

Although the perpetual under-consumption dilemma of the Marxian theory of imperialism is discarded, Neisser discerns the existence of an international capitalistic dilemma which derives from the fact that the supply of new capital must provide net new investment to absorb the workers both in industrial and in raw material countries. Two alternatives are possible; either the supply of saving is split between domestic and foreign investment, or a maximization of domestic employment is immediately aimed at, in which case investment may be concentrated in the national field by deliberate policy, despite the lower productivity per unit.

# II. THE EMPIRICAL CONTRIBUTION

## A. Mitchell and the Contribution of the Business Annals

The importance of Mitchell's pioneer work in business cycle analysis can hardly be overstated. Both the original work on business cycles, published in 1913 and its rewritten edition in 1927, *Business Cycles: The Problem and its Setting*, are landmarks in the field.

From the particular viewpoint of our interest here, namely, the international aspects, Mitchell's contribution is to be found in the introductory analysis to the volume on *Business Annals*, prepared by Dr. Willard Thorp for the National Bureau of Economic Research.

Elaborating his familiar concept of cyclical fluctuations as an upshot of a certain stage and type of economic evolution, namely, the "business" or "profit" economy, in which economic activities are carried mainly by "making and spending money" [15], Mitchell advances the hypothesis that the sensitiveness to cycles would in itself describe a cyclical pattern.

The international spread of cycles was first noted in connection with financial crises and was first studied by Juglar in his classic work *Des Crises Commerciales et leur Retour Périodique en France, Angleterre et aux Etats Unis*, published in 1889. Data collected in the *Business Annals* of the National Bureau of Economic Research show that England and the United States shared in the crises of 1815, 1825, and 1837, being joined by France in the crisis of 1847, and by Germany in the crisis of 1857, while all those countries, plus Austria, experienced in various degrees the crisis of 1873 and the mild recession of 1882–84. From 1890 on, a clean international pattern is noticeable, the annals being available for seventeen countries of which ten had recessions in 1890–01, fifteen in 1900–01, fifteen in 1907–08, twelve in 1912–13, eleven in 1918 and fourteen in 1920. Of the 34 countries covered by the Annals in 1926–31, two had recessions in 1927, two more in 1928, seventeen had recessions beginning in 1929 and nine beginning in 1930, while four other countries had had prolonged depressions since 1926. By 1931 the depression was truly worldwide.

More important, though less noticed than the international sweep of crises,

---

[15] The more highly organized a country's business, the larger the proportion of its people who live by making and spending money incomes, the more important become the recurrent cycles of activity". *Business Annals*, Introduction, p. 88. Earlier crises that occurred before the industrial age, such as those studied by W. Scott in England, show more the influence of extra-economic factors and agricultural vicissitudes than inherent disturbances of the economic system. W. C. Mitchell, *Business Cycles: The Problem and its Setting* (N.B.E.R., 1923), pp. 75-6.

is the propagation of entire phases of cycles, such as the protracted depression of the 1870's, the unstable fortunes of the 1880's, the revival of the middle 1890's, the boom of 1906–07, the prosperity of 1912, the depression of 1920 and, one may now add, the great slump of the 1930's, sometimes referred to as the "world financial crisis of 1931" or as "the great world depression".

On the basis of the experience of the countries and periods covered by the Annals, Mitchell observes that, concurrently with the development of modern money economy and the spread of industrialization, a growing tendency towards closer international synchronization of cyclical fortunes is clearly noticeable. This trend was temporarily interrupted by the economic disruption that followed the First World War.

Contrasting with this growing tendency towards parallelism of cyclical reactions, we find persistent obstructions and variable degrees of conformity to the international pattern, the final product being the result of conflict between national economic interdependence and local economic peculiarities.

Mitchell suggests the hypothesis of an evolutionary law of cyclical behavior, according to which the sensitivity to international fluctuations would historically describe, by itself, a cyclical movement. In the first phase, characterized by the predominance of agriculture, economic fortunes are governed more by harvest variations and acts nature than by the impact of world business. During the successive phase, the rise of trade and industry would create a greater dependence upon foreign finance and enterprise, increasing the share of foreign ownership and making for a greater sensitivity to foreign-induced fluctuations. The third phase would be characterized by efforts toward economic emancipation, by gradual absorption of foreign capital and enterprise, and expansion of the home market, with the result that business cycles " will diverge more widely from the international pattern".

Finally, with the modernization of economic activity, greater integration of industry and trade, and development of financial markets, the national responsiveness to world fluctuations would again reaffirm itself.

In broad outline, an international pattern of business cycles can be sketched as follows:

1st cycle: 1890–91 to 1900–01
       Recession in 1890–91; contraction in 1891–95 revival in
       1895–96; expansion in 1896–1900; recession in 1900–01.

2nd cycle: 1900–01 to 1907–08
       Recession in 1900–01; contraction in 1901–03; revival in
       1903–04; expansion in 1905–07; recession in 1907–08.

3rd cycle: 1907–08 to 1913–14
> Recession in 1907–08; contraction in 1908–09; revival in 1909–10; expansion in 1910–13; recession in 1913–14.

4th cycle: 1913–14 to 1918
> Recession in 1913–14; contraction in 1914–15; revival in 1915; expansion in 1915–18 recession in 1918.

5th cycle: 1918–1920
> Recession in 1918; brief and mild contraction em 1919; rapid revival after the spring of 1919; expansion in the rest of 1919 and early in 1920; recession.

6th cycle: early 1920–late 1929
> Recession in 1920; severe contraction in 1921–22; revival in 1922–23; oscillations around a rising level in 1924–28; recession in 1929.

7th cycle: 1929 to 1937[16]
> Recession in 1929; severe contraction in 1930–32 or 33; revival in 1932 or 1933; recession in 1937.

The general conclusion drawn by Mitchell on the evidences presented by the Annals, is that the "international similarity of phase in business cycles increased, on the whole, with the passage of time". The disruption of economic bonds in 1914 interrupted the synchronization trend, economic behavior being then dominated by non-economic factors which, although exercising at first a uniformizing effect among the belligerents, on one side, and among the neutrals, on the other, sowed the seed of great economic antinomies.

The revival and prosperity of the twenties were irregular in extent and timing, contrasting with the depression of the thirties, which showed more universality and uniformity. The great depression was most particularly severe in the United States, Japan and Canada, as well as in the countries forming the gold block, but relatively moderate in the sterling area.

That the international solidarity to behavior seems to be closer in depression that in prosperity is not a new observation. Expanding the elements of the

---

[16] In Mitchell's article in Bulletin XXVIII (1935) of the Institut International de Statistique, from which the above classification of cycles was taken, the seventh cycle of the '30-a was of course marked as incomplete. The indication of 1937 as the end of the cycle is not, therefore, Mitchell's responsibility, but is now a widely accepted interpretation.

Annals with data of last depression, Dr. Thorp adds new force to this observation. His statistical studies indicate that, except for the depression of 1901, there seems to be greater agreement of behavior in depression than in prosperity, as shown in the following table:

### Table I
### Co-Variation of Cyclical Movements[17]

| Year | AGREEMENT | | | DIFFERENCE | |
| | Number of Countries | Percentage | | Number of Countries | Percentage |
|---|---|---|---|---|---|
| | **PROSPERITY** <br> **For 16 countries** | | | | |
| 1899 | 15 | 94 | | 1 | 6 |
| 1906 | 14 | 88 | | 2 | 12 |
| 1912 | 15 | 94 | | 1 | 6 |
| 1920 | 14 | 88 | | 2 | 12 |
| 1929 | 11 | 69 | | 5 | 31 |
| | **For 34 countries** | | | | |
| 1928 | 15 | 74 | | 9 | 26 |
| 1929 | 14 | 71 | | 10 | 29 |
| | **DEPRESSION** <br> **For 16 countries** | | | | |
| 1901 | 12 | 75 | | 4 | 25 |
| 1908 | 16 | 100 | | 0 | 0 |
| 1914 | 16 | 100 | | 0 | 0 |
| 1921 | 15 | 94 | | 1 | 0 |
| 1931 | 16 | 100 | | 0 | 0 |
| | **For 34 countries** | | | | |
| 1930 | 34 | 100 | | 0 | 0 |
| 1931 | 34 | 100 | | 0 | 0 |

---

[17] For details and methods used consult *The Depressions as Depicted by the Business Annals*, by Willard Thorp, News Bulletin, No. 43, of the National Bureau of Economic Research, September 1932. Thorp's conclusions are thus summarized: "It may be suggested from this material, that domestic factors may be strong enough to prevent a country from joining the rest of the world in prosperity but they are seldom sufficient to maintain prosperity in one country in face international depression."

Another important observation of the Annals bears on the highly controversial issue of the average duration of cycles.[18] The analysis of the material contained in the Annals, supplemented by data covering the last depression (published in News Bulletin No.34 of the National Bureau of Economic Research) indicates a concentration of average duration around a three-year period. The range of observations includes altogether 187 different cycles:

**Table II**
**Duration of Cycles**

| Duration in years | Number of Observations | Duration in years | Number of Observations |
|---|---|---|---|
| 1 | 3 | 7 | 18 |
| 2 | 19 | 8 | 13 |
| 3 | 33 | 9 | 11 |
| 4 | 31 | 10 | 6 |
| 5 | 25 | 11 | 3 |
| 6 | 24 | 12 | 1 |

Dr. Thorp's work, so far published, does not go beyond 1932. It does not cover, therefore, the upswing of the thirties, after the great depression. The period is of particularly difficult analysis, because of the frequent interference of "external factors" which distort the picture of cyclical reaction by making the separation of cyclical and non-cyclical changes well-nigh impossible.

The recovery was uneven in extent and in timing, and directly influenced by revolutionary changes is monetary and governmental policies. While in the upswing of the twenties, the increases in industrial production for the several countries ranged from a minimum of the 12 to a maximum of 55 per cent, a much wider dispersion was observed in the thirties, production increases varying from 14 to 180 per cent.[19]

---

[18] Professor Morgenstern makes cogent objections to Mitchell's and Thorp's measure of average cyclical duration, on the ground of lack of comparability of the basic phenomena described, and in particular of the meaning of prosperity, depression, etc., as between different countries. He accuses Mitchell —"an institutionalist"— of overlooking fundamental structure differences in space and time. This anti-institutional approach is implied, for instance, in the attempt to compare cycles of 1790 (when a credit system would scarcely be said to have existed) with modern cycles, or in the attempt to compare data relative to completely different economic structure such as those of Great Britain and China. Cf. *International Vergleichende Konjunkturvorschung*, in Zeitschrift für die Gesamt Staats-Wissenscharft (1927), pp. 274-275.

[19] Cf. League of National, *Economic Stability in the Post-War World* (Geneva, 1945), p. 87 and diagram XII on p. 89.

According to the emphasis given to recovery policies and to the monetary behavior, we may distinguish three groups of countries:
1. The "working-program-creation" countries, which sought to stimulate recovery by monetary inflation and public investment, such as Germany, Japan, Italy and, to a certain extent, the United States. In the first three countries, recovery was stimulated by huge military expenditures.
2. The devaluation countries, including the sterling block and the dollar area (United States, Canada, and Latin America.)
3. The "gold block" countries, consisting of France, Netherlands, Switzerland, and Poland, whose recovery was greatly hindered by monetary deflation.

The unevenness of the recovery is clearly brought out in the following table (extracted from a Department of Commerce publication which indicates the volume of industrial production and national income expressed as percentage changes from 1929 for selected countries:

## Table III[20]
### Volume of Production and National Income

| Country | Physical volume of industrial production | | | | National Income | | | |
|---|---|---|---|---|---|---|---|---|
| | 1935 | 1936 | 1937 | 1938 | 1935 | 1936 | 1937 | 1938 |
| **Sterling-bloc countries:** | | | | | | | | |
| United Kingdom | 5.6 | 15.8 | 23.6 | 15.5 | 5.3 | 12.1 | 20.9 | 14.5 |
| Sweden | 23.0 | 35.0 | 49.0 | 2.5 | 10.1 | 24.2 | 29.4 | |
| Norway | 7.6 | 18.2 | 29.6 | 29.1 | 7.4 | 6.4 | 21.2 | 32.9 |
| New Zealand | 21.0 | 29.0* | 26.0* | (1) | 1.9* | 15.5* | 25.6* | 45.7* |
| **War-economy countries:** | | | | | | | | |
| Germany | 6.0 | 6.3 | 17.2 | 26.2 | 17.8 | 6.4 | 3.1 | 9.5 |
| Japan | 40.6 | 50.2 | 68.9 | 74.7 | 24.7 | 36.9 | 71.8 | 88.9 |
| Italy | 6.2 | 12.5 | 0.4 | 1.5 | (1) | (1) | (1) | (1) |
| **Gold-bloc countries:** | | | | | | | | |
| France | 25.9 | 21.7 | 18.1 | 23.9 | 30.9 | 24.0 | 14.9 | 9.1 |
| Netherlands | 9.8 | 8.6 | 2.8 | 4.1 | 26.5 | 24.8 | 20.2 | 16.6 |
| Belgium | 17.8 | 13.5 | 2.8 | 21.3 | (1) | (1) | (1) | (1) |
| **Dollar-countries:** | | | | | | | | |
| United States | 20.9 | 5.4 | 2.7 | 20.0 | 33.1 | 22.1 | 14.2 | 22.9 |
| Canada | 9.0 | 2.0 | 12.0 | 1.0 | 34.3 | 25.6 | 15.7 | 18.5 |

(1) Not available
* Fiscal year ended March 31 of following year

---

[20] United States Department of Commerce, *The United States in the World Economy* (Washington: U.S. Government Printing Office, 1934), p.184

What we have witnessed in the last decade was a gigantic process of disintegration of world economy, which, to use Ropkes's expression, amounted to a "quantitative shrinkage" and a "qualitative pathological change", deeply rooted as much in social and psychological, as in economic factors. The words "world economy" and "world cycle" have lost substance as shape. In the world economic order that is now emerging the principal deciding lines of economic response will not probably be drawn as between different modes or spheres of production, but between areas of relatively free operation of economic forces and areas in which economic reactions are shape by politico-social preconceptions.

## B. Economic Evolution and the Duration of Cycles

Professor Mills has called attention to the secular changes in the average duration of business cycles in the four countries for which long period data are available (United States, Germany, France and England) and also in some other countries listed in the *Business Annals*, and representing different stages of economic evolution. Mills' hypothesis claims substantially that the length of cyclical fluctuations is related to the stage and rate of industrial development and is affected by structural changes inherent to the industrialization process:

> The duration of business cycles in a given country is a function of the stage of the stage of economic development which that country has attained. More specifically: When the modern type of economic organization is in the initial stage of development, the average duration of business cycles is relatively long. During the stage of rapid growth, when modern types of business enterprise and modern forms of industrial organization are being applied extensively, business cycles are of relatively short average duration. With the decline in the rate of economic change and attainment of comparative stability, business cycles increase again in length.[21]

The obstacles to an adequate statistical testing of the hypothesis are of course formidable since we lack an "index of industrialization", and a precise appraisal of structural changes in time is in itself a huge task for historico-statistical investigation. The classification of countries per stages of industrial development involves of course some element of arbitrariness. The following groups are established by Mills, combining observation of the *Annals* and independent investigations:

---

[21] F.C. Mills, *An Hypothesis Concerning the Duration of Business Cycles* (Journal of the American Statistical Association, December 1926), vol. XXI, pp. 447-57.

### A - Countries in early
####    Stages of industrialization                        Annals begin in

| Country | Period | Annals begin in |
|---|---|---|
| United States | to 1822 | 1796 |
| Germany | to 1866 | 1848 |
| Italy | to 1907 | 1888 |
| Canada | to 1913 | 1888 |
| Australia | to 1913 | 1890 |
| China | to date | 1890 |
| India | to date | 1889 |
| Russia | to date | 1890 |
| Argentina | to date | 1890 |
| Brazil | to date | 1889 |

### B - Countries in the stage
####    of rapid economic transition[22]

| Country | Period | Annals begin in |
|---|---|---|
| England | to 1831 | 1793 |
| United States | 1822 to date | |
| France | to 1876 | 1838 |
| Germany | 1866 to date | |
| Austria | to 1873 | 1866 |
| Italy | 1907 to date | |
| Canada | 1913 to date | |
| Australia | 1913 to date | |
| South Africa | 1913 to date | 1890 |
| Japan | to date | |

### C - Countries in which transition
####    is going forward at a decreasing rate

| Country | Period | Annals begin in |
|---|---|---|
| England | 1831 to date | |
| France | 1876 to date | |
| Austria | 1873 to date | |
| Netherlands | to date | 1891 |
| Sweden | to date | 1892 |

---

[22] Professor Mills was writing in 1926 and since then considerable structural changes have taken place. His classification, however, remains generally valid up to date, except perhaps regarding Russia whose index of industrial growth has been rapidly increasing in the last decade, entitling her to a transfer to category B. But again, Russia presents from the viewpoint of cyclical analysis a "terra incognita" owing to its planned economy and economic insulation. The United States might also conceivably be included C, since the phase of industrial maturity is clearly in sight.

Utilizing the data of the Annals on cycle duration, Professor Mills reaches the following conclusions:

|  | Early Stages of Industrialization | Stage of Rapid Economic Transition | Stage of Relative Stability |
|---|---|---|---|
| Number of observations | 51 | 77 cycles | 38 cycles |
| Mean duration | 5.86 years | 4.9 years | 6.39 years |
| Standard deviation | 2.41 years | 1.88 years | 2.42 years |

Actual cyclical experiences in England and France seem to lend support to Mill's hypothesis. In the United States, whose cycles are characteristically of smaller amplitude than those of Great Britain and France, the experience is less conclusive, a diversion from the expected pattern being noticeable in the period 1860 to 1888, as shown below:

|  |  | Cycles | Average Duration |
|---|---|---|---|
| England | 1793–1831 | 9 | 4.22 years |
|  | 1831–1920 | 13 | 6.85 years |
| France | 1854–1876 | 6 | 3.67 years |
|  | 1876–1920 | 7 | 6.32 years |
| United States | 1798–1822 | 5 | 5.20 years |
|  | 1822–1860 | 11 | 3.50 years |
|  | 1860–1888 | 5 | 5.50 years |
|  | 1888–1923 | 11 | 3.20 years |

Despite the unavoidable arbitrariness in the dating of the cycles and in demarcation of periods of industrialization, Mills' generalization is very suggestive and "prima facie" quite plausible. Indeed, the existence of a connection, although not yet quantitatively ascertainable, between the stage and rate of industrial development and the cyclical behavior can scarcely be questioned.

Mills' hypothesis is significantly related to Kuznetz's elaboration of the principle of retardation of industrial growth, which will engage us next. The two hypothesis show interesting points of contact, one emphasizing the changes in duration, and the other in the amplitude of cycles. In Mills' scheme the "periods of rapid transition" and in Kuznetz's scheme the "periods of rapid growth", are associated with increased cyclical instability. This is a plausible interference, since during those periods the sensitiveness of the system of fluctuations is likely to be sharpened by the violent shifts required in income distribution, by the continuous re-adaptation to technical changes and by the growing uncertainties associated with the adoption of new and roundabout methods of production. With the advent of industrial maturation (the "statization period", to use Schumpter's expression", adaptation and change would tend to become longer and smoother processes.[23]

## C. The Principle of Retardation of Industrial Growth

Kuznetz's contribution towards linking cyclical changes to longer-time changes, in the broad framework of economic evolution, is to be found in his book *Secular Movements in Production and Prices*,[24] which represents a happy blending of statistical and theoretical work.

To the usual description of long period economic changes is terms of population growth, changes in demand or technology, a new hypothesis is added, namely, "the principle of retardation of industrial growth", which in turn is explained by the following structural-evolutive conditions:

I - Slackening of technical progress
II - Retarding influence of the slower growing industries upon the faster growing branches
III - Decrease in the relative size of the funds available for the expansion of industries as they grow in size
IV - Retarding effect of competition of industries in younger countries upon industries in older countries

The principle of retardation of industrial growth provides the basis for the statistical description of long time movements. The logistic and Gromperz curves are found to provide the best (although not the only possible) fit for the description of the declining rate of growth detected in the series of agricultural, industrial and mining production for selected countries. Underlying the primary trend line, represented by the Gromperz curve, there are secondary movements or long swings of more irregular pattern. These are the so-called "secondary movements of production and prices" with an average duration of 22 years for a complete swing of

---

[23] For a critical appraisal, *cf.* Mitchell, *op. cit.*, pp. 413-16.

[24] "The primary and secondary secular movements are the two quite different component parts of the complex total phenomenon called secular changes". S. Kutznetz, *Secular Movements in Production and Prices* (Hougton Mifflin, 1930), p. 325. The secondary wave occupies thus an intermediary position between the Kondratieff cycle (roughly 50 years) and the Juglar or financial cycle.

production, and 23 years for the price cycle. Some interesting observations, which have a direct bearing on cyclical analysis, are drawn from the statistical behavior of the time series analysis, to wit:

1. Precession of price movements over production movements, in the majority of the series studied;
2. Greater amplitude of secondary variations in producers' goods industries as compared to those registered in consumers' goods industries;
3. Positive correlation between the amplitude and duration of secondary and cyclical fluctuations and the rapidity of industrial growth. The retardation of industrial growth is associated with decreasing fluctuations, while rapid growth is accompanied by wide adaptive fluctuations. The correlation between primary growth movements and the secondary movements is generally greater than that between primary and cyclical movements, the latter being affected by a host of complicating influences.

We need not enter into a detailed discussion. The limitations of Kuznetz's study are those inherent to any statistical extrapolation. We might mention in particular the effects of innovation and technical changes which, as noted by Schumpeter, are sufficiently unpredictable to vitiate any extrapolation based on the principle of decreasing returns (which is more legitimately applicable to stationary rather than to dynamic conditions), or on the principle of retardation of the rate of growth. Even if the latter were a conclusive inductive truth for individual industries, as successfully shown by Kuznetz, it might not be true for industrial evolution as a whole.[25]

From our viewpoint, Kuznetz's generalization, which is moreover couched in a very guarded tone, retains its full significance as an attempt to broaden the study of cyclical fluctuations by an inductive generalization concerning the "course of economic development", and the shorter movements in time.

---

[25] *Cf.* Joseph Schumpeter, *Business Cycles* (McGraw Hill Book Co., 1939), II, p. 500.

# III - THE "CLOSED SYSTEM" THEORIES OF CYCLES

At this point, the landscape on international cyclical relations is most uncomfortable.

If against this slim background of theorization on cyclical behavior and on the general contours of economic evolution, we now project the bewildering multiplicity of particular theories of cycles[26] (mostly of the closed economy or spaceless type) and the large mass of inductive findings on static or micro-dynamic aspects of the cycle, one gets the impression that somehow, in this branch of our science, people have decided to see economic reality through a telescope or through a microscope without hardly ever exercising the normal vision.

There is a definite over-production of business cycle theories, all differentiated according to the emphasis placed on "physical, emotional, or institutional explanations" (Mitchell). A convenient classification given by Professor Haberler groups the main theories under the following heading:

1 - Purely monetary theories
2 - Over-investment theories
3 - Over-indebtedness and "error" theories
4 - Under-consumption theories
5 - Psychological theories
6 - Harvest theories

The common characteristic of all, or nearly all of the preceding theories, is that they are developed largely as a disquisition on the interdependence and causal relationships of economic magnitudes as such, independently from their organic

---

[26] Mitchell alone, in a classification aimed at being charitable to the reader, lists ten types of theories and twenty variants, but warns that twice or five times that amount could put valid claims to the reader's attention. Since the publication of *Business Cycles: The Problem and its Setting*, in 1927, the proliferation of new theories has been such that Mitchell's fears that the abundance of divergent explanations of cyclical behavior would be "confusing rather than illuminating" have proved only too justifiable. The old saying "entia non sunt multiplicanda praeter necessitatem" should apply in this case.

setting.[27] This is the so-called "closed economy approach", which again may take two different forms. The cyclical behavior may be studied in function of abstract economic magnitudes (over-investment, over-saving, etc.) taken as conceptual units isolated from environmental complications; or, alternatively, the cyclical behavior is studied within the confines of institutional or geographic units and the results of the disquisition later generalized. In both cases it happens, not infrequently, that some causal relationships are detected and given universal "validity" as "the" correct theory of the business cycle.

As a last minute concession to realism, scarcely any of the closed system theories fails to mention the need for modification of the theoretical tenets, in face of the existence of fundamental international differences in economic structure. The international factors are, however, held to be merely in the nature of " complicating factors", which do not invalidate the causal relationships discovered for the "closed" or "model" economy. Or, to use Professor Norgenstern's apt expression, "international aspects of the cycle have been developed as appendices to particular theories of causation", centered around the mechanism of business fluctuations in specific countries, considered as independent areas of cyclical movements.[28]

It might well be argued that the "closed economy approach" is nothing but a legitimate methodological device "connatural to economic thought" of isolating complicating factors one by one, before arriving at general relationships. If so conceived, there can indeed be no quarrel with the closed economy approach. In fact, international economic reactions are so complex that for the initial attack to the cycle problem we have, unavoidably, to assume simplified patterns of economic behavior.

A disquieting factor, however—and one that makes us suspect as incorrect use of that methodological device in most of the theorizing that goes under the heading of over-investment, monetary theories, etc.,—is that they propose to be theorems of cyclical causation of general validity, when in reality they describe,

---

[27] Since this study will be primarily concerned with the mechanism of cycle propagation, no systemic analysis will be attempted of the possible international applications of each individual theory, except insofar as our conclusions have a direct bearing on them. The monetary theory, for instance, will be reviewed in connection with the transmission of fluctuations through monetary ligamina, the over- investment theory in connection with cyclical movements of capital and the under-consumption theory in connection with its imperialistic interpretation. Brief notes on the international aspects of each individual theory can be found in Professor Haberler's *Prosperity and Depression* (Geneva, 1941), *passim*. The only detailed and systematic analysis, to our knowledge, is to be found in an unpublished doctoral thesis *International Propagation of Business Cycles* (Harvard University, 1941) by Svend Laursen, to whose courtesy and observation we are greatly indebted.

[28] *Cf.* the illuminating article by Professor Morgenstern, *On the International Spread of Business Cycles* (Journal of Political Economy, LI, 1943), pp. 287-309.

more or less plausibly, the mechanism of generation of trade fluctuations for one particular institutional conspectus and stage of development.[29] The very attempt to arrive at a single causation formula for the business cycle as a whole surmises a static approach to economic reality.[30]

It is quite clear that no "closed system" theory can claim sufficient generality as an explanation of the international cycle. The monetary mechanism of the Hawtreyan type, for instance, has but a limited historical and geographical validity, say, for explanation of British crises in the late 19th Century, but makes little sense if applied to the undeveloped money system of Hungary or Brazil. The overinvestment theories of the Hayekian variety presuppose a certain technological conspectus, including the possibility of selection, by the entrepreneur, of different degrees of roundaboutedness of production, an assumption clearly more appropriate for industrial than for agricultural countries. For the same country at different stages of development the causation of crises may vary. The depression of the seventies in the United States was clearly a case of under-saving (over-investment during the railway boom), while the slump of the thirties had all the characteristics of an over-saving crisis.[31]

Thus the phenomenon of the international cycle running through different and complex economic structures has all but led into discredit the feasibility of a "single causation" or single theory approach in cycle analysis, desirable as it may

---

[29] One of the weakest points in the international application of business cycle theories is the neglect to take into account international changes in economic motivation, which alter the relative importance of the "strategic factors" in business cycle. An explanation of crisis which seems plausible for a mature economy need not be equally valid for an expanding economy. The comparative unimportance of interest rate changes in the trade cycle of "new" countries is a case in point.

[30] Cf. Colin Clark, "Die Internationale Verflechtung Volkswirtscaftlicher Bewegungsvorgänge", in *Weltwirtschaftlichen Archiv* ( November 1935), p. 401: "The theoretical analysis of the problem of economic fluctuations has so far confined itself, by and large, to the study of a "closed system", instead of attacking the much more difficult problem of partly independent and partly dependent economic systems, in which each of the dominant factors is, to an unknown extent, subject to foreign influences".

[31] Cf. E. Lundberg, *Studies in the Theory of Economic Expansion*, (London: 1937), pp. 252-55.

be from the purely scientific standpoint.[32] To judge from the empirical and theoretical work so far erected, the wisest approach might be to interpret the closed economy theorems as fragmentary theories of causation, applicable to particular structural groups, the international cycle not admitting of a uniform explanation but being rather the result of a "Sukzession der Ursachen" ( to use Professor Morgenstern's expression). The closed system theories would thus fall into their proper places as subspecies of a more general theory of economic change and evolution.

But this throws us into the moot question of causation in social sciences. Should we be concerned at all with causation of economic behavior or should we be concerned merely with the discovery of functional relationships or of a "hierarchy of influences", at the most?

The tragedy of the situation is that while only a causal explanation would ultimately satisfy the scientific instinct and provide a firm basic for cycle-control policies, it is fairly obvious, from the abundance and contradiction of the theories, that the variables are too numerous and too complex to allow any definite conclusion as to a precise causal nexus. There is, thus, something to say in favor of a modest functional approach, which concerns itself merely with establishing organic relationships, without passing judgments on the "primus movens" of the system. This is especially true in the international field. In fact, the attempt to formulate theories of causation has been made by using the extremely diluted raw material of abstract models in which the process of isolation of variables via the "coeteris paribus" clause has gone as far as a complete castration of economic reality. Or, when some degree of concreteness is allowed in the theoretical laboratory, it seldom goes beyond the closed domain analysis, in which the actions and reactions are studied within the confine of an artificially isolated economic unit.

In our particular field, the causal approach is further made difficult by the frequent confusion between causes and symptoms of cyclical behavior, or between co-variation and causality. We must keep in mind that in the business cycle, to use

---

[32] Mitchell diverges on this point: "In the progress of knowledge, causal explanations are commonly an early stage in the advance of analytic description. The more complete the theory of any subject becomes in contrast, the more mathematical in form, the less it invokes causation. "...the idea of causation has pragmatic rather than scientific warrant". *Cf. op. cit.*, p. 55. But Mitchell contradicts himself in another page: " ...complexity is no proof of multiplicity of causes. Perhaps some single factor is responsible for all the phenomena. An acceptable explanation of this simple type would constitute the ideal theory from the practical as well as from the scientific viewpoint. " *Ibid.*, p.180. The question is largely a terminological one. If we can define causation broadly as an invariant relationships between two phenomena, or a "necessary and sufficient condition" (Schumpeter), it will clearly be a prerequisite of any scientific knowledge. But if causality is taken as usually to imply a genetic connotation, its applicability in the field of social sciences becomes limited.

Schumpeter's paradoxical expression, the effects may actually precede the causes. To exemplify: The cost increasing feature of the upswing cycle, no clearly brought out by Mitchell, may be divergently interpreted as symptoms of a growing maladjustment of production, or as the cause itself of the maladjustment. The parallel downward movement of international prices in the downswing, while generally considered merely a symptom of a deterioration in real economic factors, may in some circumstances (say in the case of primary producers greatly dependent upon foreign trade) be the primary causal factor in starting a depression. If further refinements are added by the distinction between "causa per quam", or "causa sine qua non" or between "causa efficiens" and "causa cooperans", we risk a futile plunge into social metaphysics that makes very justifiable indeed the unrestrained apology (by the historical and organicist school) of the "functional" and "morphological" approach to economic science.

The importance of the problem should not, however, be exaggerated. To a large extent the functional and causal approaches differ merely in terminological refinement. Although the methodological and conceptual cleavage seems deep, the practical results do not differ in yield. What really matters is the discovery of positive relationships. Whether they exert a causal influence or merely describe an organic interdependence may be, for many purposes, a secondary question.

Another pitfall in business cycle analysis is the crucial concepts of equilibrium. Explanations in terms of under-consumption, over-investment and what not, clearly imply deviations from an optimum equilibrium position, but usually little care is taken in elaborating the concept.

Yet the notion of equilibrium is by no means a crystalline one. The business cycle itself and the recurrence of prolonged depressions have largely done away with the familiar "automatic equilibrium" of the classical theory (based on compensatory movements of factors towards an ideal combination), while the formalistic Walrasian apparatus of general equilibrium has lost determinateness with the development of the theory of imperfect and monopolistic competition. Additional complications have been introduced by the seemingly perpetual disequilibria resulting from technological lags, stickiness of prices, or rigidity of factors, now studied under the name of cobweb theorem.[33] Also it should not be forgotten that some schools of thought, such as the Historical School, and the recent German organicism, deny altogether the usefulness of an equilibrium approach, while oth-

---

[33] *Cf.* Mordecai Ezechiel, "The Cobweb Theorem", in *Quarterly J. Economics* (Feb. 1938), pp. 253-80. *Cf.* also Schumpeter, *op. cit.*, pp. 30-71.

ers, such as the Marxian socialism, see capitalistic evolution as a growing tendency towards disequilibrium.[34]

The sphere of application of equilibrium analysis is also a subject of controversy. From the viewpoint of business cycle theorizing, the general equilibrium analysis would be the only one theoretically satisfactory since the ultimate goal of the theory is to express the movements of the system by the inter-relationships of a few macro-dynamic variables. It often turns out, however, that in order to become mathematically manageable, the general equilibrium approach risks engaging in sterile abstractions or excessive simplification of variables. Thus a more modest approach through the application of the Keynesian aggregative equilibrium analysis, or even of the Marshallian partial equilibrium analysis, might commend itself in some cases as a compromise between imperfection and realism.[35]

At any rate, if the equilibrium concept proves to be an indispensable tool of business cycle analysis, how should it be defined?

The fact that there is not, in a dynamic economy, as noted by Mitchell, any <u>normal</u> state of business, compels one to think in terms of a moving equilibrium, and even so in an accounting sense (profits and losses) rather than in a theoretical sense (factoral equilibrium). But one may chose to keep within theoretical premises and then, following Schumpeter, visualize business cycles as fluctuation not around an imaginary equilibrium point but around zones of equilibrium, so that the system would be at discrete points on the time scale touch "neighborhoods of equilibrium".

The great: emphasis recently placed on practical problems of employment has resulted is a tendency to define equilibrium in relation to an optimum or full employment level (exclusive of frictional or voluntary unemployment). But if, as noted by Neisses, some degree of unemployment is quite compatible with prosperity, should not the equilibrium position be defined merely with relation to total costs (including normal interest on owned capital) and total receipts? Prosperity would then be characterized by an excess of receipts over total costs, and depression by an excess of costs over receipts either in the producer's (under-saving) or

---

[34] Karl Pribam contends that the Marxian reasoning in terms of a <u>declining</u> rate of profit or of <u>underconsumption</u> imply a re-introduction of the normal or equilibrium concept by the back door. For an interesting discussion of the problem, *cf.* his *Equilibrium Concept and Business Cycle Statistics*, Institut International de Statistique, 22nd session (London, 1934).

[35] The general equilibrium approach, based on variation method of the Lausane School (which examines the reaction produced in the whole system by variations in one elements) is considerably more ambitions but frequently less enlightening than isolation method of the English and Austrian School (in which the analysis is confined to the interdependence of certain economic magnitudes considered as relevant).

in the consumer's goods sphere (over-saving). We have, thus, the root of a distinction between an income-equilibrium and an employment-equilibrium concept. They are not, as noted by Professor Williams, invariantly related since, due to the progress of technology, world income has risen relatively to world employment. Technological developments have rendered human labor a relatively, less efficient instrument of production than alternative methods, so that an optimum equilibrium level, in strict theoretical sense, might be better defined with relation to aggregate income rather than to full employment of labor.[36] But since we cannot escape the social painfulness of unemployment, strict theoretical impartiality in the selection of an equilibrium criterium for business cycle policy is well-nigh impossible.

The imprecision and pragmatical character attached to the concepts of "normal" and "equilibrium" cannot be wholly overcome by theoretical refinement and remain a constant reminder of the limitations of business cycle analysis.

A fourth obstacle to the development of an international cycle theory is the deficiency of the empirical basis. The available statistical material on international cycles is heterogeneous and incomplete, both spatially and temporally (covering few countries and relatively short periods). This lack of comparability multiplies the dissension in interpreting empirical data and explains in part the profound disagreement on the etiology and physiognomy of even those individual cycles which have been most thoroughly studied.

We may, at this point, summarize the shortcomings of the conventional business cycle theory, from the international viewpoint:

1. Assumption of a closed system, within which the branches or spheres are analyzed in total or as blocks;
2. Neglect of the impact of national differentiation and structural composition upon the cyclical behavior of economic magnitudes;
3. Loose utilization of the equilibrium concept;
4. Inadequate empirical basis.

It is easier, however, to diagnose errors than to discover correct solutions. And this study, while pointing out the meagerness of the achievements on an international aspects of cycles, is at the same time, a confession of inability to attack the problem on the scale and with the intensity required. We recognize that the speculation is not mature enough nor the ground sufficiently broken for the formulation of a general theory of economic change.

---

[36] John W. Williams, "Deficit Spending", article reprinted in *Post-War Monetary Plans* (New York: Alfred A. Knopf, 1944), pp. 78-9.

There is, nevertheless, an intermediate analytical step, which may bring a significant contribution to future theoretical development: It is the study of the conditions and mechanism of propagation of cycles.[37] The process of percolation of cycles through different economic structures in space and time may indeed throw some light on the two crucial problems of our field of inquiry; the relation of cyclical changes to the stage of economic development and the differentiation of cyclical reactions according to economic structures.

It is to this task that we shall now address ourselves. Our inquiry on the international aspects of economic fluctuations will be divided into three parts:

The first one will deal with the general process of economic propagation and with the international differentiation of economic types.

The second will analyze the three principal vehicles of cycle diffusion, namely, the money system, capital movements and foreign trade. In each case the theoretical aspects will be discussed with a view to determine the fitness of the theory for the cyclical analysis. The actual experience in the transmission of fluctuations will be briefly reviewed.

In the third part we shall discuss the international behavior of two different groups of economic magnitudes; those which exhibit an approximately uniform international cyclical behavior, and those which are to be considered as irregular variations.

In a final chapter the results of the inquiry will be summarized.

---

[37] There are, to my knowledge, only two systematic studies on the theoretical aspects of international economic fluctuations; both are unpublished doctoral dissertations written at Harvard University in 1941. One by Svend Laursen, called *International Propagation of Business Cycles*, and the other by Shang-Kwei-Fong, under the titles *Business Cycles and the International Balance of Payments*.

# PART ONE

## PROPAGATION AND IMPULSE PROBLEMS IN THE ANALYSIS OF INTERNATIONAL CYCLES

# CHAPTER I

# CONCEPTS AND DEFINITIONS

In order to cover a broad range of phenomena we entitled this inquiry a study on the "International Aspects of Economic Fluctuations". This will avoid commitment either to the notion of periodicity or to any particular time-shape of cyclical behavior.[1] To escape cumbersome repetitions, the words "cycle" or "cyclical" frequently replace the less wieldy term "fluctuations". Whenever it is so done, they should be understood in their etymological connotation of "recurrent movements". In some cases the word "fluctuation" will be broadened to cover also structural changes which are so frequently inseparably intertwined with cyclical movements.

Most of the international experience, on which statistical material is available, refers to the major or Juglar cycle. On national and specific cycles, by far the richest collection of statistical data is that of the National Bureau of Economic Research, which refers mostly to the shorter Kitchin or Mitchellian cycles. Recently, thanks to Professor Schumpeter's powerful work, the contours of the Kondratieff, Juglar and Kitchins cycles are rendered more clearly discernible, as far as the three major industrial countries, United States, England and Germany, are concerned.

Our study is, however, quite independent from any particular theory of cycle generation or time-projection. What we are concerned with is to study the general conditions of propagation of fluctuations and the extent to the cyclical behavior is affected by international structural contrasts. In other words, we take for granted the occurrence of cycles in the Mitchellian sense of "alternations of prosperity and depression". The four-phase model—revival, prosperity, recession, and depression—which has won wide acceptance, is also assumed to furnish an appropriate description of cyclical behavior. "Crisis" and "boom" are used to indicate the degree of intensity rather than separate typical phases.

The whole field of business cycle analysis is still with considerable conceptual difficulties, and unfortunately all the attempt to reach very precise definitions and mensurations have yielded so far diminishing returns.[2]

There are two problems at the outset. One concerns the distinction between

---

[1] We are indebted to Professor Donaldson for enlightened suggestions and pointed criticisms on the matter.

[2] For careful methodological discussions, *cf.* Haberler, *op. cit.*, pp. 5-13; Schumpeter, *op. cit.*, pp. 3-29; and Morgenstern, *loc. cit.*

structural and cyclical changes. While prima facie the distinction by the criteria of <u>continuity</u> and <u>recurrence</u> seems obvious, the line of demarcation, in actual observation, is sometimes uncomfortably blurred. The recurrent problem of causality adds fuel to the fire. Are structural change wholly independent phenomena, or are they the affect of cyclical changes? Are they not, per chance, subject to a peculiar long-term cyclical movement of their own? Or, conversely, are not cyclical changes the effect and result of structural shocks?

Much has been made of the distinction between structural and cyclical changes.[3] Structural depressions (resulting from physico-objective conditions, such as exhaustion of mineral resources, acts of nature, etc.) are contrasted with cyclical depressions derived from internal factors of change.[4]

The methodological value of this procedure is unquestionable. The separation of non-rhythmic and constructional changes from rhythmic and functional changes, helps considerably in delimiting and clarifying the problem.[5] It is important, however, to keep in mind the relativity of the two concepts, to realize that both are subspecies of a common dynamic manifestation and that, from broader secular perspective, structural changes may well be but episodes of a cyclical of law of growth and decay. We have thus, at this point, to resort to the question already mentioned at the outset of whether the theory of a particular change makes sense at all if not integrated with a general theory of economic development.

The recent popularity of the "nature economy" or "stagnation" theories, born largely from the striking severity of the last depression, has drawn attention to the persistent disequilibrium tendencies that exist in some of the wealthier industrial societies, afflicted by a milder form of chronic depression or unemployment. This <u>chronic depression</u>, or secular stagnation, is largely traced to oversaving tendencies caused either by the lack of investment opportunities or by under-consumption. Such factors as the "closing of the frontiers", the decline of the rate of population growth (and attending changes in the composition), the increas-

---

[3] Schumpeter distinguishes between "the problem of explaining the mechanism of the cycle" and the "problem of a theory of a concrete factor of individual cycles". *Cf. The Theory of Economic Development* (Harvard University Press, 1934), p. 277.

[4] *Cf.* League of Nations, *Economic Stability in the Post-War World*, pp. 42-4.

[5] Professor E. Wagemen has, to our knowledge, offered the best and most elaborate presentation of the several types of economic changes which he classifies as follow: 1/<u>isolated or structural changes</u> which may be either (a) <u>discontinuous</u> (expansion, transformation, etc.), and 2/<u>periodical fluctuations</u>, which again may appear in a <u>fixed rhythm</u> (seasonal fluctuations), or in a <u>free rhythm</u> (Konjunktur proper). *Cf. Economic Rhythm*, English translation (New York, McGraw Hill Book Co., 1930), chap. 3.

ing share of goods of deferrable demand in total production, changes in income distribution, rigidities of prices and factors, state intervention and war-induced maladjustment in agriculture plus shifts in the geographical location of industry, are all given a share of responsibility for the decline of economic vitality. We thus have three types of depressions, the structural, the cyclical, and the chronic, the latter being defined as the superimposition or coincidence of structural and cyclical changes.[6]

Closely related is the distinction between partial and general depressions (or partial and general over-production, to use Professor Neisser's terminology). The partial depression may be simply the result of lags and unevenness of recovery from a general cyclical depression or may assume structural character, afflicting either particular firms (affected by changes in tastes or technological displacements), or entire areas (exhaustion or destruction of natural resources). The partial depression is always a consequence of lack of mobility of factors of production or rigidity or productive techniques.[7]

The second question concerns the distinction between <u>external</u> and <u>internal</u> factors, which is at the core of Bouniatian's famous dichotomy of exogenous and endogenous factors. From the viewpoint of the closed economy approach, most of the international factors are external. They are listed among the "disturbing" or "complicating" elements and do not form an integral part of the explanations of cycle generation. For the study of propagation of fluctuations, this procedure is obviously unsatisfactory. The line of distinction has to be drawn not in relation to the geographical origin the phenomenon (national or international) but merely with reference to its economic or extra-economic nature.

There always remains, however, an element of arbitrariness since the separation of economic and extra-economic factors depends in itself upon the particular philosophy adapted as to economic evolutions. The discovery of new territories and technological innovations, for instance, are usually regarded as "external factors". There are, nevertheless, good reasons, as pointed out by Schumpeter, to list them among the factors "acting from within the economic sphere", since they are inherent elements of the process of economic evolution. Population changes present a similar problem. They are generally considered as a "datum" of the system and as such listed as "external" factors for the cyclical analysis; but if the population

---

[6] *Cf.* League of Nations, *Economic Stability in the Post-War World*, p. 42

[7] *Ibid.*, chapter II.

changes are due to migrations (i.e., migrations induced by employment fluctuations and not by religious or political oppression) they are clearly bound up with cyclical process itself and cannot be treated as independent "data".[8]

Borderline cases can be multiplied ad infinitum and, thus, it appears that the arbitrariness and conventional character of the old catchword distinctions between the <u>data</u> (or constants) of the system (natural, institutional and technical conditions) and the (variable) economic magnitudes (Tinberghen), or of the Schumpeterian distinction between factors "acting from within or from without the economic sphere" cannot, at this stage, be escaped.

A world may finally be said concerning the, for a while, fashionable expression of "world cycle".

While there have been widely spread fluctuations, truly international in scope, there is no world cycle[9] <u>stricto sensu</u>, since (1) there remain isolated economies more of less cushioned from depression, and (2) there is no exact time-coincidence between crises or revivals in the different countries, so that no economic fluctuation is actually world-wide.

Moreover, the economic disintegration that took place since the First World War, with the emergence of contrasting capitalistic and non-capitalistic areas, and of controlled as against free economies, broke the previous trend towards a world economic order and considerably reduced the meaningfulness of the related concept of "world equilibrium".

---

[8] *Cf.* Harry Jerome, *Migration and Business Cycles* (National Bureau of Economic Research, 1926), *passim*. The study in question shows a significant, though by no means, perfect correlation between fluctuations in the rate of immigration and cyclical undulations in employment opportunity in the United States, the turning point in migration cycles ordinarily following with a certain time-lag that of cycles in industrial activity.

[9] It might be safer to speak of <u>interregional</u> cycles (fluctuations spread between countries belonging to the same production unit), or interstructural cycles (fluctuations spread between complementary economies).

# CHAPTER II

# THE ORIGIN OF INTERNATIONAL FLUCTUATIONS

While there is a wide area of agreement on the empirical fact of high parallelism of cyclical behavior on an international scale, especially among the western industrial nations, which are linked by what Juglar called "la solidarité des grands marchés", there is much less agreement on the question of the origin and location of the disturbances.

Three hypotheses can be advanced:

1. The existence of "Konjunkturfaktoren" acting autonomously and simultaneously on an international scale.
2. The generation of cycles by the process of international friction and structural shocks between conflicting economies.
3. The spreading or diffusion of cyclical movements, or cycle-generating shocks, from a single region throughout the world economy.

## A. The Hypothesis of International "Konjunkturfaktoren"

"The notion of international cyclical factors (International "Konjunkturfaktoren") capable of generating autonomous cycles on an international scale, is, by and large, an upshot of the exogenous cycle theories and especially of the meteorological theories (Jevon, Moore), but is also implied in some interpretations of the innovation theory".[10] The endogenous theories, which as a rule are less sanguine about the single-cause theorem and rely more on a multiple-

---

[10] It is open to question whether the "innovation" theory in Schumpeter's formulation can be regarded as an exogenous theory in Bouniatian's sense. As noted before, Schumpeter himself describes innovation as an inherent feature of the capitalist system and regards it as an internal factor (acting from within the economic sphere). *Cf. Business Cycles*, p. 8. We prefer, however, to follow the general usage in classifying innovations as an exogenous force involving, to use Tinberghon's expression, changes in the "data of the system". The question is, however, one of terminological choice, since "what is to be called an economic and what a non-economic factor or circumstances is frequently rather a matter of convention than of argument". *Cf.* Haberler, *op. cit.*, pp. 8-9.

causation or functional approach, have made little effort to explain the operation of an international cycle mechanism.[11]

In the case the meteorological theories the universality and periodicity[12] of cycles can be logically explained in terms of a cosmic factor—sunspot (Jevons), rain cycle (Moore), cosmic radiation (Garcia-Mata)—acting on an universal scale. The problem would then be not so much to explain the international parallelism of cyclical behavior, but on the contrary to explain the lack of universality of many historical crises and the time-lags between expansion and contraction in several countries.

In the case of the innovation theory one could conceivably explain the international spread of cycles by waves of innovation of international span, which might induce simultaneous and autonomous cycle generation.[13]

Even if we granted the validity of the two theories, the explanation of the international parallelism of fluctuations by the assumption of "Konjunkturfaktoren" would still rest on weak foundations. For, such an explanation faces the fundamental objection that the alternations of prosperity and depression, both nationally and internationally, are not merely a function of the "originating factors" but also

---

[11] A good discussion of the methodological position of the endogenous and exogenous theories, as regards the international comparison of cyclical behavior, can be found in an articles by Morgenstern Ïnternational Vergleichende Konjunkturforschung", in *Zeitschrift für dis Gesamte Staats-Wissenschaft* (Sept. 1928), pp 264-80). *Cf.* also Muhlenfels, "International Vergleichende Konjunkturzusammenhunge", in *Jahrbücher für Nationalaekonomie und Statistik* (June, 1929), pp. 801-05.

[12] The assumption of strict periodicity is another secondary distinction between the exogenous theories ( of the meteorological type) and the endogenous ones. Throughout the more recent literature on cycles, the concept of periodicity has been replaced by that of recurrence. To use Schumpeter's expression, we should envisage cycles as an "irregular regularity " of the economic system.

[13] The innovation theories are under no logical compulsion to claim the existence of universal "Konjunkturfaktoren" as it is the case for the meteorological theories. The cyclical process started by innovations can be just as well simultaneously generated as transmitted from country to country. It even appears that historically the latter has been the case, as one can gather from Schumpeter's masterful array of historical material on the Kondratieff and Juglar cycles. It is possible, however, to interpret the innovation theory as implying cycle generation by the working of a single mechanism operating on an universal or international scale. Some of Schumpeter's statements (otherwise carefully qualified) certainly lend themselves to this interpretation: "Not only do cycles in different countries systematically affect each other, so much so that the history of hardly any one of them can be written without reference to simultaneous cyclical phases in other countries. But cycles really are, especially as regards the great innovations that produce the Kondratieff, international phenomena. That is to may, such a process as the railroadization or the electrification of the world transcends the boundaries of individual countries in such a way as to be more truly described as one world-wide process than as the sum of distinct national ones". *Cf. op. cit.*, vol. II, p. 666.

of the "responses of the business system", to use J.M. Clark's expression. Even if we assume as uniformity of the stimuli or impulses (either meteorological or technological) to cycle movements, there is no reason to assume co-variation of responses, given the difference in structural types and stages of development. Thus, the international parallelism of cyclical behavior—to the extent that such parallelism exists—would still have to be explained.

There are, however, more specific objections to both versions of the international origin of fluctuations.

As regards the meteorological theories, it may be noted that the significance of harvest variations in cycle generation is in itself a controversial matter. It suffices to mention the basic controversy on whether agriculture plays an active or passive role in the origination of fluctuations.[14] Whatever the theoretical viewpoint adopted, three facts are unquestionable: a) the decreasing share of agricultural output in total world output, subsequent to the spreading of the industrialization process, tends to decrease the weight of harvest variations in cycle generation; b) the development of a world market for agricultural produce and the improvements made in techniques of conversation tend to average out the effects of weather induced local variations in crops[15]; c) there is no international pattern or periodicity but rather a wide differentiation of harvest behavior, owing not only to regional and temporal differences in atmospheric conditions but also to different stages of agricultural techniques.[16]

The claim of innovations to the role of "international-Konjunkturfaktoren" meets with similar difficulties. The speed and type of reaction to innovating impulses (and the meaning of innovation itself) are closely related to institutional factors and to stages of economic development, and will therefore differ widely in intensity and direction as between industrialized and agricultural countries, capitalistic and non-capitalistic economies. As an explanation of the international parallelism of cyclical behavior the innovation theory, could at best, claim validity for the limited circle of mature capitalistic countries, within which the institutional resistances to technical changes derive from social and traditional motives rather than from economic and environmental hindrances.

---

[14] For a discussion of the divergent viewpoints, *cf.*, Haberler, *op. cit.*, chapter 7.

[15] *Cf.* Keynes, *The General Theory of Employment, Interest and Money* (New York: Harcourt Brace and Co., Inc. 1939), p. 331

[16] G. Müehlenfels, *loc. cit.*

## B. The Hypothesis of International Attrition

A second possible line of approach is to explain the international co-existence of cyclical fluctuations as a form of economic shock and attrition. Cycles would not be caused by internal maladjustment but rather internal fluctuations would be the repercussion of international shocks.

Under this group fall the theories that link industrial fluctuations to wars and revolutions. It is a matter of common notices that the great depressions have come in wake of wars. The crisis of 1825 followed the Napoleonic wars, the depression of the seventies the Franco-Prussian and Crimean wars, and the great slump of the thirties, the first World War. Ciriacy Wantrup has pointed out the interesting association noticeable in the nineteenth century between warlike expansion and the upswing of the long wave, while depression seems to be the natural outcome of the structural changes and adjustments that follow in the wake of wars and revolutions.[17] Others point out the association of the rising wave with wars, and of the falling wave with revolutions and social disturbances.

It is, moreover, quite possible, as pointed out by Professor Donaldson, to construct a consistent and self-perpetuating scheme of cycles on the basis of the social phenomenon of war. The phase of warlike expansion would bring about an upward fluctuation, while creating at the sometime serious disruptions and dislocations in the international productive structure resulting from the war-produced imbalances in trade and in the international debt structure. The subsequent readjustment and absorption of structural changes would in itself bring about a downward movement. The depression, in turn, would sharpen economic conflict, aggravate social instability and plant the seeds of a new war with the familiar chain of expansions and contractions.

The broad range of social phenomena affecting business life and business psychology makes it impossible either to prove or to refute conclusively any of those historical hypotheses. As it is often said in social phenomena more than in any branch of sciences correlation is no proof of causation. By a careful selection of <u>external</u> factors it is indeed possible to construct a plausible explanation of any international fluctuations. But the case for an "International" rather than "national" origin of economic fluctuations, by the process of attrition, cannot be demonstrated until it is proved that business cycles are purely accidental phenomena and not <u>an inherent mode of behavior</u> of individual economies operating on a profit system and utilizing roundabout methods of production.

---

[17] For a critical discussion of this, as well as of the monetary (Cassel) and innovation (Spisthoff, Schumpeter) hypotheses on the long waves, *cf.*, A. Hansen, *Fiscal Policy and Business Cycles* (New York: W.I. Norton & Co. Inc., 1941), pp. 27-41.

Now, all the available evidence points to the fact that, quite independently from international attrition, economic fluctuations may occur within single economies, simply by the cumulative effect of production disadjustments,[18] although it is quite true that external factors may influences the strength or the transmission of the shock and may even, in certain cases, play a causal role.

We hold, therefore, that there is a great deal of plausibility in the contention that trade fluctuations have a national or regional origin, as point of start, the shock being afterwards transmitted internationally. The fact that the international cycle in seldom perfectly synchronous but always occurs with certain leads and lags, plus the prevalent differences in intensity and duration, seems to indicate that the international cycle can best be explained by the propagation of local movements. This, of course, is not meant to deny the possibility of simultaneous operation of cyclical starters in more than one country or region. We claim merely that the international cycle is a composite of autonomous and induced national cyclical movements and not necessarily the result of an international "Konjunkturfaktoren", be it meteorological, technological or social.

It has been possible in some cause to identify historically the epicenter of fluctuations. Thus, the crisis of 1873 was of German origin, is that of 1921 started with the silk speculation in Japan, while the Stock Exchange crash of 1929 in the United States is generally considered the starting point of the last depression.

Thus, by way of exclusion, we come to accept the third hypothesis of diffusion of cycles or shocks. This will introduce us to the study of the mechanism of propagation of fluctuations.

---

[18] The micro or macro-dynamic models of cyclical oscillations (Samuelson, Kalecki, etc.) are predicated on this assumption. *Cf.* Haberler, *op. vit.*, p. 473.

# CHAPTER III

# THE PROCESS OF PROPAGATION OF CYCLES

We assume as a working hypothesis that cycles or cycle-inducing shocks originate in particular strata, nations or regions, and irradiate from those epicenters, or "center of diffusion" (to use Mitchell's phrase) to other economic areas. The basic problem to be investigated will be therefore the mechanism of propagation of economic fluctuations.

## A. Psychological and Economic Transmission

In broad terms, we may speak of economic or psychological processes of transmission. In the first case, the process of diffusion will be made either through impersonal market relationships between two countries, or through direct links between economic units in different areas, independently from market phenomena.[19] In the second case, through purely psychological contamination of individuals from within different economic spheres.

Actually, the economic transmission involves, in the majority of cases, inextricably interwoven psychological elements, some spheres being more and others less vulnerable to the vagaries of mess psychology. The most conspicuous examples of psychological transmission are the financial markets which, as it is well known, act in response to a variety of motives, either economic or extra-economic, and are subject to what one may call "imitation cycles" that cannot be readily accounted for, at least in their inception, by any disproportionality of real economic magnitudes. The relative importance of psychological or economic elements will depend, of course, on the type of shock transmitted.

If we adopt Bouniatian's morphology, i.e., crises of exchange media (money and credit), commercial crises (commodity and capital) crises of production (industrial and agricultural), it will be readily seen that the psychological transmission is much more important in the credit and capital type of crisis than in the trade or production crises. In Spiethoff's scheme, psychological elements are comparatively more important in the transmission of "stock market "crises than of the commercial crisis proper.

---

[19] Here the concepts of "international affiliation of enterprise" discussed by Professor Donaldson comes to mind. Cyclical shocks can be directly transmitted between affiliated companies in different countries before and independently from their reception in the national markets. An autonomous depression, say, in the United States, may star a contracting movements in affiliated branches of industrial enterprises abroad, even before the impact of cyclical shocks is felt in the markets of the countries of operation.

## B. Direction of Transmission

Borrowing the concept of horizontal and vertical maladjustments, familiar to the over-investment theories, we can speak a vertical or horizontal propagation of the cycle either nationally or internationally, since the mechanical process is substantially the same. The vertical diffusion is the normal process of propagation between vertically integrated economies, connected by relations of complementariness, while the horizontal spreading would operate principally among regions of similar structural composition. The two oscillations usually operate simultaneously in both directions.

The international diffusion of economic fluctuations in the vertical sense may originate from the interdependence created by:

a) Division of the same productive process among several countries, or regions (Produktionserteilung), such as exists between the higher and lower stages of production, semi-manufactures and finished products.[20]
b) International division of production, lato sensu, resulting from the specialization of labor, such as between the industrial and the agrarian sphere, or between the producers' and consumers' goods industries.
c) Financial complementarity such as exists between capital-surplus and capital importing countries.

## C. The Area of Cyclical Fluctuations

1. Autonomous and Induced Changes. According to the nature of the originating impulse, we should distinguish between autonomous and internationally-induced fluctuations. While the theoretical distinction is obvious, the actual separation of the autonomous from the international elements of change is an almost hopeless task for the investigator. As pointed out by Professor Morgenstern, an unambiguous or quantitative separation of national and international influences will have to remain for the moment a distant goal.

Statistical data show merely the composite phenomenon but do not allow us to detect, except grosso modo, the autonomous or induced nature of the cyclical components. The question of timing presents an additional complication. An autonomous change in period I may be propagated to other countries and may be

---

[20] This feature of the present economic organization, which has been called the "internationalization of industrial structures" is a major factor in spreading booms and depressions, and explains to a large extent the parallelism of cyclical fortunes of western industrial nations. Cf. A. Mühlenfels, "Internationale Konjunkturzusemmenhänge", in *Jahrbüsher für Nationaloekonomie und Statistik*, (CXXX, 1929), p. 803.

received back and give rise to induced movement in subsequent periods. This involves the perplexing problems of "leads and lags", which complicates "ad infinitum" the possible direction of cyclical forces.

2. <u>Regional and Functional Relationships</u>. It would be pertinent to explore here some basic concepts which have been transplanted uncritically from the "closed economy" approach to the international analysis of business cycles.

One of the most common assumptions is that the countries set one upon another as <u>economic blocks or units</u>. Those units are made to coincide with the actual geographic areas, which are thus conceived as starting points for business cycles.

To a certain extent, the utilization of the concepts of geographical units as "independent areas of cyclical variations" is a methodological necessity since, as pointed out by Pribram, "time-series of economic magnitudes and indices are more or less the by-products of administrative statistics".

If we take, however, a deeper view of the block-economy concept, its inadequacy becomes obvious. It is, in particular, open to objections on two counts; lack of a functional and of a structural approach.

a) The several strata of a single economic system are not a compact unit but show a variable degree of coalescence. Some of the economic spheres, specially the financial markets, show a functional rather than a geographical behavior. There is a more intimate connection, for instance, between the money markets of London and New York, than between the latter and the wheat market of Chicago. International cycles in specific industries, cutting across national frontiers, are now historically and statistically identifiable. The economies come in contact through a wide variety of channels, exchange markets, capital movement, raw material prices and stocks, investment, etc., which are different per countries and per periods of time, and which react with variable degrees of sensitivity.[21] In some cases, it is not the general cycle of one country that counts for the projection of international effects, but rather one specific cycle. The relevant international component of economic fluctuations in Chile, for instance, is the activity in the copper-using electrical industries in the United States and elsewhere, which may or may not show a high degree of agreement with the general reference cycle.

b) From the viewpoint of the cyclical behavior, the structural regions or structural types are much more relevant than geographic units. The assumption of geographic areas (identified by the criteria of language, monetary system, culture or political sovereignty) is borrowed from the traditional international trade theory

---

[21] As an institutionalist, Mitchell is quite aware of the problem (witness his very balanced statement on p. 456 of the 1927 edition of *Business Cycle*, although he seems sometimes to loss sight of the heterogeneity of structural composition, which restricts considerably the comparability of economic fluctuation and the validity of the measurements of average duration attempted in the "Annals".

but is no more adequate for cycle analysis than it is for international trade theory. Berteil-Ohlin's reformulation widened considerably the horizon of the international trade theory: zones of endowment of productive factors (localization principle) rather than administrative units become the point of departure for the analysis. A similar approach is required for the development of international cycle theory: the <u>multiple-market</u> analysis would have its counterpart in a <u>multiple-strata</u> cyclical transmission. The regions of productive factors would have their counterparts in structural relationships. While in international trade theory, at least in its earlier formulation, the predominance of commodity trade and the importance of transportation costs rendered necessary a more or less strict adherence to regional markets in the territorial sense, in the cyclical theory, owing to the enormous variety of transmission channels—trade, investment, migration, finance, mass psychology—one may conceive of regions in a wider sense, so as to include functional relationships (by structural similarity or complementarity) rather than purely locational connections.

# CHAPTER IV

# PROPAGATION AND IMPULSE PROBLEMS

## A. The Type of Shock

Besides the question of the areas and origin of economic changes, we have to consider the fundamental problem of the type of change transmitted.

As pointed out by Professor Morgenstern, the concept to "international spreading of fluctuations" is susceptible of several interpretations. There may be transmissions of:

1. <u>Erratic shocks</u> (panic, war, inflation) transmitted by one country and absorbed by another. A host of problems present themselves in this connection, such as the magnitude and duration of the shock, part of the economy affected, phases of the cycle, etc.
2. <u>Isolated shocks</u>, which are not absorbed and which give rise to cyclical movements. Random shocks not absorbed may generate a cyclical process in the receiving country. We would then have a shock-induced cycle.
3. <u>Complete cycles</u>, this phenomenon will occur especially in the case of complementary or closely related economies (say Great Britain, and Denmark). In this hypothesis there would be a close correspondence of phases either with simultaneity of movements or with leads and lags.[22]

## B. The Swinging Mechanism

Professor Frisch has called attention to the important distinction between propagation and impulse problems, which was first adumbrated by Wicksell.[23] The propagation problem is essentially a study of the structural properties of the <u>swinging system</u>, which determine the "length of the cycle and the tendency towards dampening", while the intensity (amplitude) of the fluctuations is deter-

---

[22] *Cf.* O. Morgenstern, "On the International Spread of Business Cycles", in *Journal of Political Economy* (August, 1943), LI, p. 292.

[23] Wicksell devised the famous illustration which gives a humorous description of the difficult problems connected with the stimulus to, and reactions of the economic mechanism: "If you hit a wooden rocking horse with a club, the movement of the horse will be very different from the movement of the club." "Wicksell mentions innovations and inventions as irregular shocks capable of generating cyclical fluctuations. *Cf.* Ragner Frisch, "Propagation and Impulse Problems", in *Economic Essays in Honor of Gustav Cassel* (London, 1933), p. 121.

mined primarily by the external impulse. The impulse problem involves, on the other band, the consideration of the erratic shocks capable of disturbing the normal dampening tendencies. Firsch's study gives new emphasis to the usual distinction between the external impulses and "response of the business system" and opens wide vistas to the infinite complexity of impulse propagation combination. If the present development of analysis is inadequate even for an isolated single swinging system (there is not as yet in fact any quantitative analysis of the determinant elements in macrodynamic terms), the difficulties are a fortiori greater in the international field. The initial task to be undertakes, as a crude approximation, would be classification of economic structure and of their degree of functional inter-relationships.[24] <u>Faute de mieux</u>, this effort has to confine itself modestly to the analysis of the groups relations of similarity and complementarity, from the viewpoint of cyclical behavior. Within each swinging system there would be, of course, a wide differentiation of structural composition (such as relative importance of producers' goods, proportion of foreign trade to national income, composition of foreign trade, phases of industrial development, etc.) but certain general patterns of cyclical behavior could undoubtedly be discerned.

A more ambitious task would be that of supplementing the classification of spatial relationships with a scheme of temporal relationships. The aim would then be not only to compare simultaneous cycles of several countries, but to draw a "cross section of time", and compare the cyclical behavior according to the stage of economic development. In this way, for instance, a cycle undergone by the United States in the early stages of industrialization (1860) would be compared with a current cycle in Brazil, which is now traversing approximately the same phase of development. An investigation of this sort really exceeds, however, the possibilities of statistical and historical verification by any individual investigator.

1. <u>Economic Typology as a Starting Point for the Study of Transmissions</u>. The physiognomy of the international economic fluctuations will thus depend not only on the intensity of the impulse but also on the peculiar reactions of the swinging mechanism. In other words, we may describe a transmitted cycle as the final outcome of the interplay of factors of affinity (which tend to facilitate and uniformize the spread of cycles) and factors of resistance (which tend to localize and differentiate). The ratio between the factors to affinity and factors of resistance will determine the degree of <u>openness</u> or sensitiveness of a country to foreign-induced fluctuations.

While, from the viewpoint of the closed system, analysis, structural conditions may be taken as constant and ignored, the situation is altogether different

---

[24] Professor Morgenstern has pointedly called attention to the lack of a method for classification of economic types and forms ( Wirtsohaft typen, Wirtschaftsformen), which is an indispensable analytical tool for international comparisons of cyclical behavior. *Cf.* Morgenstern, "Internationale Vergleichende Konjunkturforschung", in *Zeitschrift für die Gesant Steats-Wissenschaft* (1927), p. 273.

from the international viewpoint. The analysis of structural composition and structural changes is basic for the understanding of the international cyclical behavior, under two respects:

(a) as an <u>initiating</u> factor; structural changes may in themselves originate business fluctuations. Witness the effects of the artificial stimulation of agricultural production during the last war on the commodity crisis of 1921. (b) as a <u>conditioning</u> factor. The same impulse may provoke different cyclical responses according to the structural composition of the country. A decrease in the export demand for products of a mining country is, for instance, reflected in a relative fall of both prices and output; a decrease in demand for agricultural products provokes a fall in prices but usually does not elicit a fall in output and may even increase the total agricultural effort.

Furthermore, it is of interest to note that the structural composition itself may be subject to changes during the business cycle, because of the latter's influence on the specialization of production. While in the long run, barring artificial tariff effects, specialization is governed by comparative costs and localization of resources, in the short run it may be affected by course of the cycle itself. For instance, depression in one agricultural country, accompanied ordinarily by exchange depreciation and deterioration of the terms of trade, may render profitable industries which would not be competitive given a more favorable export-import ratio. In some countries, such as Brazil and Argentina, the last depression, characterized by a violent slump in the prices of exported raw materials and only a slight fall in prices of imported manufactures, acted as a stimulate to local production of previously imported goods. The reverse phenomenon occurs in luxury goods industries, which become sub-marginal in depression and intra-marginal in prosperity. The migration of populations from city to country in depressions, and vice versa in prosperity, with the subsequent shift in regional specialization, is a well known phenomenon. The influence is therefore bi-directional; the economic structure conditions the course of the cycle, and is in turn affected by it.

The study of economic structure will bring realism and precision to the spaceless and abstract magnitudes that abound in cycle theory. It places under new light both the theoretical question of whether there is any point at all in the attempt to formulate a theory of cycles on basic of conditions prevailing in a particular type of capitalistic evolution, and the practical questions of whether a general cyclical control policy is at all possible. Economic typology introduces an element of relativism in the cycle theory. For countries of different economic structures, different theories of causation will apply. Thus the monetary theory of the Hawtreyian type, or the over-investment theories of the Hayekian variety will appear as rationalizations of economic behavior of certain financial and industrial structures. The possibility of different cycle generating shocks in different countries and in different times will become clear. In this way harvest variations, over-investment and under-consumption can be envisaged as equally plausible modes of cyclical reaction for different economic organisms, or for different stages of development. Along these lines Professor Neisses has suggested that the American depression of the 1930-ies may well have had over-saving as the causal factors; the same crisis in Germany assumed the forms of an under-saving, while in England the deflation was imposed by foreign trade factors. Lundberg has also suggested that in the course of time both scarcity of capital and inadequate consumer spending may take turns in cyclical generation, according to the current institutional conspectus.

2. <u>Classification of Economic Structures</u>. Any essay on economic typology is rendered difficult by the multiplicity of criteria that may be adopted according to whether one chooses an economic, historical, or geographical viewpoint. The most elementary but still useful category is the standard differentiation between industrial and agrarian economies, or between industrial and frontier economies.[25] Although the terms are dangerously loose and fail to express finer shades of development, they still retain usefulness as indicators of broad structural contrasts. Starting from a socio-psychological viewpoint we might, with B. Harms, speak of consumption economies (Konsumptionswirtschaften), or profit (Erwebswirtschaften), or following Sombart's classification, enterprises (Unternehmung, Erwerbprinzip) economies, and handicraft or subsistence economies (Bedarfsdeckungprinzip). Politico-economic considerations are likely in the future to affect cyclical behavior a great deal more than heretofore, so that a distinction between free and controlled economies is imperative. The latter might still be more finally differentiated as between orientated, planned and directed economies.

We shall subsequently discuss two of the most suggestive sketches of economic types, one laying stress on the intensity of economic development and form of organization, and the other on the historical evolution of economic types.

(a) <u>Wageman's Classification</u>. The first classification, suggested by E. Wageman, taken into account both the evolutive and the structural criteria. The basic economic structures are differentiated according to degree of intensity of development and to the form of organization as shown below:

Intensity of development:
    1. The non-capitalist
    2. The neo-capitalist
    3. The semi-capitalist
    4. The mature-capitalist
Form of organization:

---

[25] *Cf.* John Donaldson, *International Economic Relations* (1928), where examples of both historical and structural classifications can be found.

1. Consumptive economies - free
                              - controlled
2. Lucrative economies - free
                              - controlled

The first group refers to the intensity of development and is linked to the inter-relationship of productive factors. So, in the mature capitalistic economies both capital and labor are applied intensively per unit of territory; in neo-capitalistic countries both capital and labor are extensively applied, while in semi-capitalistic countries labor is intensive but capital extensive.

While the line of demarcation is far from neat, a fairly accurate delimitation of the main groups can sketched. In the following table Wagemen outline a possible scheme of classification, the _intensiveness_ or _extensiveness_ of labor being measured by proportion of population per square kilometer, and the degree of capitalization by the money value of machinery consumption per capita, foreign trade and proportion of finished articles in export and import.

## Table IV
### Economic Types, Classified According to Intensity of Development

|  | Population per sq.Km | Consumption of Machinery | | Foreign Trade Turnover RMks | Finished Articles as Percentage of Total | |
|---|---|---|---|---|---|---|
|  |  | Per Capita Index | Per sq.Km. RMks |  | Imports | Exports |
| **1. MATURE CAPITALISM** <br> a. Europe (excluding Russia & Turkey) | 85 | 20 | 1706 | 376 | 28 | 61 |
| b. United States | 15 | 125 | 1845 | 326 | 21 | 33 |
| c. Japan | 162 | 6 | 997 | 131 | - | - |
| **2. SEMI CAPITALISM** <br> a. Russia (European) | 20 | 5 | 97 | 24 | 37 | 5 |
| b. Asia (excluding Japan and Asiatic Russia) | 40 | 0.5 | 20 | 35 | 54 | 9 |
| **3. NEO-CAPITALISM** <br> a. Central & South America | 4.4 | 6 | 27 | 222 | 67 | 2 |
| b. Australia | 0.8 | 47 | 36 | 981 | 81 | 8 |
| c. South Africa | 6.1 | 1.3 | 81 | 387 | 76 | - |
| **4. NON-CAPITALIST COUNTRIES** (Asiatic Russia, Belgian Congo, French West Africa, Sudan, etc.) | 2.1 | - | - | - | - | - |

These countries represent:

|  | Population in Millions | Area in Million Square Kilometers |
|---|---|---|
| Mature-capitalism | 554 | 23 |
| Semi-capitalism | 1018 | 30 |
| Neo-capitalism | 106 | 30 |
| Non-capitalism | 58 | 58 |
| **Total** | **1736** | **110** |

Source: E. Wageman, *Economic Rhythm* (New York: Mc Graw Book Co., 1930)

In mature capitalistic countries, economic fluctuations are usually reflected in larger fluctuations in employment and output than in prices. In semi- and neo-capitalistic countries output is less elastic and is comparatively irresponsive to price changes. Depression is usually manifested by a drastic fall in export prices, while output (except in forestry and mining) may prove fairly stable. The drop in employment will not be spectacular but will take the form of "disguised unemployment" by an increase of labor surplus in farming areas. The working out of fluctuations in income levels is also different for capitalistic areas, which possess mechanized instruments of production, and for semi-capitalistic countries. In the former, due to the availability of technological apparatus, production is much more elastic, its value depending largely on the ebb and flow of the monetary stream; in the latter due to the lack of technological equipment, the monetary expansion is likely to reach much earlier the inflationary point. The reagibility to interest rates is also much more marked in capitalist than in semi-capitalist countries, for, in the latter, the scarcity of capital stock renders the marginal productivity of capital much greater than in countries where capital is plentiful.

In general, the modes of reaction are governed by the position of the economy in relation to the two extreme types; the economies geared to profit (accumulative) and the economics geared to consumption (subsistence type). The same country, of course, can have different regional morphology. The phenomenon of isolated coastal towns (e.g., in China, Brazil, Argentina, or India) which have price reactions and general cyclical behavior quite different from backward inland areas, is quite well known.

The emergence of the planned and controlled economies has led Wageman to emphasize still another aspect of economic organization that affects profoundly the modes of economic behavior. It will suffice to note the comparative unimportance of the price stimulus in the export trade of Russia or in the trade of Japan and Germany within their spheres of influence, to realize the import of the difference in economic motivation between free and controlled economies. These considerations are, of course, outside the scope of the conventional cycle theory, which postulates a certain institutional atmosphere of the capitalistic type. It remains true, however, that any international theory of cycles would have to include also the study of fluctuations in semi-or neo-capitalistic areas or even in controlled economies as a sub-species. It is, for instance, quite conceivable that the controlled economies, which claim to have eliminated the cyclical disease, might well be subject to peculiar cycles of their own. The errors of optimism and pessimism of entrepreneurs which generate fluctuations in free capitalistic economies, might have their counterpart in errors planning. Or else, a cumulation of <u>random</u> shocks might induce periodical oscillations according to the Slutsky's model. Or, still the recurrent ebbs and flows of economic activity in free economy areas may exert their impact and cause recurrent disturbances of economic planning, not to speak of meteorological and climatic factors which are continuously impinging upon the economic organism.

(b) <u>Colin Clark's Classification</u>. Another interesting analysis of economic types has been recently presented by Colin Clark. He defined economic types with relation to the distribution of population among different groups of productive activity; primary, secondary, and tertiary industries. Primary industries are defined as agriculture, forestry, and fishing; secondary industries as manufacturing, mining, and building; the tertiary industries, in turn, include commerce, transport, services and the balance of economic activities.

The growth of the tertiary is not directly related to the extent of industrialization but to the level of income. In the United States, Great Britain, Canada, Australia and New Zealand, roughly one-half of the population is engaged in tertiary industries, while for other European countries and Argentina the share is from 33 to 40 per cent.

A temporal law of development is formulated; the proportion of population engaged in agriculture is hold to be constantly declining and that of tertiary increasing. The proportion of population devoted to secondary industries is found to rises to a maximum and then to begin falling off, indicating apparently that each country reaches a maximum industrialization point beyond which industry begins to decline relatively to tertiary production.[26] Primary, and especially secondary industries, have in the course of time showed a larger increase in productivity than tertiary industries. The Malthusian theory which implies an inverse relationships between the trend of real income per head, and the rate of growth of population, finds some measure of confirmation only for agricultural countries, while for industrial countries it does not hold, and even the reverse may be true.

---

[26] *Cf.* Colin Clark, *The Conditions of Economic Progress* (London: McMillan, 1941), p. 7.

## Table V
### Percentage Distribution of Occupied Population Current Figures
### (Most Recent Census)

|  | Primary | Secondary | Tertiary |
|---|---|---|---|
| United States | 19.3 | 31.1 | 49.6 |
| Canada | 34.5 | 23.2 | 42.3 |
| Argentina & Uruguay | 22.6 | 43.0 | 34.4 |
| Great Britain and Northern Ireland | 6.4 | 43.9 | 49.8 |
| Eire | 49.6 | 16.2 | 34.2 |
| Rest of America | 37.9 | 27.9 | 34.2 (Chile*) |
| Norway | 35.3 | 26.5 | 38.2 |
| Sweden | 32.3 | 29.2 | 38.5 |
| Denmark & Iceland | 35.7 | 27.5 | 36.8 |
| Finland | 51.0 | 39.4 | 18.6 |
| France | 25.0 | 39.7 | 35.3 |
| Spain | 57.0 | 24.6 | 18.4 |
| Portugal | 47.6 | 52.4 | |
| Holland | 20.8 | 39.2 | 40.0 |
| Belgium-Luxembourg | 17.1 | 47.8 | 35.1 |
| Germany-Austria | 24.3 | 38.5 | 37.2 |
| Switzerland | 21.3 | 44.9 | 32.8 |
| Italy | 42.9 | 31.1 | 26.0 |
| Baltic States | 57.7 | 19.8 | 22.5 |
| Poland | 61.6 | 18.0 | 20.3 |
| Czechoslovakia | 27.3 | 43.6 | 29.1 |
| Hungary | 54.1 | 24.8 | 21.8 |
| Balkans | | | |
| Greece * | 44.2 | 33.9 | 21.9 |
| Bulgaria * | 67.3 | 17.4 | 15.3 |
| Australia | 24.4 | 29.4 | 46.2 |
| New Zealand | 27.1 | 24.2 | 48.7 |
| U.S.S.R. | 74.1 | 15.4 | 10.5 |
| Japan | 50.3 | 19.5 | 30.2 |
| India & Burma | 62.4 | 14.4 | 23.2 |
| China | 75.0 | 5.0 | 20.0 |
| W. Asia | | | |
| Thailand * | 84.1 | 2.2 | 13.7 |
| Turkey * | 73.1 | 11.5 | 15.4 |
| Palestine * | 52.6 | 17.9 | 28.5 |
| S.E. Asia | | | |
| Java | | | |
| The Islands | | | |
| Africa | 85.0 | 15.0 | |

\* Only countries for which Census data available.

For sources, *cf.* Colin Clark, *The Economics of 1960* (London: McMillan Co. 1944), p. 71.

Although Colin Clark, being primarily interested in secular trends, does not attempt to link his structural classification to shorter cyclical undulations, some interesting inferences for the cyclical analysis can be drawn, along the Keynesian line of thought, from his observations on the capital exponent and on the relationships between income and consumption. In this description farm capital is the first one to be accumulated, followed by capital for railways. Industrial and commercial capital form the next stage but in mature wealthy communities new accumulation consists primarily of building construction. When manufacturing industries reach the point of capital maturation, only housing, public utilities and replacement will offer an outlet for savings.[27] Investment and replacement waves would, then, in industrial societies constitute an equivalent to the element of periodicity introduced by variations of crop yields in agricultural societies.

Another important observation concerns the well known fact of a low income-elasticity of demand for food products (Engels' law), contrasting with much higher elasticities for manufactures and services. Since the growth in demand for products bears no proportion to the relative growth in productivity of each of the three industries, the economies are bound to suffer from violent maladjustments and increased instability.

Wageman's and Colin Clark's classifications are both relevant by drawing attention to structural characteristics, which have a direct bearing upon economic fluctuations, and which have been largely neglected in the study of business cycles. Obviously, the differentiation of cyclical reactions among the several economic types is of such a nature that the methodological device of studying cycles separately from the "international complications" presents grave dangers.

It is a familiar observation that the growth of industry and the maturation of capitalistic institutions, by widening the margin of economic choice (or the "space of economic maneuver") and increasing the deferrability of expenditures, as well as the role of anticipations, have added to the vulnerability of the system to economic fluctuations. Along this line of thought, Mitchell envisages business cycles as by-products of the money economy, while Sombart has attributed their emergence to the liberation of modern industry from the limitations of organic production.

Granted that the typical business cycle is primarily a phenomenon of certain types of capitalistic development, the question that now presents itself is whether, and to what extent, neo- and semi-capitalistic economies share in the cyclical fortunes of mature industrial societies. Now, it is generally agreed that the

---

[27] *Cf.* Colin Clark, *ibid.*, p. 13. This amounts actually to a pessimistic theory of economic growth, in mechanical terms, as compared to the Malthusian theory formulated in biological terms. By contrast, Schumpeter's interpretation would be described as an optimistic theory of capitalistic evolution.

progress of transportation, the "internationalization of capital" and the development of channels of trade have increased the vulnerability of agrarian economics to shocks originating not from meteorological factors, but from fluctuations in the foreign demand for their products. In addition to autonomous cycles, resulting from variations in crop yields, they are increasingly subject to fluctuations of the passive or adaptive type. That much is clear.

More controversial is the question of the relative intensity of economic fluctuations. It has been contended, for instance, that industrial economies, deeply affected by the highly volatile investment magnitude, are inherently more unstable than agrarian economies of the consumptive type. Now, it is true that the sensitiveness to, and the relative intensity of, economic fluctuations is closely related to degree of capitalization and financial organization. The violence of fluctuation cannot, however, be measured in absolute terms and the typical severity of agricultural depressions would seem to indicate that the difference lies less in the degree of intensity than the form of manifestation.[28]

As noted before, crises in the agrarian sphere are primarily price crises; output is relatively stable and unemployment does not assume spectacular proportion but is rather concealed under the form of "disguised unemployment", or periodical surpluses of farm labor. The capitalistic "Expansionskonjunktur", on the other hand, is largely an output-employment phenomenon. This, however, does not tall us anything concerning the severity of the depressions. Even small fluctuations, in absolute terms, may represent in semi- and neo-capitalistic countries an appreciable narrowing of the margin between real income and subsistence level, implying in relative terms a much more severe disturbance than the wide swings of manufacturing activities and incomes.

---

[28] Data of the League of Nations showing percentage income falls in various industrial and agrarian countries, during the last depression, do not offer conclusive evidence as to the relative degree of stability:

**Percentage Fall in National Income (1929–1932)**

| Industrial Countries | | Agrarian Economies | |
|---|---|---|---|
| United States | 40 | Hungary | 48 |
| Great Britain | 12 | Roumania | 47 |
| Germany | 39 | Australia | 34 |
| Japan | 21 | New Zealand | 34 |
| France | 16 | Greece | 30 |

(Adapted from the League of Nations, *World Economic Survey* (1935–1936), p. 104.

# CHAPTER V

# INTERNATIONAL STRUCTURAL RELATIONSHIPS AND PROPAGATION OF TYPES

## A. Complementary and Similarity Relationships

We are more directly concerned, at this point, with general structural relationships, insofar as they the propagation of economic fluctuations. All of the several possible methods of classification of economic types, mentioned before, are relevant to our study at one stage or another, but we shall for the moment confine ourselves to the broad group-relationships, from the viewpoint of their degree resistance or conductivity to the spread of cycles.

The international spread of cycles follow the line of least resistance. Under this criterium, the countries may be related to one another by:
- structural complementarity
- structural similarity
- structural dissimilarity

As noted before, the case of structural complementariness presents the most propitious ground for cyclical propagation. This complementarity may stem from the division of the <u>same productive process</u> between two or more countries, from the international specialization in branches of production (e.g., the raw-materials and the industrial sphere), or still, from financial relationships (debtor-creditor, exchange reserve and member countries, connections, etc.)

The most obvious case of complementary between dissimilar economies is the implied in the usual dichotomy of industrial countries and agrarian countries (agriculture and mining). But, within the industrial sphere, there are complementary relations extremely conducive to synchronization of cyclical fortunes, such as for instance the phenomenon of division of same productive process among several countries (internationalization of the productive structure). The vertical integration of industrial enterprises, which places centralized control different stages of production developing outside the national boundaries, is a good example of the growing importance of functional relationships.

The financial complementariness creates also an additional element of cyclical outsides. Debtor countries are immediately affected by the cyclical behavior of creditor and nations and by fluctuations in the rate of capital imports. In this sense, it is possible to speak of lending and borrowing cycles. The case of special exchange relationships (reserve and member countries in the gold exchange system) is less obvious but nevertheless important.

Complementarity relationships may exist between economies completely dissimilar in organization, resources or stage of development, or between countries dissimilar in productive resources but similar stage or development, such as for instance, Great Britain and Denmark. The complementarity of relations that exist between industrialized countries themselves are, of course, less obvious; they refer to specific markets and branches of production rather than to the aggregate economic structure. In this case it is not the general cycle but rather specific cycles that are important from the international viewpoint.

For countries connected by relations of complementarity, lato sensu, the industrial and financial center usually sets the pace for (or at least has a predominant influence on) the cyclical behavior of the smaller country. Business conditions in Argentina, Denmark, or South African are, to a large extent, a reflex of conditions of British business. As noted by Professor Morgenstern,[29] it might be possible, by enlarging the application of the concept of reference cycle used by National Bureau of Economic Research, to consider the general cycle of the former as the international reference cycle or chief international influence upon the behavior of the latter. If the complementariness relation is confined to certain lines of production or markets, the specific cycles rather than the reference cycle would have to be considered as the dominant international influence.[30]

The possibility of transmission of cycles between complementary economies are obviously numerous. Not only cycle-inducing shocks but complete cycles can be transmitted through changes in the balance of trade, in the rate of capital movements, etc. The cyclical behavior in the receiving country may be parallel or inverse, synchronous or lagged.

The case of similarity between economic structures presents also a favorable, though less direct, vehicle of propagation. The similarity may be in productive resources and techniques, geographical conditions, financial organization or degree of development. The vehicles of transmission will of course be different in each case. In countries with highly developed financial markets, psychological reactions may form an important element of transmission, which accounts for the high solidarity of cyclical behavior in exchange rates, interest rates and stock prices detected by some investigators (Neisser, Colin Clark) in historical studies of the

---

[29] *Cf.* Morgenstern, "On the International Spread of Cycles", in *Journal of Political Economy* (1943, LI).

[30] A tentative list of reference countries could easily be drawn up, by measuring the degree of dependence of raw material or food producing areas upon the major industrial countries. Thus for Argentina, Australia or New Zealand, the British trade cycle could be taken as the reference cycle; for Brazil, Cuba or Canada, on the other hand, business conditions in the United States are the major conjunctural factor, the same role being played by Germany in the pre-war period for Poland and Hungary.

American, French, British and German financial markets. For countries not connected by financial links, the main vehicles of propagation is the competition in world markets. A decline in industrial demand for raw materials, or fall in world prices of food products, may start a competitive price-deflation in commodity markets. This seems to be the usual vehicle for the spreading of depression (in the horizontal sense as compared to the vertical propagation in the case of complementarity) among agricultural areas, whose production is inelastic and highly competitive. A slackening of industrial demand leads to accumulation of unsold stocks and intensification of competitions, within the limit of transportation coast. The geographical factor is here a more important element than in the case of structural complementarity.

The case of structural dissimilarity, such as exists between a predominantly mining and a predominantly agricultural country is, of course, neutral from the viewpoint of cyclical propagation. In the absence of trade and financial links, the transmission can only be indirect, i.e., through psychological reactions or through a general shrinkage of world trade.

## B. The "Degree of Openness"

Each business cycle is ordinarily a congerie of national and international components. The strength of the international component is determined by the ratio between the elements of affinity or transmission (similarity or complementarity in relation to the origin of the shock) and the elements of <u>resistance</u>, which in turn may be either natural (transportation costs) or artificial (tariffs, exchange, restrictions, etc.) The interplay between elements of resistance and of transmission determines the "degree of openness" of a country the foreign business cycle.

The sensitiveness to international cyclical influence is quite uneven as between different countries, depending on their size, structure of production, degree of monetary autonomy but also on the geographical location of the original disturbance.

The width of the "international margin" of the business cycles of any individual country may be roughly measured by:

1. Its <u>dependence of foreign trade</u> – The proportion of foreign trade to national income would provide a reasonable criterium for the "openness" to trade fluctuations. It should be kept in mind, however, that the real dependence on foreign trade may be much greater than a simple percentual relationship to national income would indicate. In fact, the export trade, even if percentually unimportant, may constitute precisely the "marginal" output, without which an optimum size of industry and

optimum scale of output could not be maintained. Similarly, if imports consist mainly of "bottleneck" items in the industrial production, their statistical smallness may grossly underestimate their total influence on income fluctuations. Thus foreign trade may have a <u>functional</u> importance out of proportion to its quantitative import. As noted by Wilherlm Roepke, <u>quantitative</u> factors must also be taken into account, foreign trade being important not only by its actual but also by its virtual or potential repercussions.[31]

2. <u>Composition of foreign trade</u> – Account should also be taken of the degree of concentration in specific products, and also of the proportion of cyclical <u>sensitive</u> items (durable or raw materials) in the total foreign trade. The degree of monopoly or competition in the export trade is also relevant. The balance of trade will be negatively elastic if the country enjoys an export monopoly and positively elastic if the export products are substitutable.

3. Its <u>dependence on foreign finance</u> – The proportion of foreign investment in relation to national income would provide a satisfactory criterium to determine the internal vulnerability to fluctuations in the international supply of savings.[32]

---

[31] *Cf.* Wilhelm Roepks, *International Economic Disintegration* ( New York, MacMillan, 1942), pp. 30-5.

[32] Some authors see in the financial inter-dependence, rather than in foreign trade the main reason for the growing parallelism of international cycles. Wageman, for instance, attribution the quick spread of the last depression to the "fact that the financing of production and trade was being done more and more on an international basis, so that collapse of the credit system in one country quickly spread to the banking systems of other countries and from there on influenced production and consumption all over the world". *Cf.* Policy Currency Management, in supplement to the weekly report of the German Institute of Business Research (Dec. 27, 1937), p. 4. Of the two possible alternatives of anti-cyclical policy, namely, autarchy in the production of goods and financial autarchy of the national credit systems, Wageman condemns the first as leading to impoverishment and compression of the standard of living, and rates the second as a successful remedy against the occurrence of world depressions.

4. <u>Exchange rates and size of the monetary reserves</u> – Exchange rates affect the competitive trade position, and the monetary margin governs the degree of monetary autonomy.[33]

In addition to the "international margin" which determines the resistance of the receiving mechanism, account must also be taken of the "shock" factor. The intensity of the shocks, and their impact upon individual economies will, as noted by Professor Morgenstern, depend on such elements as:

a. Magnitude of the disturbance
b. Place where it occurs
c. Phase of the cycle

Thus a disturbance originating in a large country, which plays a large role in the world economy will have a larger spread than fluctuations originating in smaller areas. Received shocks may superimpose themselves on internal fluctuations or may counteract them. The sensitiveness to shocks is again more pronounced in certain phases of the cycle than in others. The possible complications are infinite but the analysis of cycles in individual countries may throw significant light on the possibilities and limitations of anti-cyclical policies.

The goes without saying that the openness or closeness to the world cycle does not tell us anything as to the intensity of <u>autonomous</u> fluctuations (such as those started in agrarian economies by weather factors, or in industrial countries by technological displacements). The resistance to foreign cycles is determined by the "international margin" in the economic activity of a given country, while the internal stability is determined by the degree of structural elasticity of the system. Thus, countries comparatively independent from foreign factors, such as the United

---

[33] Some statistical measurements of the "degree of openness" have been attempted although on a more limited basis than the above suggested. An interesting attempt towards a quantitative expression of the degree of openness has been made by J.J. Polak (*Cf. Review of Economic Studies*, vol. II, 1939, p. 79). Applying the multiple correlation calculus to data on industrial production, mining and exchange rates of nine countries, Polak found a positive correlation between their cycle and the "world cycle", and a negative correlation between the prices of their currencies and the currencies of other countries (indicating the beneficial influence of low exchange rates). For small European countries of similar structure, he found an average coefficient of openness to the world cycle of 0.80, and a negative coefficient of 0.64 as regards exchange rates. The results are, however, only partial significance in view of the limited set of factors taken into account.

States, may present a high degree of internal instability. Others countries, like Sweden, may enjoy a great deal of internal stability but are particularly vulnerable to fluctuations in international trade.

So much for the study of the <u>conditions</u> of cyclical transmission. In the next part, we shall address ourselves to the study of the strategic factors or main vehicles for the propagation of economic fluctuations.

# PART TWO

## THREE VEHICLES OF PROPAGATION OF CYCLES:

## MONETARY INTERDEPENDENCE, CAPITAL MOVEMENTS AND INTERNATIONAL TRADE.

# INTRODUCTION

In this second of our inquiry, we confront the task of analysis the operation of the three principal vehicles of cyclical transmission. Although the diffusion of economic shocks and fluctuations, be it inflationary or deflationary, may be influenced by a great variety of factors—economic, social and psychological—all of them find an ultimate expression in the interaction of international economic ligamina—exchange relationships, capital movements and international trade.

The preceding chapters have shown that the three different diffusion mechanism may operate between regions or areas connected by relations of complementarity or of similarity. In the trading sphere, we have a <u>commodity complementarity</u>, manifested in the international exchange of industrial products for raw materials, of producers' for consumers' goods, or of goods of the same type but in different stage of manufacture. The usual process of transmission, in this case, are fluctuations in the relative price and quantity of goods traded, in response to changes in the level or direction of international demand. But trading fluctuations can also spread horizontally between countries producing similar commodities, the mechanism of transmission being in this case the competitive price deflation.

In the exchange and capital movements sphere, we have the case of <u>financial complementarity</u> that finds its expression in debtor-creditor relationships between capital surplus and capital-importing countries. Prosperity and depression may be transmitted through constant fluctuations in international investment, through debt collection or merely through changes in the rate of capital flows. But the mechanism operates also between <u>similar strata</u>, as evidenced in the solidarity of cyclical movements of the great financial markets.

The importance of each diffusion mechanism will of course very as between different countries, different cycles or even different phases of the same cycles. In some cases, it is a fall in export prices that initiates the deflationary pressure, in others the cessation or decline in capital imports, in others still the disequilibrium created by exchange rate movements. Or simultaneous interaction between the three strata may occur, with a dampening or aggravation of the shocks.

The analysis of the mechanism of transmission will be broadened by a brief survey of the theoretical aspects of exchange ligamina, of capital transfers and of international trade, the existing doctrines being examined from the viewpoint of business cycle theory. Attention will also be paid to the influence of structural contrasts on the cyclical behavior. Finally the propagation of booms and depressions will be analyzed in the light of the recent international experience.

# SECTION I

# MONETARY SYSTEMS AND THE INTERNATIONAL PROPAGATION OF BUSINESS FLUCTUATIONS

That the interdependence of monetary standards is an important factor contributing to the synchronization of business fortunes is scarcely open to doubt. Direct monetary transmission may take place between (1) countries having the same or closely related monetary standards, or (2) countries having highly organized and sensitive financial markets. We shall be primarily concerned, at this stage, with the cyclical conductivity of monetary standards, which presents some interesting theoretical problems. The close interdependence and receptivity of the great financial markets—revealed by the occurrence of psychologically transmitted mimetic cycles—is, on the other hand, an already well studied phenomenon which will not concerns us here. While the occurrence of direct monetary transmission is widely recognized, there is much less agreement on the extent of its influence and on the allocation of responsibility as between the several possible patterns of international monetary relations.

In broad terms, we may distinguish two extreme positions; that of the <u>monetary nationalistic</u>, who emphasize the need for exchange flexibility, and that of the <u>internationalists</u>, who emphasize the advantages of exchange stability. In between, there is a wide range of shades of opinion, a successful compromise between the two attitudes being recently attained in the agreement for the establishment of the International Monetary Fund.

The extreme Monetary nationalists hold internal stability to have primary over, and to be frequently incompatible with, exchange stability. The internationalists, on the other hand, question both the advisability and the possibility of attaining internal stability through independent national monetary policies. Much of the discussion was centered around the conductivity of the gold standard to the business cycle, a subject that will engage us next.

# CHAPTER I

# THE CONTROVERSY ON THE GOLD STANDARD

The discussion raised by the world-wide attempts for restoration of the gold standard in the late twenties, and by its breakdown in the early thirties, serves to illustrate conveniently the areas of agreement and disagreement.

One of the conflicting tendencies, which later developed into the school of monetary nationalism, attributed to the gold standard a large measure of responsibility for the propagation of cycles. It is not always clear whether the objections voiced related to the gold standard, qua talis, or to the imperfections of its operation, resulting from the conscious or unconscious failure of the monetary authorities to observe the "rules of the game".

There are, within this group, several shades of opinion. Hawtrey emphasized especially the cyclical influence of gold flows and outflows on the size of the reserves and on credit policy. Keynes chose to stress the subordination of the domestic rate of interest (as manipulated by Central Banks) to foreign monetary factors, as the main factor making for interdependence of economic fluctuations. Irving Fisher, on the other hand, ascribed the principal role in the transmission of booms and depressions to the international solidarity of price-level movements under the gold standard.

A second group of theorists is inclined to deny the responsibility of the gold standard in the spreading of instability, claiming rather that the gold standard never in fact operated internationally. What existed was a "hybrid system", characterized by the existence of national reserve systems.[1] It is said, in this sense, that the best possible defense of the gold standard is that it never really existed.[2] Professor Hayek, who can be taken as the leading representative of this group, allocates the responsibility of international monetary instability to short-term capital movements instead:

---

[1] Compare F.A. Hayek, *Monetary Nationalism and International Stability* (London, 1940), p. 74. "The Monetary Nationalists condemn it (the gold standard), because it is international. I, on the other hand ascribe its short-comings to the fact that it is not international enough."

[2] Professor Williams has called attention to the often overlooked fact that the principle of Central Banking is in direct contradiction to that of the gold standard. In fact, due to Central Bank policies, the " rules of the game" were never observed. Neutralization of gold flows, either by design or unintentionally, was a normal occurrence even before the establishment of Equalization or Stabilization funds as shown by Ragnar Nurske in *International Currency Experience* (League of Nations, 1944), chapter IV.

The ultimate source of difficulty is the differentiation between moneys of different degree of acceptability or liquidity, the existence of a structure consisting of superimposed layers of reserve of different degrees of liquidity, which makes the movements of short term money rates, and in consequence the movements of short term funds, much more dependent on the liquidity position of the different financial institutions than on changes in the in the demand for capital for real investment.

Still other authors base their defense of the gold standard on the advantage of the self-adjusting mechanism which, at least in its pure form, provided an automatic anti-cyclical device, prosperity being dampened by gold outflows and depression attenuated by gold inflows brought about by the operation of the price-specie-flow mechanism.

## A. Hawtrey's Theory and the Cyclical Conductivity of the Gold Standard

The effects of the gold standard on the international cyclical behavior have been dealt with in detail by Hawtrey. He ascribed the flagrant phenomenon of close synchronization of international fluctuations, in pre-war times, to the operations of the international money mechanism, and implied that the breakdown of the gold standard had led to the disappearance of international cycles:

> Since the war there has been no trade cycle of the old type. Fluctuations in productivity there have been irregular and mostly short, and have not been synchronized in different countries... There could not be a trade cycle, so long as there was to link between the price-levels in different countries.[3]

Hawtrey's description of the international behavior of the gold standard is couched in the familiar lines of the price-specie-flow mechanism and its effects on money and credit. Hawtrey points out that the self-regulating mechanism of gold movements, which would tend to put a brake on prosperity and attenuate the downswing, holds only true if the expansion or contraction of one country is out pace with that of other countries. The mechanism, however, does not operate if we regard the entire gold-using world as a single economic unit. We quote:

---

[3] R.G. Hawtrey, *Currency and Credit* (London, 1919), p. 95.

The general employment of the gold standard, combined with the systematic regulation of credit, does not prevent expansions and contractions of credit but merely decries that they should be approximately equal and simultaneous everywhere. A movement of gold from one country to another is merely a sign that they are not exactly keeping pace. One lets credit expand a little faster than the others and loses gold; another legs behind and receives gold... But if the whole gold using world be regarded as a single economic unit, it suffers from just the same dangers as we already traced in a single country. It is threatened by the inherent instability of credit, and when a credit expansion occurs, the dangerous latent demands for cash and credit come into being in a greater or lesser degree in every country which participates in the movements. When the latent demand for cash becomes actual, the turning point is reached... in coping with this situation no country can expect help from any other since all are in difficulties.[4]

A high degree of parallelism in the cyclical behavior is thus the normal pattern under the gold standard. Hawtrey acknowledges, however, several possibilities of departure from this parallelism. A country may expand or contract out of unison if any of the following conditions occur:

a. Existence of <u>surplus gold reserves</u>. Any one country that possesses them may prolong the expansion or delay the contraction independently from foreign business cycles;
b. Temporary disturbance of production: a bumper crop or harvest failure may cause a favorable or an adverse movement of foreign exchanges and entail an uneven rate of expansion or contraction. Also, the process of expansion itself may induce abnormal shifts in demand in favor of certain groups of products, such as luxury goods, special raw materials and manufactures, enabling the country that produces them to expand faster without losing gold, but risking also a severer strain in depression;
c. Uneven rate of progress as between lending and borrowing countries and disparities in the demand for fixed capital. The export of capital takes place from "old" countries to "new" countries where the demand for fixed capital is greater. Capital movements are stimulated when credit expands in creditor countries and shrinks when there is a credit contraction:

---

[4] Hawtrey, *Currency and Credit*, pp. 94-5.

...When credit is expanding and the new countries borrow more than usual, they find their exchanges favorable, and have the choice of importing gold or indulging in a greater expansion of credit than their neighbors When credit contracts and they borrow less than usual, they lose gold and have to effect a greater contraction of credit than their neighbors... Thus it may happen that the foreign borrowings of a particular nation are at a maximum when those of others are at a minimum.

The intrinsic limitations of the purely monetary theory, as a closed system explanation (in view of the possibility of disturbances on real side of economic phenomena), have been clearly expounded both by the under-consumption and the over-investment theories. We will at present limit our considerations to the validity of the theory for the explanation of the international propagation of cycles.

The first limitation is, obviously, that Hawtrey's mechanism is directly dependent upon the existence of the gold standard and of a world money market. It is of scarcely any value to explain the international cycle after the disappearance of the pre-war integrated money system. The second limitation derives from the price-specie-flow assumption, which presupposes a mechanism of speedy reaction of commodity trade to price-level changes that, under present conditions, is quite unrealistic. While it is true that losses of gold and the subsequent fall in domestic price level (or a rises in the foreign price-level) are likely to provoke an equilibrating reduction in imports, the second side of the adjustment mechanism, i.e., the stimulation of exports, may be frequently impeded by economic frictions, insufficient elasticity of foreign demand or imperfection of competition.

The third weakness of the theory lies in the postulated connection between the central bank rate and the general level of prices. It is clear that this relationship is not always operative. In fact, the recent analysis casts very serious doubts on the effectiveness of the discount rate policy of central banks for the control of the money market, and on the very role played by changes in interest rates in governing the behavior of investors and trades during the cycle.

It follows that the theory of the international money mechanism, on which Hawtrey based his explanation of cycle propagation, is valid only for a certain rage of institutional conditions. He succeeded in demonstrating the high conductivity of the gold standard of economic fluctuations. There is, however, room for disagreement both as regards the amount of responsibility to be ascribed to it in the generation of booms and depressions, and as regards the role played by gold movements in the determination of the volume of credit and commodity trade.

In the inter-war period we have seen a complete reversal of the traditional role of gold, to which Hawtrey ascribed so much importance. As pointed out by Nurske, gold and other international reserves instead of acting as "conveyors" or "transmitters", came to serve more and more as cushions or "buffers".[5] The "rules of the game" were replaced by an open policy of neutralization of gold flows, the growing need for internal stability having led to a general revolt against "rigid exchange". Moreover, the growing fluidity of short-term funds disrupted the operation of the price-specie-flow mechanism. Time and time again (such as in the case of the dollar and franc devaluation), the rise in internal prices, far from provoking a corrective outflow of gold, attracted capital, in the expectation of profits, and added to the maladjustment by causing a new inflow of gold and further disequilibrating price movements.[6]

## B. The Gold Exchange Standard

The mechanism of propagation of fluctuations under the gold exchange standard does not present great difference from that of the gold standard, except that the brakes to monetary expansion (i.e., outflow of gold or decrease in exchange reserve) are likely to be more operative for member countries than for the center or reserves country. When the former expand too rapidly, their balances in the reserve country tend to be depleted. If however, it is the reserve country that has a higher rate of expansion, it need not lose gold or feel the pinch of credit stringency (as it would occur under the pure gold standard), except insofar as money is withdrawn from circulation in the form of higher demand deposits in favor of member countries.

But, on the other hand, the "spilling over" of an expansion started in a reserve country is likely to be greater since it will tend to increase the balances (or basic money supply) of the member countries, while an expansion in the latter does not provoke, by itself, any increase in the basic money supply ( gold reserve) of the nuclear country.[7]

---

[5] *Cf.* Ragner Nurske, *International Currency Experience* (League of Nations, 1944), p. 213

[6] See John H. Williams, "Monetary Stability and the Gold Standard", reprinted in *Post-War Monetary Plans*, p. 181

[7] *Cf.* Haberler, *op. cit.*, pp 432-433; also Nurske, *op. cit.*, pp. 41-46.

# CHAPTER II

## IRVING FISHER AND THE PRICE-LEVEL MECHANISM

The importance of monetary standards in cyclical transmission has been particularly stressed by Fisher. He is perhaps the most uncompromising defender of the view that monetary standards are primarily responsible for the international transmission of booms and depressions through the mechanism of correlated changes in price-levels.

Investigating the price behavior of 27 countries, classified into three monetary groups—gold standard, sterling block and miscellaneous—he reached the conclusion:

1. That countries on the same monetary standard have the same price movements;
2. That countries not on the same monetary standard do not have similar price movements;
3. That any country changing from one monetary standard to another, changes its price level accordingly, a result that makes the case for monetary transmission of price level changes fairly complete.[8]

Fisher's conclusion is in keeping with his general view that cycles are primarily monetary phenomena.

Even discounting his exaggerated optimism about the statistical significance of international comparisons of price-level indexes (constructed under different techniques), it may readily be granted that the consonance of price variations is likely to be much grater between countries on the same monetary standard. This is particularly true for the gold standard, since in a system of rigid exchange no wide price discrepancies can exist for any prolonged period.

One can, however seriously question the significance of this finding for the explanation of the international cyclical behavior. We need not go, for instance, so far as to admit that the similarity of monetary standard is the cause of the similarity of price movements (the latter could well be explained by co-variation of underlying real factors), or that "without the monetary conduit there would be very little danger for infection". In fact, once it is admitted that cyclical movements may

---

[8] See I. Fisher, *Are Booms and Depressions Transmitted Internationally*, communication for the International Statistical Institute; also printed in separate, New York, 1934, pp. 1-32.

originate from disproportionalities in the real side of the economy, even a complete independence of monetary standards would not impede the spreading of fluctuations.[9]

There is one further step in Fisher's analysis that is open for criticism, namely, his reliance upon general price-level movements as indicators of cyclical fortunes. In fact, it is now widely admitted that fluctuations may be set under way merely by changes in relative prices. Thus the solidarity of changes in the general price level alone cannot by itself be taken as an evidence of solidarity of cyclical fortunes. Conversely, as noted by Professor Hayek:

> The fact the averages of (more or less arbitrarily selected) groups of prices move differently in different countries, does not of course in no way prove that there is any tendency of a price structure of a country to move as a whole relatively to prices in other countries.

To sum up: It is scarcely questionable that monetary interdependence plays a significant part in the contamination of a country by a foreign boom and depression; that, however, monetary standards are the cause or the most essential elements in the internalization of cycles, is a controversial question which cannot be demonstrated by simple price-level comparisons. The causal nexus suggested—from monetary standards to price-level changes and from those to general business conditions—cannot be easily accepted unless one is inclined to discount other cyclical influences than the monetary ones in cycle generation.[10]

---

[9] Fisher is quite aware of this possibility although be tends to discount its importance. He mentions, however, specifically that in the 1931–1932 depression other than monetary factors were operative.

[10] Compare Fisher's sanguine conclusion: "... if, by monetary control, booms and depressions can be forestalled or mitigated within a nation, the international transmission of them can be forestalled by any nation through monetary means, that is, by cutting loose from the standards which transmit or threaten to transmit the booms and depressions from it to other countries". *Op. cit.*, p. 19.

# CHAPTER III

# THE MONETARY NATIONALISM AND ITS THEORETICAL BASIS

## A. The Keynesian Influence

The emergence and present popularity of the school of monetary nationalism in Britain and in the United States is in large measure traceable to the influence of Lord Keynes' writings. His caustic denunciation of the conventional Central Bank policies as instruments for sacrificing domestic interest rates to the operations of "blind forces" and his forceful commendation of the primacy of internal over external stability had a wide repercussion.[11] Harrod in England and Whittlesey in the United States may perhaps be singled out as the most ardent apologists of monetary nationalism. On the continent, the prevalence of nominalist theories of money and especially the influence of Knapp's "state theory of money" had rendered monetary thinking much less orthodox than in the Anglo-Saxon countries, dominated by the classical tradition.

The discussion between monetary nationalists or internationalists is not a technological but rather a methodological one. The point in question is not the need or desirability of achieving a large measure of international economic stability, on which all agree, but whether it can best be achieved by striving primarily for internal or for external stability.

It is not easy to give precise contours to the notion of monetary nationalism—an expression borrowed from Professor Hayek—and still more difficult to translate into specific terms the general set of ideas that is known as monetary internationalism. The concepts have to be rarified in order to encompass the broad tendencies of monetary thinking. <u>Faute de mieux</u>, we may resort to broad fundamentals following Professor Hayek, who defines monetary nationalism as: "the doctrine that a country's share in the world's supply of money should not be left to be determined by the same principles and the same mechanism as those which determine the relative amounts of money in its different regions or localities." By contrast, "a truly international monetary system would be one where the whole world possessed a homogeneous currency such as obtains within separate countries and where its flow between regions was left to be determined by the results of the action of all individuals."[12]

---

[11] J.M. Keynes, *The General Theory of Employment, Interest and Money*, pp. 338-9.

[12] F.A. Hayek, *Monetary Nationalism and International Stability* ( London, 1939), p. 4.

Although within the group of monetary nationalists there are varying shades of opinion, there is a firm ground of common agreement; the maintenance of internal stability and of a high level of employment should be "the" criterium of monetary policy, rather than the preservation of exchange parities. It is claimed that under the "rules of the game", or for that matter under any regime of fixed exchange, the quantity of money, the domestic price-level and interest rates are controlled by the balance of payments position, thus subjecting the economy to the full impact of vicissitudes abroad.[13]

Stress is laid on the fact that internal equilibrium is not unfrequently incompatible with external equilibrium. The rigidity of wages and prices makes the adjustments necessary to maintain the exchange parties impossible, unless through painful deflation and unemployment. It is held that exchange rates and not prices should bear the burden of adjustment and that the gold standard principle and indeed the entire classical theory neglected the cumulative effect of price level changes, by assuming a too smooth mechanism of adjustment.

The growing preoccupation with internal stability and the growing awareness of cyclical employment problems is clearly illustrated by the evolution of the never-satisfactorily-defined concept of <u>equilibrium rate of exchange</u>. Casual described is as the rate which would equate the purchasing power of two currencies; Keynes, as the rate which would eliminate gold flows. A frequently resorted to criterium held the equilibrium rate to be the one which would ensure equilibrium in the balance of payments. Since, however, the equilibrium in the balance of payments was found to be quite compatible with internal deflation and unemployment (as evidenced by the case of Great Britain from 1925 to 1929), a further elaboration was needed to takes full account of the internal stability viewpoint. Thus Ragner Nurske suggested that the equilibrium rate be defined as the one "that maintains the balance in equilibrium without the need for mass unemployment at home, or at any rate, without a degree of unemployment greater than in the outside world".[14]

Thus, at present the main emphasis of the monetary nationalists centers around the business cycle, it being freely admitted that internal instability is too great a price to pay for unhampered international trade.[15] The monetary internationalists, on the other hand, lay stress on the greater freedom of trade and devel-

---

[13] Compare Keynes: "...with as international system, such as gold, the primary duty of a Central Bank is to preserve <u>external</u> equilibrium. Internal equilibrium must take its chance, or rather, the internal situation has to be forced sooner or later into equilibrium with the external situation".

[14] *Op. cit.*, p. 126.

[15] See Williams, "International Monetary Organization", reprinted in *Post-War Monetary Plans*, p. 202.

opment of capital movements historically associated with the operation of the international monetary standard.[16]

It behooves to note that the psychological and economic attitude towards exchange policy is in itself subject to cyclical changes. In periods of prosperity, with booming incomes and rising trade, the need for exchange stability is more intensely felt, while in depression exchange flexibility tends to be resorted to out loose from deflationary drags and stimulate home trade.[17]

For young countries depending on a few exports of inelastic supply-demand, adherence to a rigid international standard becomes impossible in depression. The sequence of events is familiar to us. Lack of diversification of output and long crop periods make it impossible to curtail output when prices fall. To meet debt and interest payments and to pay far imports, exports increase in volume, what tends to depress prices further. The drag on exchange reserves and gold render the resort to depreciation imperative sooner or later.

## B. The Haynekian Position

The most elaborate criticism, on an abstract level, of the postulates held by the monetary nationalists, is due to Professor Hayek. In his view, the attempt, by use of monetary means, to overcome difficulties resulting from rigidity of wages and prices creates new disturbances of the self-reversing kind, by entailing misdirection of production. Production is then governed not by fundamental or real changes but by wrong expectations created by an artificial level of prices. The effort to resist necessary adjustments of productive factors and of incomes, by variations in exchange rates, would bring about a redistribution of spending power

---

[16] As noted by Keynes, the importance of exchange stability is greater for capital movements than for international trade. For the latter, the inconveniences of unfettered exchanges could be adequately obviated through the market of forward exchange, not available in the case of capital movements. *Cf. Treatise on Money* (1930), vol. II.

[17] Paradoxically enough, it is precisely in depression, i.e., when international trade is small, that the corrective virtue of exchange adjustment is both most needed and less effective. In fact, under a depressed trade and investment outlook, the price-elasticity of demand of any country for other country's exports is likely to decrease, so that the principal effect of exchange depreciation may be, as noted by M.E. Bernstein, to turn the terms of trade against the depreciating country, without any compensatory improvement in the balances of trade and of payments. This experience was common to a number of raw material countries in the last depression. After depreciating, they raw their terms of trade worsened, without experiencing any equilibrating increase in foreign demand for their exports. This explains, in part, the paradoxical fact that Great Britain, even after devaluating, continued to enjoy cheap imports of primary products, which fostered her recovery. *Cf.* E.M. Bernstein, Scarce Currencies and the Monetary Fund, *Journal of Political Economy*, March 1945, p. 11.

and a temporary stimulation of certain industries in a way which is not based on a corresponding change in the distribution of demand and productive power.

In Hayek's view it is the delay in effecting, or the attempt to avoid internal adjustment to international forces that make the adjustment itself more painful and difficult than it would be otherwise.

Under the hybrid or traditional gold standard (gold nucleus with a superimposed multiple credit structure), the lag in the outflow of gold induced by excessive credit expansion, the tardiness of monetary authorities in reducing circulation in proportion to the gold lost, and especially the off-setting of gold losses by new credit creation, resulted in increasing the international disequilibrium and in rendering necessary a much larger gold flow than it would have been needed had not the normal redistribution of purchasing power been interfered with. The postulate, frequently advanced by monetary nationalists, that any rise in the domestic rate of interest should be prevented is also assailed by Hayek, on the ground that, if the capital outflow which provoked the rise in interest is due to a fundamental disequilibrium, any attempt to prevent it by compensatory credit expansion would further increase the pressure on exchange and lead to an increase in domestic prices and in the demand for loans, with a subsequent rise in the equilibrium rate of interest and attendant inflationary consequences. Furthermore, an autonomous national rate of interest could not be maintained without complete control of international capital movements. But even an effective control of international capital movements would not guarantee the stability of interest rates, due to possible repercussions on the side of commodity trade. For, if wide inequalities of interest rates prevail between countries, the price of capital goods would tend to fall in the countries having high interest rates and this price change would in turn be transmitted to those countries tying to maintain stable interest rates. These would then experience an increase in the profitability of investment, the resulting demand for funds thus creating a new upward pressure on interest rates.

On the practical side, Hayek has two main objections against the policy of monetary nationalism; government intervention in the money market and the inflationary bias concomitant to exchange flexibility. Its anti-cyclical insulation value, according to Hayek, is moreover limited:

> For a country which is sharing in the advantage of the international division of labor it is not possible to escape from the effects of disturbance in these international trade relations by means short of reversing all the trade ties which connect it to the rest of the world.

There is undoubtedly a great deal of truth in Hayek's contention that the national independence of monetary supply creates an artificial distortion of the structures of production and demand, and impedes the natural adjustment to international changes in productivity. But the question is whether exchange stability does not present a similar danger. For, if the monetary supply and interest rates in a country are made obedient to changes in its international position, the adjustment may be, and is likely to be, carried too far, especially if the structural changes are drastic and rapid. The free fluctuations in internal prices and costs, preconized by Hayek, may again outrun changes in basic or real factors, entailing a deflationary cumulative process.

Hayek is right in pointing out that the modern Anglo-Saxon monetary theory, partly no doubt because of the influence of Irving Fisher's writings has exaggerated the inflationary or deflationary character of general price-level-changes (as against the much more significant changes in individual and relative prices). But the classical habit (to which Hayek shows unmistakable sympathy) of considering general price-level changes as natural is also quite ever-simplified.

Granted that exchange depreciation is a blunt weapon, in the sense that it affects uniformly all export and import prices and cannot therefore insulate against deflationary influences transmitted by shifts in relative prices, it does not follow that, by maintaining exchange stability, the adjustment will act only upon those industries directly affected by changes in international demand and in relative costs, leaving the rest of the system untouched.

Hayek's light dismissal of the case made by monetary nationalists in favor of exchange adjustments, when a country suffers a deterioration of its competitive position and deflationary pressure because of a higher rate of technological growth in a competitor country (to wit, Great Britain and United States during the interwar-period) cannot thus be accepted.[18] We may concede to Hayek that exchange depreciation will, in this case, spread the burden of adjustment among other industries that do not suffer technological disadvantages. But so would exchange stability, if deflation in the industries directly affected generates pessimistic anticipations.

Moreover, it is difficult to see why the depreciation process is of necessity more painful and less sound than the alternative of allowing, by exchange rigidity, contraction and unemployment in individual industries, an adjustment that may easily star a deflationary wave throughout the economy. Admittedly, in the long run, it is not feasible nor desirable to effect, by exchange manipulations, the competitive advantage of countries or industries enjoying a faster rate of technological advance. The long-run remedy is of course structural adjustments in the least favored countries or industries. In the short run, however, the choice is not so easy; in many cases the use of depreciation to prevent wholesale unemployment may be

---

[18] *Cf. op .cit.*, pp. 38-40.

a better course than exchange stability and certainly a much less dangerous one than Hayek would lead us to believe.

The question is not one that can be settled on purely abstract grounds. As in many other sectors of economic theory, the discussion between extreme internationalists of the Hayekian type and extreme nationalists of the whittlesey variety is largely bound up with the difference between short and long-run viewpoints.

Hayek's reasoning is deeply imbedded in the classical full-employment, long-run equilibrium analysis. The difficulties of adjustment are minimized. Business cycles, to be sure, are taken into account, but although theirs social painfulness is recognized, they are given credit for performing a necessary economic catharsis.

The problem of cyclical unemployment is, on the other hand, at the very core of the analysis of the monetary nationalists. Their aversion towards adjustments involving wage deflation reveals that social factors are given as much as purely economic considerations.

Against the long-run advantages of exchange stability for the development of trade and foreign investment we have to weigh the great losses of cyclical slumps, which are aggravated by exchange rigidity. This dilemma has nowhere been expressed than by Sir William Beveridge:

> The virtue of international trade is that it saves labor; the virtue of a full employment policy is that it uses labor. It would be senseless to save labor through international trade only in order to waste labor in unemployment.[19]

---

[19] William H. Beveridge, *Full Employment in a Free Society* (New York: Morton and Co., 1945), p. 211.

# CHAPTER IV

# THE GOLD STANDARD AND THE FREELY FLUCTUATING EXCHANGES

In a sense, the pure gold standard—homogeneous international metallic standard—and the system of freely fluctuating exchange are both two extreme hypothetical cases. Both presuppose complete absence of interference with, and management of, the exchange market.

In practice, the periods of automatic and unregulated exchanges have been temporary exceptions. The choice has usually been between different degree of monetary management. In fact, the Central Bank principle represented, intrinsically, a denial of the automatism of the gold standard.[20] The freely fluctuating exchanges, on the other hand, would imply complete independence of currencies one from another, a situation hardly likely to obtain in practice.

The transmission of cyclical shocks through the gold standard, and the high degree of parallelism that it brings about, have already been discussed in connection with Hawtrey's theory. Several possibilities of divergence in the cyclical movements, within Hawtrey's scheme, have been briefly dealt with. A word should, however, be added concerning the policy of neutralization of gold flows so widely practiced by Central Banks in the last two decades.

The possibility, for any country of pursuing an independent anti-cyclical policy, depends upon:
1. Size of the international "buffer", i.e., amount of gold reserves (in case of an outflow) and stocks of salable assets ( in case of an in-flow);
2. Degree of localization of credit:
3. Degree of closeness of trade connections , as determined by the localization of resources and transportation costs;
4. Direction which is given to the flows of money by its successive recipients;
5. Average income-propagation period.[21]

---

[20] The recent League of Nations study on "International Currency Experience" prepared by Ragner Nurske, calls attention to the fact that, quite apart from Central Bank action, there has been throughout the period in review an undesigned and almost automatic neutralization of the supposedly automatic effect of gold flow. Nurske notes that the tendency to neutralize has been much more automatic than the operation of the "rules of the game".

[21] Cf. Haberler, op. cit., p. 428

There has been in the twenties considerable over-optimism regarding the effectiveness of Central Bank policies in insulating the domestic money flow against the impact of international fluctuations. In reality, however, the discount rate mechanism has proved much more successful to check expansions than to prevent depressions. While the neutralization of the inflationary effect of gold flows on the volume of internal cash and credit has been more or less successfully achieved by the Equalization Funds, it did not prove an adequate defense against external deflationary forces, except insofar as the latter derived merely from temporary disequilibrium in the balance of payments provoked by capital exports or decline in capital imports. The mechanism fails, however to be operative, as pointed out by Professor Haberler, when deflationary forces is due to a switch-over of demand from home-produced to foreign goods, in which case not oven a liberal credit policy will compensate for the "deflationary consequences of a worsening of anticipations of business men."[22]

Just as the managed gold standard had its faithful adherents, the system of flexible exchanges is now ardently advocated as a recipe for escaping imposed deflations. A detailed discussion of the problem would take us far afield and we shall limit ourselves to cursory observations.[23]

The chief limitation of the flexible exchange technique is that, while it may neutralize general price level effects and avoid painful deflationary adjustments, it cannot disequilibria originating from changes in relative prices (other than export-import prices), in which many theorists see the root of cyclical disturbances. The resort to depreciation may sometimes affect unfavorably the inducement to invest, by increasing the price of imported capital goods and raw materials, thus aggravating the deflationary pressure that it purported to avoid.[24]

Thus, while from the viewpoint of anti-cyclical policy, the "straight jacket" of the gold standard imposes a constant danger of inflationary contagion for countries living on a thin margin of international reserve, the freely fluctuating exchanges (which are the case limit of exchange flexibility) involve serious drawbacks, which are thus summarized by Nurske:

a. They create an element of risk that discourages international trade.
b. They render necessary constant shifts of labor and resources as between

---

[22] *Cf.* Haberler, *op. cit.*, p. 429. For a thorough discussion of the failure of "external currency management" to restore international economic equilibrium, *cf.* John Donaldson, *The Dollar* (New York: Oxford University Press, 1937).

[23] The literature on the possibilities and limitations of exchange manipulations is very rich and constitutes one of the best developed fields in economic theory. For illuminating discussions, cf., particularly John Donaldson, *op. cit.*, pp. 164-192, and Juan Robinson, *Studies in the Theory of Employment*, pp. 182-3.

[24] This unfavorable affect may, however, be neutralized by a parallel shift in demand from foreign to domestic goods.

production for home markets and for export, which tend to create frictional unemployment.

c. They give rise to speculative anticipations of further changes of exchange rates, creating explosive conditions of instability.[25]

This extreme form of exchange flexibility, the freely fluctuating exchanges, constitutes a theoretical case of considerable interest.[26] By definition, the monetary standards would be completely independent, no international flow of money taking place, all adjustments being made by variations in exchange rates and in exports and imports. The cyclical contagion through international money flows would be non-existent. Some paradoxical effects, as noted by Professor Haberler, would take place; contrarily to the conventional mechanism of the gold standard, capital exports would be inflationary for the paying country and deflationary for the receiving country, since the only channel of transfer would be the merchandise trade.

A major factor in current day monetary theory and policy is the International Monetary Fund, whose basic document is a successful attempt at compromise between a satisfactory degree of exchange stability (needed for the restoration of trade and international investment) and the need for a minimum degree of monetary autonomy and exchange flexibility (indispensable to obviate balance of payments disequilibria without sacrificing internal employment policies.)

The Bretton Woods agreement on the International Monetary Fund has given rise to a voluminous literature that need not be reviewed here. From the theoretical angle it represents but a compromise, and as such it is considered too rigid by the monetary nationalist and dangerously lax by the advocates of a truly international monetary standard. Objections have been voiced against some of the mechanism features of the plan (the quota system, devaluation and scarce currencies provisions), or against its over-ambitious idea of wholesale international stabilization.[27] Perhaps the best augur for the success of this new attempt in monetary cooperation lies in the sober view and realization of the potentialities and limitations of monetary stabilization. It is now increasingly recognized that monetary policies attack usually symptoms rather than causes and that they need to be supplemented by a program of revival and orientation of international investment (entrusted to the International Bank) and by some sufficiently flexible scheme for prevention of erratic fluctuations in prices of primary products. As monetary standard, trade and investment are three principal vehicles for cyclical propagation, so the problem of stable employment has to be attacked in all three sources of deflationary contagion.

---

[25] *Cf.* Nurske, *op. cit.*, p. 20.

[26] For a detailed discussion cf. Haberler, *op. cit.*, pp. 441-50; also P.B. Whale, "The Theory of International Trade in the Absence of an International Standard", in *Economica* (February, 1936).

[27] Professor Williams, in particular, has suggested a more modest bilateral approach in his "Key Currencies Plan".

# CHAPTER V

# THE MONETARY EXPERIENCE IN THE INTER-WAR PERIOD

The inter-war period has been marked by the great devaluation cycle of the thirties, starting with the devaluation of the sterling in 1931, and ending with devaluation of the franc in 1936. Or, covering a broader period, the complete cycle be described as beginning with the de fact stabilization of the franc in 1926, at an unduly low level, and ending with the second devaluation of the franc in 1936.

It is generally agreed that the stabilization of the franc at an undervalued level was a major disequilibrating factor that played a significant part in thwarting the world-wide efforts for restoration of the gold standard. By draining gold away from the world market, both as a result of current surpluses in the balance of payments and repatriation of capital, France exerted a deflationary influence just as disequilibrating as the one later created by the huge capital inflow in the United States market, during the thirties. England's position, on the other hand, was already considerably weakened by the deterioration of her competitive expert position subsequent to the over-valuation of the pound in 1925. The devaluation of the sterling was, however, preceded by that of currencies of agricultural countries, such as Australia, New Zealand, Argentina and Brazil, whose exchange reserves could not withstand the impact of the crash in raw material prices in 1929.

It is often suggested that exchange depreciation is the normal adjustment-reaction of raw material countries, lacking international reserves and highly dependent on a narrow range of unstable export prices. While this proved true by their exchange behavior at the outset of the depreciation, it behooves to note that by 1935 the devaluation of "creditor "currencies had outrun that of agricultural areas. In many cases, exchange depreciation had to supplemented by structural adaptations (diversification of production and industrialization), and the latter, no less than the former, soon became standard features of governmental policy of primary producing areas.[28]

Various criteria have been advanced as to what exchange adjustments should be considered expansionary or deflationary. The most obvious and simplest criterium would, of course, be to measure deviations from the "equilibrium rate of exchange". The imprecision and variety of the interpretations of the equilibrium rate concept—diversely defined with relation to purchasing power (Cassel), gold

---

[28] For a detailed review, *cf.* Seymour Harris, *Exchange Depreciation, passim,* and also League of Nations, *International Currency Experience.*

flows (Keynes), balance of payments (Haberler), employment (Nurske), etc.,— render, however, its application for practical policy extremely difficult. A more general concept has been suggested by Professor Haberler; from the world point of view currency devaluation will be expansional if it corrects a previous overvaluation and deflationary if it makes the currency undervalued:

> The criterium for an international equilibrium being the absences of persistent gold movements and of abnormal capital movements motivated by anticipation of a fall or rise in exchange rates.[29]

A third criterium recently advanced to determine the economic legitimacy of exchange depreciation, resorts both to the balance of payments and to the employment criterium. A line of demarcation is drawn between a "buffer" exchange policy, which aims purely at cushioning deflationary or inflationary shocks, and a "beggar-way-neighbor" policy, characterized by the attempt to divert a larger share of demand from international trade to national output.[30]

Some interesting lessons can be derived from the experience of the thirties. Not the least among them is the fact that, in the process of recovery, trade increased more between depreciated currencies themselves than between then and the gold standard or stable currencies. This result is in direct contradiction to what one should expect in the light of the traditional international trade and gold standard theories, with their emphasis on terms-of-trade affects, i.e., premium on exports and burden on imports of the country with depreciating currency.

This seems to suggest that the mechanism of internal monetary expansion was much important in the process of recovery than the "competitive-export-position" aspect emphasized in previous discussions of exchange depreciation.

Another interesting inference is that the so-called anti-cyclical exchange policy tended to be curiously one-sided. Exchange depreciation was liberally resorted to prevent deficits in the balance of payments. But its counterpart—exchange appreciation (to prevent inflationary shocks or disequilibrium surpluses in the balance of payments)—was very seldom applied, the only conspicuous example being the appreciation of the Swedish Kroner after the last war. Neutralization or sterilization of gold or money in-flows, rather than exchange appreciation, was the normal reaction of creditor countries, with the result that no corrective action was exercised on the balance of trade. Thus, one of the major short-comings of any anti-cyclical exchange policy seams to be the danger of one-sidedness, inherited from the depression bias of the thirties.

---

[29] *Cf.* Haberler, *op. cit.*, p. 439.

[30] *Cf.* Nurske, *op. cit.*, chapter IX.

For agricultural countries, lacking an international reserve margin, the cushioning against periodical shocks in the exchange market is a particularly pressing problem. A successful anti-cyclical exchange policy has been recently pursued by Argentina, through the absorption by the Central Bank of surplus exchange in 1936 and early part of 1937, and gradual release of exchange to attenuate the contractionary impact of a sudden fail in export prices in the latter part of 1937. In other countries, such as Peru, the building of reserves during the boom of 1935–1937 was inadequate, so that the deflationary impact of the 1937 recession could only be mitigated through a twenty per cent exchange depreciation.

Strangely enough, throughout the troubled conditions of the inter-war period, no country revealed desire for freely flexible currencies, the spreading of depreciation being, by and large, traceable to lack of coordination of attempts to relieve deflationary pressures, rather than to an urge for monetary independence or trade autarchy .

The melancholic conclusion that we cannot escape at this juncture is that neither the refinements of theory nor the lessons of practical experience have succeeded in bringing sight a solution for the crucial problem of international monetary experience which, as Professor Williams said, consists in:

> How to prevent the occurrence of world booms and depressions, and how to enable individual countries to protect themselves from such disturbances arising in the outside world, while at the same time retaining the advantages of international trade and capital movements.[31]

---

[31] *Cf.* "International Monetary Organization and Policy", reprinted in *Postwar Monetary Plans* (New York, 1944 ), p. 202.

# SECTION II

## CAPITAL MOVEMENTS AND THE PROPAGATION OF CYCLES DEFINITION AND CONCEPTS

Fluctuations in international capital movements bear a large share of responsibility for the international transmission of cycles, since they determine the level of international investment. The influences on the cyclical behavior is, in general, greater for the long-term or "disturbing" capital movements than for the short-term flows which, at least under gold standard conditions, were primarily "equilibrating" in nature. The importance of the latter is, moreover, restricted to highly development capital markets. It must remarked, however, that the erratic behavior of short-term capital movements in the last two decade increased ponderably their share of responsibility in the propagation of economic fluctuations.[32] The short-term movements have aptly been called "the ungrateful children of the gold standard"; their mobility and development was rendered possible by the existence an international monetary standard, and yet, through an historical irony, they not only robbed the balancing role of gold flows, but actually delivered the coup-de-grace to the gold standard.

The several classifications of foreign investment, according to motivation, ownership, and political aspects, such as direct and portfolio, governmental and private, etc., are too well known to deserve mention. The empirical material available frequently reveals only the composite phenomenon and, <u>grosso modo</u>, the basic distinction between abort-term and long-term, so that definitional refinements have more of a theoretical than of a statistical interest.

Viner speaks of "disturbing" (long-term) and "equilibrating" (short-term) capital movements. Ragnar Nurske contrasts long-term (or independent) with induced capital movements, that result from changes in "other" items in the balance of payments. Iversen talks of "short-term equalizing capital movements, while Kindleberger distinguishes between" income short-term capital movements" and "speculative short-term capital movements".

A careful conceptual discussion of the case been recently offered by Professor Machlup, who contrasts <u>autonomous</u> capital movements ("transactions on capital account which are not in response to any other change in the balance of payments") with <u>induced</u> or <u>accommodating</u> capital exports, which are "responses"

---

[32] *Cf.* J. Donaldson, "The International Balances", in *Annals of the American Academy of Political Science*, No. 170.

rather than "forces" in the markets of foreign domestic funds. Autonomous capital exports are always, ex-definitions, autonomous capital imports of the borrowing country but the <u>spontaneity</u>, (i.e., the initiative in the demand for funds) of the movement may be one-sided, as it frequently happens in our age of "security capitalism".

The different types of capital movements are analyzed according to their impact on primary disbursements (investment and consumption in the borrowing and lending countries) and the problem of transfer is reviewed in the light of the relative income effects, a point that will engage us presently. Another useful contribution of Professor Machlup is to call attention to the tautological concept of equilibrium of the balance of payments, as contrasted with genuine equilibrium:

> In the one sense (tautological) the balance must always "balance", credit and debit entries can never be unequal. In the other sense, thee balance of payments is called "favorable" if a credit item, through counterbalanced by a debit item, is not neutralized in its effects on exchange rates, circulation and income flow.[33]

Another distinction that deserves mention is that between short-term capital movements induced by differential interest rates and those induced by fluctuations or expected changes in exchange rates; the latter tend to be for the most part speculative or, to borrow Professor Haberler's expression, "irregular" in the sense that they flow upstream from debtor and high rate of interest countries to creditor and capital exporting countries.[34]

The present discussion will start with a review of the controversy on the theory of capital transfer, with special reference to the new income approach and its contribution to business cycle analysis. From the theoretical discussion, we shall proceed to consider the mechanical aspects of cycle transmission through capital movements. In the third part attention will be called to the international investment experience.

---

[33] *Cf.* Fritz Machlup, *International Trade* (Philadelphia: The Blakiston Co., 1943).

[34] Nurske defines disequilibrating short-term movements alternatively as "a transfer which proceeds in such a direction that the discount or interest return on comparable assets is bigger in the country of provenance than in the country of destination", or as a transfer "from a country with a deficit to a country with a surplus in current payments and transactions combined with any commercial or investment loans. *International Currency Experience*, p. 72.

# CHAPTER 1

# THE THEORY OF CAPITAL TRANSFER FROM THE VIEWPOINT OF BUSINESS CYCLE ANALYSIS

## A. Development in the Theory of Capital Transfer. Price, Demand Income Aspects of Foreign Lending. The Savings-Investment Theory

The theory of international capital movements is but an aspect of the theory of international trade, the main development of which, from the viewpoint of modern cyclical analysis, will be discussed at a later stage.

It seems pertinent, however, to deal now with some controversial aspects of the relationship between capital movements and commodity trade, and with the discussion that centered around the nuclear problem of the <u>real transfer</u> and of the gain or loss from foreign investment. The main points of disagreement between the "modern" and the classical schools concern the "trade-follow-loan" theorem, the importance of price or demand changes in the mechanism of real transfer, and the course of the terms of trade. All these question are familiar in the modern international trade literature, and will be briefly dealt with. A further question, however, will warrant more detailed discussion. It concerns the contribution of the modern savings investment analysis to the general theory of capital movement and of the business cycle.

(a) <u>The cause or effect controversy</u>: The classical or neo-classical theories attribute an initiating role to capital movements, the balance of trade being the passive or adjustable item. The Keynesian or neo-mercantilistic school, on the other hand, sees capital movements as the effect rather than the cause of trade.[35] Still third compromise view claims that there is no theoretical necessity for the exclusive precedence of either capital movements or trade, all depending on particular historical or economic factors.[36] The discussion has often been obscured by the failure to distinguish between autonomous (long-term) capital exports and not capital exports. That the second adjust themselves to the balance of

---

[35] The matter is fully discussed by Viner, *Studies in the Theory of International Trade* (Harper & Brothers, 1937), pp. 292-304; Carl Iversen, *Aspects of Theory of International Capital Movements* (Copenhagen: 1935), pp. 68-9.

[36] Viner claims, for instance, that although there is a strong historical presumption in favor the classical mechanism, there are other cases in which the Keynesian mechanism seems a plausible one.

trade (or better to the balance of current accounts) is obvious, since they are induced by it. As to autonomous or long-term movements, nothing can be advanced a priori. The balance of trade may well play a passive role, as contended by the "trade-follow-loan" theorem, which is backed by considerable historical evidence. But it is also quite conceivable that autonomous changes in the balance of trade (say an increase in exports) may, by increasing the income level and the rates of savings in creditor countries, induce long-term capital exports.[37]

(b) <u>The course of terms of trade</u>: The traditional theory assumed that the terms of trade would turn against the lending country and in favor of the borrowing country, the real transfer being affected through the export surplus of the former, subsequent to changes in price level. Ohlin, however, by analyzing the possible consequences of changes in demand and shifts in the relative scarcity of productive factors, and of changes in sectional price levels, was able to demonstrate that the course of the terms of trade is not univocally determined[38] and may also turn in favor of the paying country.

(c) <u>The income effects of the capital transfer and the modern cyclical analysis</u>: Although aware of the risk of over-simplification, we believe it would be useful to distinguish three different steps in the theory of capital movements and international trade, according to whether emphasis is laid on price level changes (classical theory), demand changes (modern or new classical theory) and total income effects (neo-mercantilistic theory).

In spite of the partisan fervor which attended the discussion, the theories are complementary rather than conflicting. They worked on different assumption and differ in degree of realism and approximation to actual conditions. It could not, for instance, be said that the classical theory wholly neglected income effects. For, as pointed out by Professor Haberler, price-level changes obviously affect money incomes. It is true, however, that the assumption of necessary and proportional price changes in opposite direction in the paying and receiving

---

[37] A closely related question is that of whether there exists a direct link between capital and commodity exports. The empirical material available reveals that the efforts made by creditor countries to insure a purely bilateral transfer (the proceeds of loans being spent directly in the lending country) have not been on the whole successful. The general philosophy behind the tied-in investment idea seems to be: (a) to foster employment in export industries in the lending country, and (b) to prevent a deterioration of its terms of trade. The data available for French, American and British capital exports seem to indicate that the multilateral transfer has been much more frequently operative than the bilateral one, no direct link being observed between the source of supply of capital and the actual imports of borrowing countries. *Cf.* Iversen, *op. cit.*, pp. 89-97.

[38] *Cf.* Ohlin, *Interregional and International Trade* (Cambridge, Mass. 1933), pp. 152-58. Iversen, *op. cit.*, pp. 510-11.

country is hardly a realistic one if we start from a situation of elastic supply and under-employment equilibrium.[39] The modern emphasis on output rather than on price changes is thus justifiable. The <u>demand analysis</u> is of course more refined and can easily be developed into the income-investment approach, provided multiple and not merely proportional repercussions of changes in purchasing power are taken into account.[40] Both the classical and the demand school are, however, static in the sense that they are mostly concerned with the final equilibrium position rather than with the sequence of changes and transitional positions, which are of major importance for the theory of economic fluctuations.

But, despite the fact that the income-investment analysis can hardly claim novelty, it represents, nevertheless, a most significant contribution to the theory of capital transfer. The attention is deviated from the traditional problem of the mechanisms of the real transfer through changes in export-import prices or in relative demand, to the consideration of the total income effects (investment, consumption, exports, imports) which may be quite different from the original transfer. Much of the current analysis had its roots in the problem of net gain or less from foreign investment, to which we shall now turn.

## 1. The Early Keynesian Analysis.

The problem of the net gain or less from foreign investment was first discussed at length by Keynes in this *A Treatise on Money*. His argument runs substantially as follows: Historically the volume of foreign investment tends to adjust itself to the balance of trade; now, if profitability aspects abroad elicit foreign lending in excess of what is justified by the trade balance,[41] exports of gold will take place and, unless production costs fall sufficiently to yield a compensatory addition to the export surplus, the domestic rate of interest will rise, discouraging investment and employment.[42] These potential unfavorable effects of foreign lending must be

---

[39] *Cf.* Haberler, *op. cit.*, p. 471.

[40] Ohlin's emphasis on the readjustment of productive factors, subsequent to the transfer, contains implicitly the whole nucleus of the modern income approach: "Capital movements, as previously stated, involved (1) the monetary transfer of purchasing power, (2) the real transfer of commodities and services, and (3) a change in the supply of the productive factor called capital which insures after the transfer in the countries concerned; in the importing country such a change appears only if the capital is not consumed as it flows in. *Interregional and International Trade*, p. 39.

[41] Keynes holds that the foreign balance and foreign lending are governed by different factors; the first by relative price levels at home and abroad, and the second by differential interest rates.

[42] Keynes assumes, of course, all along that the terms of trade move against the lending countries. *Cf.* Iversen, *op .cit.*, pp. 166-171; also Svend Laursen, "International Propagation of Business Cycles" (Unpublished Ph.D. dissertation, Harvard University, 1941), pp. 228-381.

weighed against the favorable foreign repercussions, namely, a stimulation of exports to the borrowing country, interest receipts and final redressment of the terms of trade when the loan is repaid.

While over a long period the question of net gain or loss cannot be settled a priori, the solutions depending on the inter-action of the above mentioned factors, there is, according to Keynes, a strong presumption that in the transition period immediate difficulties are created for the lending country which not be entirely offset by the possibility of a future net gain.[43] The above analysis has been ably criticized by Iversen on the following grounds:

(a) The terms of trade needs not necessarily move against the lending country.
(b) The gain from foreign investment cannot be measured simply by the difference between the yield from the capital exported as compared with the yield that would be realized from the same amount of capital if applied at home, for foreign lending is likely to increase also the marginal productivity of that part of the capital which was not exported.
(c) Considering the whole cycle of the transaction, from the original transfer to the repayment of the loan, there is a strong likelihood that the outcome will be favorable rather then neutral or negative for the lending country, since its eventual losses due to unfavorable terms of trade will be more than neutralized by:
   i. a final redressment of the terms of trade,
   ii. net interest payments by the borrowing country.[44]

The question is not one that can be easily settled. The factors involved are complex. Much will depend on whether the exported capital gives rise to cooperative or competing industries in the receiving country. Again, the results may be different according to whether one thinks of the <u>net gain</u> in terms of improvement of the world income that has historically attended the growth of capital exports (and which, as Keynes realizes, involve always an indirect gain for the lending country), or whether one thinks in the narrower terms of direct again for an individual capital exporting country.

Mr. Svend Laursen, in his paper already referred to, raised a very interesting point concerning the two opposite interpretation of the impact of exportation

---

[43] *Cf.* Keynes, *A Treatise on Money*, p. 347: "If the demands of home investment are elastic and the foreign trade position is inelastic the troubles and inconveniences of the transition may be very great".

[44] *Cf.* Iversen, *op. cit.*, p. 169.

of capital on the lending country. He holds that Keynes and the imperialistic theory of crises stressed both two particular aspects of a more general theory of transfer. Keynes emphasized the effects of the transfer on the paying country through the direct impact on domestic investment and seems to have underestimated the possibility that the expansionary movements in the receiving country might stimulate the export industries of the paying country to an extent sufficient to offset or even to exceed the initial deflationary movements. In other words, be over-emphasized the direct domestic income changes, neglecting the foreign repercussions.

The Imperialistic theory of crises is still more one-sided. Foreign investment is appraised merely from the viewpoint of the creation of export balances that enable the capital exporting country to stave off chronic under-consumption tendencies. The impact of the capital transfer on the level of domestic investment is completely ignored.

Those two extremes can be neatly, even if too simply, expressed by the use of the familiar multiplier equations for two countries:

$$Y = (V + x - M) \frac{1}{1-\alpha}$$
$$Y' = (V' + X' - M') \frac{1}{1-\alpha'}$$

in which Y stands for income, V for net home investment X – M for the export balance and $1/1-\alpha$ for the multiplier, expressed as the reciprocal of the marginal propensity to save. Keynes laid stress on the impact of the capital transfer on V and neglected the counteracting effect of changes in X – M. Clearly both are particular cases of a general solution. Whether the final effect of a capital transfer will be inflationary or deflationary in the paying and receiving countries depends on the relative intensity of changes in V and in X – M, which are governed by the marginal propensities.[45] The gain or loss from foreign investment cannot be settled on a priori grounds.

## 2. The Modern Keynesian Analysis

Since many of the basis postulates of the *Treatise on Money* have been

---

[45] Strictly the above observation should refer only to the earlier Keynesian formulation. The new literature on the foreign trade multiplier that sprang after the publication of the *General Theory* has a definite mercantilistic slant and tends to overemphasize the stimulating role of the export surpluses, rather than the other way round. Professor Machlup has some interesting comments on what he calls the neo-mercantilistic and the imperialistic interpretations of the multiplier. He approaches the question from a different angle from that envisaged by Mr. Laureen. But more of it later.

formulated in the *General Theory*, the earlier Keynesian analysis of foreign lendings calls for a re-examination. The earlier argument laid special stress on the effects of a rise in the rate of interest upon the level of home investment and employment. In the *General Theory*, Mr. Keynes called attention to the mutual determination of the level of investment by the rate of interest and the marginal efficiency of capital. The alleged danger of encroachment of foreign lending upon the supply of savings has also to be revised in the light of the liquidity preference concept. These qualifications, plus the recognition of the institutional weakness of the incentives to invest in wealthy societies (lending nations), would to borrow Mr. Lausen's phrase, lead one to:

> Expect Keynes now to with less skepticism on foreign investment than in *A Treatise on Money*, because of his theory of unemployment which arises from the insufficiency of inducement to new investment.[46]

It is regrettable that Keynes did not re-examine the question at any length. The somewhat cursory allusions to the problem in the *Notes on Mercantilism* seem again to stress unduly the unfavorable repercussions of foreign lending upon the rate of interest,[47] when a more promising and realistic line of approach would

---

[46] Laursen, *op. cit.*, p. 230.

[47] *Cf. General Theory*, p. 337: "Great Britain in the pre-war years of the 20th century provided an example of a country in which the excessive facilities of foreign lending and the purchase of properties abroad frequently stood in the way of the decline of the domestic rate of interest which was required to insure full employment at home." If we consider, however, the favorable effects of foreign lending on the marginal efficiency of capital, and the institutional stickiness of the rate of interest (which has more to do with the liquidity preference than with foreign lending). Keynes seems to overemphasize the interest rate side of the investment function. He seems to have projected into the past an analysis of foreign investment which is less applicable to the pre-war period than to the troubled conditions of the post-war period, namely decreasing international specialization, and trade restrictions that inhibited the response of British export to capital flows. The point is well expressed by Professor Williams: "British economists complain that capital which should go into home investment goes abroad. That any Englishman should make such an outcry is a striking commentary on how times have changed. Before the war of 1914 British foreign investment was quickly reflected in the export trade. Foreign investment meant more and cheaper food and raw materials and an increased market for British goods. As I have said, investment and trade were dual aspects of a virtually simultaneous process. The cumulative effects upon England were extremely beneficial. She was enable to specialize at home in industries operating at a decreasing costs as output increased, while developing abroad cheaper products of increasing cost industries. Armed with these advantages, and intellectually fortified by her doctrine of free trade as a universal and eternal truth, England played at will upon the economic world, with enormous advantage to it as well as to herself. The more capital she exported, the more she had for home investment. In this way she piled up capital and labor upon her small island, and earned excellent rewards for both". *Post-War Monetary Plans*, p. 169.

suggest itself by focusing the question from the viewpoint of the marginal efficiency of capital and of the propensity to spend[48] of lending and borrowing countries.

This has been, in fact, the line of approach pursued by the contemporary savings-investment analysis developed along Keynesian lines, Contrary to the traditional assumption that a capital transfer implies always disinvestment in the lending and investment in the borrowing country (what in fact amounts to a disguised formulation of the law of conversation of purchasing power), the present day discussion suggests an ampler range of possible outcomes.

For, remarks Professor Machlup, primary disbursements in the paying country, as a result of capital movements, may fall more than rise in the receiving country; they fall less in the paying country then they rise in the receiving country; they may fall in the paying country by the same amount by which they rise in the borrowing country.[49] It might be helpful at this point, to single out the salient conceptual modifications, introduced by the modern income analysis over the traditional and over the Keynesian formulation.

The first point concerns the behavior of interest rates and investment. It is now commonly admitted that lending tends to, but does not necessarily bring about, a reverse and equalizing movement of interest rates in the borrowing country and in the lending country; this movement need not be proportional and need affect investment proportionally in the two regions. For loanable funds may come out of dishoarding (fall in liquidity preference) or credit expansion without any encroachment upon the domestic rate of interest or upon primary disbursements for invest-

---

[48] In the sense used by Angell, i.e., as the sum of the marginal propensities to consume and to invest.

[49] *Cf.* Machlup, *op. cit.*, p. 154. Strictly, as pointed out by Lloyd Metzler, there is still another possibility; that primary disbursements in either country may remain unchanged, e.g., through a transfer of savings from domestic to foreign securities. *Cf. Review of Economic Statistics* (February 1945), p. 41. Shan-Wei-Fong (in "Business Cycles and International Balance of Payments", unpublished Ph.D. dissertation, Harvard University, 1941) points out also a limiting case in which the immediate stimulating effect will be confined entirely to the paying country, such as when the loan is taken entirely in the form of imports of investment goods. This is, however, true only for short and not for long-run income effects.

ment and consumption in the paying country.⁵⁰ Conversely, borrowed funds may be partly dissipated into hoards (rise in the liquidity preference) or be absorbed into bank reserves, without provoking a proportional credit expansion and a decline of the rate of interest in the receiving country. Depending upon the shape of the liquidity preferences curve in both countries, the rate of interest may rise less in the paying country than it falls in the lending country—or vice-versa. Only when the supply of funds in the lending, and the demand for then in the borrowing country, are perfectly inelastic, as it is likely to occur during a boom, capital exports (imports) are followed by proportional disinvestment (investment).⁵¹ The response of investment to interest rate has been grossly over-rated as shown by the studies of Tinberghen and the Oxford-Harvard Investigators. Both in the open and in the closed system theorizing, more attention is now being given to the demand side (marginal efficiency of capital) than to the supply side of investment function.

Attention should also be called to a limiting case in which, in the short run, capital transfer may lead to a greater disparity than to an equalization of interest rates. This occurs when the export of capital to new countries opens up the possibility of new combinations of productive factors and of utilization of previously idle resources (ris-

---

⁵⁰ Havek, however, offers a different analysis. He claims, substantially, that reverse changes in interest rates and investment need not occur under a homogenous international standard, but that under a hybrid gold standard system (with Central Bank and fractional reserves) both interest rates and investment in the paying country are likely to be affected. In his view, an international money-flow (unless the balance of payment reverse itself very quickly either by off-setting short-term capital movements or by changes in the balance of trade) will, owing to the organization of the banking system, encroach upon the reserve margin. This leads the banks to cancel loans (which are used mostly for investment) and to raise the bank rates even if no basis changes have occurred in the rate of profitability or in the supply of savings. This raising of the bank rate over the equilibrium rate, by virtue of purely monetary rather than real reasons, will of course be reflected in a decline of investment. Hayek's analysis is based, however on somewhat rigid assumptions. It would hold true only (a) if there were no dishoarding by private individuals, and b) if the banking system were loaned up. Moreover, the contention that contraction will always alter the "customary proportions between the different parts of the credit structure and that the only way which to restore these proportions is to cancel loans made for investment purposes" is scarcely tenable in our modern era of consumers' credit. The truth is that credit contraction, if it occurs, may affect primary disbursements for consumption just as well as investment outlays. Aside from that, however, it must be noted that even under a fractional reserve Central Banking system, credit contraction need not necessarily occur and the probability of its occurrence is in itself subject to cyclical changes. One cannot escape the impression that the assumption of full employment is still pervasive in Hayek's theorizing. *Cf.* his *Monetary Nationalism and International Stability*, pp. 16-34.

⁵¹ J. Mosak's concise remarks in Chapter IX of his *General Equilibrium Theory in International Trade* (Bloomington, Ind., 1944) are substantially in agreement with this viewpoint, although couched in different terminology. He seems, however, to accept the traditional view on the movement of interest rates in lending and borrowing countries, or at least fails to express the necessary qualifications. *Cf.* pp. 171-72.

ing of the marginal efficiency of capital). The rate of interest may then rise rather than fail in the receiving country as a result of the importation of capital.

The organization of the banking system and the length of the income propagation period are of obvious importance in this respect, since they determine to a large extent the degree of expansion or contraction of credit subsequent to the monetary transfer. Viner has pointed out that if as a result of changes in the balance of trade funds are transferred from a country with inelastic credit structure to one with a highly developed credit organization, the net world effect will be inflationary. Balegh and Neisser have reminded us that a sudden transfer of funds provoked, for instance by violent shifts in international demand or by a fall in prices of raw materials, is likely to have a net world deflationary effects since the receiving country is not prepared to expand credit until structural adjustments are made and new investment plans concerted.

These observations yield two important results that have a bearing on the preceding discussion:

> (a) foreign investment does not always compete with domestic investment and consumption, but may sometimes involve merely "parting with liquidity". It follows thus that not all capital exports (imports) are deflationary (inflationary) but rather that several types of capital movement should be distinguished.[52] Following Shang-Wei-Fong, we can classify capital movements as:
> 
> i. Inflationary in nature, e.g., granting of bank credit for purchase of foreign securities;
> 
> ii. Deflationary in nature, such as transfer of funds from active circulation for hoarding purposes (capital flight);
> 
> iii. Deflationary in one market and inflationary in the other, as in the familiar case of transfer of savings.[53]
> 
> (b) The relationship of capital movements to interest rates and investment is in itself subject to cyclical changes. During depression, capital exports (if the

---

[52] We are neglecting for the moment the complications presented by unstable exchange rates upon capital movements and the rate of interest. Clearly, however, exchange rates are not neutral elements since they are likely to affect the liquidity preference schedule. In an open system, the instability of exchange rates leads to a higher demand for funds both for the precautionary and the speculative motives. The rate of interest will be accordingly affected. The limiting case of perfectly free exchanges may in fact lead to paradoxical results. In the absence of international money transfers, capital exports would affect only the relative price of the currencies and the balance of trade, the results being always inflationary in the paying and deflationary in the receiving country. *Cf.* Haberler, *op. cit.*, pp. 441-451.

[53] Compare Shang-Kwei-Fong, *loc. cit.*, pp. 180-83, who reaches the following conclusion: "(1) not all of an influx of capital is invested; (2) not the whole amount of capital outflow is at the expense of domestic investment; and 3) when a certain amount of capital flows from one country to another, the loss of investment in one may larger or smaller than the increase in investment in the other."

pessimistic psychology of investors does not eliminate them altogether) are not likely, given the liquidity of the money market, to compete with domestic investment or consumption, and they may exert but little influence on the domestic rate of interest if there is a shift to the left in the liquidity preference schedule. The liquidity of the banking system may of course be unfavorably affected, lending ultimately to credit deflation; but this need not necessarily occur, since the stimulation of exports to the receiving country, reverse short-term capital flows, and new savings induced by the rise in the income level may replenish reserves in time to prevent credit contraction.

During the upswing and especially in the boom, the domestic supply of funds becomes progressively inelastic. Capital exports may than either check the expansion or accelerate the crisis by affecting primary disbursements for home investment and consumption.

These observations suggest that the attempt to assess abstractly the net gain or loss of foreign investment, without taking into account cyclical factors, is an idle one. For an export of capital during periods of slack business activity and increasing propensity to hoard is clearly a net gain. In revival and recovery the outcomes may be indefinite, depending on whether there is encroachment upon domestic consumption and investment and also on the intensity of the favorable foreign repercussion.[54]

The second point, which leads to similar results, concerns the distinction between the direct and the indirect affects of the transfer. The main attention of both the traditional and the "modern" school has concentrated on the direct affect of the transfer on price levels, exchange and interest rates, and purchasing power, which are supposed to move in opposite direction in the lending and borrowing countries. The same does not hold true, however, for the induced changes in investment, consumption, exports and imports, which usually tend to reserve the original investment. Once one considers not only the primary but also the secondary or tertiary disbursements, it becomes clear that the total effects of the transfer, or in other words, the net gain or loss from foreign investment, are directly dependent not only on the original transfer but on the marginal propensities of the lending and borrowing countries. An exports of capital from a country with a high marginal propensity to save and low marginal propensity to invest to another in

---

[54] Compare Malchup, *op. cit.*, p. 150: "If the acquisition of foreign assets for some reason appears more affective, it may well take the place of home investment. Thus in all spontaneous export capital cases, home investment may be encroached upon. However, in times of easy money, a large part of the funds for the acquisition of foreign assets will probably come from liquid reserves and new bank credits. To the extent that this takes place without a stiffening of interest rates the level of current home investment will not be reduced".

which the marginal propensity to invest exceeds the marginal propensity to save has a <u>net inflationary</u> effect for both of them.[55]

Equilibrium will be re-established at a higher income level. In this hypothesis, as pointed out by Lloyd Metzler, it is likely that the balance of trade will move in favor of the lending country by more than the amount required to effect the real transfer. Then, continues Metzler, "it actually pays the country with a low propensity to invest to transfer a part of his income to the country with a high propensity to invest". The reverse will take place if the paying country is the one in which the propensity to invest exceeds the propensity to save. Income will fall in both countries. The expansionary effect of the income flow upon the receiving country is more than neutralized by the induced reduction of exports to the paying country. The balance of trade will move against the receiving country by more than the amount of the transfer.[56]

The relevance of the preceding section for the cyclical analysis is clear; were the direct effects of the transfer the only ones to be taken into account, the hypothesis of an inverse cyclical behavior between creditor and debtor countries, as a result of capital movements, would seem plausible indeed. If we take into account, however, the total effects of the transfer, there is no reason to expect an inverse rather than a parallel cyclical movement. The latter, in fact, is the more likely to occur, as noted by Svend Laursen, the higher are the marginal propensities to consume and to import in the receiving countries; this condition has been often historically fulfilled, since capital tends to flow from wealthy and highly developed countries to young countries, in which a large proportion of each increment of income is spent for consumption and imports, with a net expansional effect on world incomes. This mechanism of parallel expansion has its counterpart in the vicious solidarity of deflation. Debt collection and repatriation of capital, in the downturn of the cycle, force a contraction in debtor countries, often without eliciting an equivalent expansion in creditor countries, thus creating a parallel downward movement.

## 3. Practical Implications of the Savings-Investment Analysis

While the savings-investment analysis throws considerable light on the

---

[55] *Cf.* also Mosak, *op. cit.*, p. 171. Who express very concisely a similar viewpoint although using different terminology.

[56] *Cf.* his review of Machlup's book in the *Review of Economic Statistics* (February 1945), pp. 39-41. Metzler's observations refer to income transfer subsequent to changes in the balance of trade brought about by an expansion of domestic investment. But the same analysis can be applied without change of substance to the case of capital exports.

complex relationships of capital movements, its practical value is much less definite. It constitutes an excellent analytical tool to interpret ex post facto a given situation but it cannot furnish but tentative indications of policies. For until the unstable marginal propensities can be rendered amenable to statistical determination (and there is small hope that a satisfactory degree of precision will ever be reached), there is no way to make capital movements responsive to anything else (aside from political considerations) than to profitability prospects, an determined by differential interest rates and by the modifying factors of risk and friction. The operation of the multipliers cannot be taken into account by the individual investors.

In the practical world, the long-run income affects on the borrowing and lending countries are a relatively abstract problem, as compared to the more concrete ones of the balance of payments, and foreign exchange. The best investment from an income and welfare viewpoint may not be the best one from the balance of payments viewpoint. This has led to the heated controversy on productive and unproductive use of the loans. The well known discussion which centered around the utilization of German loans for social and welfare projects (held as unproductive) has done good service in sharpening the issue, although beclouded by the failure of some writers to realize at least the possibility, if not the probability, of an indirect productivity of welfare loans, i. e., by freeing local capital for investment or by increasing the efficiency of workers. The issue is, however, an extraneous one to our purpose here. It will suffice to note that, given the relevant propensities, the income-energizing power of investment is not univocally related to, nor accurately measured by, its foreign exchange yielding power.[57]

The second question bears on the relative merit of domestic and foreign investment for the stimulation of income and employment. An optimistic school would suggest that domestic and foreign investment present an alternate and equivalent use for idle funds on excess savings, the difference being only one of a direct as against an indirect stimulation. It is also advanced that foreign investments may often be more advantageous since they are made on a profitability basis, while domestic investment will at least partly consist of non-profit public projects which increase the burden of public debt. It appears that barring the above mentioned possibility of wide difference in the propensity to invest as between lending and

---

[57] The relationship between foreign investment and income, from the viewpoint of the balance of payment position and of the maximization of foreign exchange has been ably discussed by J. J. Pollack in an article on "Balance of Payments Problems in Countries, Reconstruction with the Help of Foreign Loans", in *Quarterly Journal of Economic* (February 1943), pp. 208-40. Pollack distinguishes three types of investment according to their income creating power and their contribution to the foreign exchange balance. *Cf.* also Norman Buchanan, *International Investment and Domestic Welfare* (New York: Henry Holt & Co., 1944), pp. 102-8.

borrowing countries, domestic investment should be considered more energizing, because foreign investments benefit the domestic economy only through the incentive to export industries and whatever secondary expansion may occur in related industries. Domestic investment, however, affects also the goods that do not move in international trade, especially the construction industries and building trades, which are precisely the ones responsible for sharper fluctuations in employment and income, and which are by nature non-exportable.[58]

This argument will, however, lose cogency if, given the institutional stickiness of interest rates, the marginal propensity to save is too high and the marginal efficiency of capital chronically low at home. In this case, it would pay to take advantage of the higher foreign multiplier. This provides a good argument in favor of a generous or "imperialistic interpretation of the theory of the multiplier", of which Professor Machlup has offered a well-balanced and enlightening discussion.[59]

## B. The Over-Investment Theory and the Propagation of Cycles[60]

A valuable attempt to explore the international applications of the Austrian over-investment theory and the role played by international capital movements in the diffusion of trade fluctuations has been made by Ragnar Nurske in *Internationale Kapitalbewegungen*, which develops the ideas contained an his earlier article on the *Ursachen und Wirkungen der Kapitalbewegungern*.[61]

The limitations of the over-investment theory for a closed or spaceless system, either in the original Hayekian formulation in *Prices and Profits*, or in his new approach *Profits, Interest and Investment*, are well known. Outside of the full employment assumption which excludes the possibility of a parallel expansion of consumers' and producers' goods industries, and allows only for expansion by subtraction of resources—a limitation which Hayek himself recognized—two pertinent and damaging criticisms have been made by Professors Hansen and Neisser. The first questioned the actual occurrence of a shortening of the structure of pro-

---

[58] *Cf.* Buchanan, *op. cit.*, pp. 143-49.

[59] *Cf.* Machlup, *op. cit.*, pp. 214-18.

[60] We are indebted to Mr. Laursen's paper (*International Propagation of Business Cycles*, unpublished Ph.D. dissertation, Harvard University, 1941) for most of the suggestions on this topic which in fact amounts to little more than a resume of this exposition. *Cf.* also Haberler, *op. cit.*, pp. 70-1. Professor Neisser offers a similar discussion in connection with "under-savings as a cause of crises". *Cf.* his *Some International Aspects of Business Cycles* (Philadelphia, 1935), pp. 44-51.

[61] *Zeitschrift für Nationalaokonomie*, 1934, p. 86.

duction in depression, as well as the inevitability of a break-down if the credit system is sufficiently elastic. The second pointed out the inadequacy of the explanation of the upper turning point via restoration of the consumption saving ratio, in the case that the round-about process of production has been brought to completion.

The weakness of the over-investment postulates are transplanted by Nurske into the international field. He succeeds, nevertheless, in bringing out some interesting relationships valuable for the explanation of the propagation of cycles through capital movements. Nurske stresses the fact that the inadequacy of internal savings to finance investment in debtor countries renders them doubly vulnerable. The boom may be brought to an end not only by fluctuations in the rate of savings (either voluntary or forced) but also by fluctuations in the rate of capital imports. If the inflow of funds stops at a late phase of the upswing, it may be impossible for debtor countries to prevent rupture of equilibrium, since even a considerable rise in the rate of interest may fail to induce capital movements, which have to surmount psychological and institutional resistances ("elements of Friction").

From the viewpoint of the lending country, the process of transfer will not be disturbing if only new savings are exported, while, if the amortization quota is encroached upon, the structure of production is likely to be distorted, since the most mobile form of capital (working capital) is likely to be exported first, thus depriving the fixed equipment of the complementary means of production.

Nurske suggests the possibility of both a parallelism or a divergence of cyclical fluctuations as a result of capital movements, all depending on the relationship between the natural and the market rate of interest. If, in a financial center, the market rate of interest is lowered in relation to the equilibrium rate, an expansion of credit will take place, and capital will flow out, provoking a parallel cyclical expansion in related markets. If, however, it is the equilibrium rate than rises, the expansionary effect in the first country is the same but the effects on borrowing markets may be different. The expanding country may draw away funds, causing a loss of capital and divergent cyclical developments in dependent markets.[62]

The mechanism of transfer is different under gold standard and under flexible exchanges. In the first case, the export surplus (real transfer) presupposes a deflationary policy in the lending country. Under flexible exchanges, the foreign

---

[62] *Cf.* Laursen, *loc. cit.*, p. 108. In his earlier paper, on the causes and effects of capital movements. Nurske has a very interesting point concerning the relationship between capital movements and changes in the technique of production. He assumed that a technical improvement occurs in one country, (thus raising the marginal productivity of capital) and concludes that the effects on capital movements will depend on (a) whether the improvement is of labor or saving type, (b) on the elasticity of demand for that country's products. The inflow of capital will be greater: (a) the more labor-saving is the invention, (b) the more elastic is the demand. *Cf.* Iversen, *op. cit.*, p. 132.

investment will tend to provoke an appreciation of the currency and subsequent stimulation of the exports of the lending country, decreasing the need for deflationary price adjustments.

The general limitations of the over-investment theory, in abstract, are aggrandized when account is taken in its international application of disparities in structural composition. For, capital importing countries are mostly agricultural areas, in which the "technical coefficients of production" have a much smaller elasticity of substitution than in industrial structures and the concepts of shortening or lengthening of the period of production, a much narrower field of application. Since in the first stage of industrial development the inflow of capital is usually directed to the financing of railroad and transportation undertakings, it is the Cassel rather than the Hayekian model of crisis that finds its most frequent historical verification.

Svend Laursen draws also attention to two specific faults in Nurske's presentation. One concerns the static character of the treatment, which neglects the bearing on the cyclical prospectus in the borrowing and lending countries as it affects (and not as it is affected) capital movements. The second deals with the familiar simplification of considering only the direct effects of a capital transfer (inflationary in the paying and deflationary in the borrowing countries) neglecting the induced effects (via the balance of trade), which generally act in opposite sense to the direct ones and may entirely reverse the expansionary and deflationary tendencies and, of course, the entire cyclical behavior of the countries concerned.[63] Whatever the measure of agreement may be, in relation to the main tenets of the over-investment theory, Nurske's work re-emphasized the peculiar vulnerability of debtor countries to cyclical shocks.

The impact of fluctuations in capital movements on the terms and volume of their trade already quite well known. But the difficulties added by the dependence of their investment activity on an international margin of saving is a further element of instability that deserves closer attention.

---

[63] Sometimes a further simplification is made, namely, that the two movements are opposite in direction and proportional in strength. This is clearly wrong, since the cumulative process originated by the transfer may be quite out of proportion to the transfer itself. *Cf.* Laursen, *op. cit.*, pp. 113-14.

# CHAPTER II

# EMPIRICAL AND STRUCTURAL FACTORS

## A. Localization of Credit and the Cyclical Behavior

The influence of localization of credit and capital on cyclical movements is, as noted by Professor Harberler, much less definite than the influence of natural and artificial obstacles to foreign trade. The latter tend unequivocally to localize booms and depressions and disturb the uniformity of cyclical movements. What affects, however, limitations to the mobility of capital will have on the cyclical behavior cannot be decided <u>a priori</u>. We shall subsequently analyze the complications which are introduced by the imperfect and sectional mobility of capital, by the existence of different degree of mobility and by cyclical fluctuations in the mobility of credit.

### 1. Imperfect Mobility of Capital

The imperfect mobility of capital renders possible the persistence of differential international interest rates. If perfectly mobile, capital flows would lead to a perfect equalization of the rates of interest. Physical and institutional obstacles lead, however, to persistent inequalities in capital distribution, capital flowing only when the differential margin is sufficient to overcome the elements of friction. The international demand for, and the supply of, savings is thus unevenly distributed. While there is a long-term <u>gravitational force</u> away from countries where capital is abundant relatively to labor and land, to neo-and semi-capitalistic countries where the relative scarcity of production factors is the reserve, the existence of technical, psychological and institutional barriers to foreign investment causes the international co-existence of chronic over-savings in certain areas and capital scarcity in others.

The possible effects of localization of credit on the cyclical transmission are difficult to trace. There are counteracting forces at work. Let us suppose, for instance, that an autonomous expansion takes place in one country. If credit is mobile, funds will flow in, feeding the boom and delaying the rise in interest rates. Otherwise, the shortage of funds would prove an early check on the boom. The mobility of capital may thus help in prolonging the expansion. But in depression the localization of credit also may be an advantage, since the impossibility of exporting capital would cause a quicker reduction in interest rates than it would be possible if capital were exported. If several countries are expanding simultaneously at an uneven rate, the mobility of capital may prolong the prosperity of one at the expense of the others, all depending upon the relative attractiveness of the investment market. Localization of credit would then promote a more even expansion. "Similarly", says Professor Haberler, "localization of credit may put a brake on depression in the most depressed countries, while prolonging it in the less depressed." Thus mobility of capital may feed as well as hinder a boom, and conversely relieve as well as aggravate a depression, all depending on the elasticity of the supply of funds in the market, or its rate of expansion and on the reaction upon commodity trade.[64]

Switching to the question of long-term trends, it may be well to recall the already mentioned possibility, to which Keynes and the French School have called attention, namely that in the long run, were it not for the excessive facilities for capital export and the bias in favor of foreign investment, localization of capital might bring about the following results: (a) the domestic rate of interest of the capital exporting country would fall more rapidity to the level compatible with full employment (Keynes), (b) the investor psychology would suffer a radical change in favor of home investment (French School). While this speculation on hypothetical economic behavior is legitimate, neither of the inferences does full justice to foreign investment. For, even aside from the probability that part of the unexported funds would be sterilized into hoards (without affecting the rate of interest, it must be recalled that foreign investment would tend to increase the marginal productivity of the non-exported capital and counteract the potential evils of an unhampered mobility of funds.

The above analysis is, however, purely formal in nature. Capital mobility or immobility has to be considered not in abstract but in relation to commodity trade and, for that matter, to the organization of the banking system. Whether the mobility of capital tends to synchronize or differentiate booms or depressions is a question that cannot be settled on general grounds, without a consideration of the total affects of each individual capital transfer. Little more can be said than that capital movements transmit shock which may induce divergent cyclical movements, depending on the general economic prospects of the paying and receiving countries.

## 2. Sectional Mobility

In the actual world, we find different degrees of mobility of different type of claims and debts. There are in effect several sub-markets for money of different degrees of liquidity. Government obligations and industrial loans, for instance, have different salability and yields. The prevalence of regional and sectional differences in mobilities and interest rates is thus easily understandable.

---

[64] This analysis is largely based on Professor Haberler's notes on *International Aspect of Business Cycles*, chapter 12, pp. 415-25.

## 3. Cyclical Mobility

The next question is of greater interest. In the mobility of capital itself subject to cyclical variation? An affirmative reply is given by Professor Haberler:

> It may be possible to make the generalization that during the downswing of the world business cycle, when the confidence of the investor is at low ebb, foreign lending is especially avoided as more dangerous than domestic lending, so that the brunt of depression falls on the borrowing country, while countries which are usually capital exporting, obtain some relief through the improvement of their balance of payments.[65]

This observation is plausible enough on general grounds, but data of actual experience, so far gathered, are not conclusive, the correlation between the business cycle and capital movements varying in significance and importance between countries and between successive cycles. The matter will be discussed at length at a later stage.

We may mention, at this point, because of its bearing on the problem of cyclical mobility of capital, the "theorem of the incline" suggested by Professor Wageman. In his explanation, which has close affinity with the rate-of-profit version of the Imperialistic theory of crises, capital and labor, under the impact of depression, would flow to neo- and non-capitalistic countries "owing to the gravitational force generated by the incline between the various structural groups".[66] A revival might then be set in motion in the latter countries, increasing their ability to absorb industrial products and giving the mature capitalist countries an initial impetus towards recovery. As full prosperity is reached, the incline in the world economy would level off, and the upward movements brought to a standstill. On this showing, the increased mobility of capital would be a phenomenon of the downswing rather than of the upswing.

As regards the short-term capital movements, a detailed investigation has been conducted by Professor Neisser on the pre-war experience under the gold standard. He contends that the mobility of short-term capital displays a cyclical pattern, increasing in depression and decreasing in prosperity. Neisser finds a close correlation between fluctuations in exchange rates and interest rates for the principal European markets (a smaller degree of consonance being noticeable between

---

[65] *Cf.* Haberler, *op. cit.*, pp. 424-25.

[66] *Cf.* E. Wageman, *op. cit.*, pp.262.

London and New York) and resorts, for explanation, to a "principle of solidarity" that would link maximum fluctuations in interest rates to the maximum risk of changes in exchange rates, within the gold points. He surmises that short-term capital flows, for the period reviewed, showed as a rule lower mobility during expansion, this being explained by, (a) decreased liquidity of the banking system, (b) pessimistic expectations of the investor regarding the course of the balance of trade and of the exchange rates during the expansion process.

While Professor Neisser's explanations do not sound convincing, they serve to indicate that no generalization is possible. On one hand, the psychological resistance to capital exports tends to grow in depression (despite the low rate of return at home and the attractiveness of rates of interest abroad). On the other hand, the liquidity of the banking system would tend to increase the mechanical mobility or capital. Whether it is the psychological or institutional factors that will shape the investors' behavior cannot be predicted on theoretical grounds. In the absence of an international money standard, such as the one prevailed in the pre-war period, short-term capital movements are of course expected to show a still more erratic behavior. The widening of the margin exchange fluctuations reduced considerably their sensitiveness to changes interest rates.

The matter has to be left unsettled. There are changes in mobility of capital during the course of the cycle, but the direction of these changes cannot be confidently predicted.

# CHAPTER III

## THE INTERNATIONAL INVESTMENT EXPERIENCE

The international impact of fluctuations in investment was dramatically evidenced by the experience of the last depression. The rapid propagation of deflationary movements between countries connected by financial complementary (creditor-debtor relationships) rendered clear the need for the adoption, on an international scale, of anti-cyclical investment policies.

The international investment experience in the last decade is thus summarized by Colin Clark:[67]

> In the five years before the depression (1925–1929) the average annual amount to long-term foreign loans in the four most important exporting countries (United States, Great Britain, Netherlands and France) was 2.1 billion dollars (in 1928 it even valued 2.8 billion dollars). By 1932 its amount had fallen off 334 million dollars. In the first years of the upswing, capital exports increased somewhat. In 1936, however, they amounted to only 311 million dollars and were not even as high as in 1932.

This drastic decline in foreign lending created adjustment problems of first magnitude. The rigidity of the loan contracts, in face of wide income fluctuations, forced the debtor countries, grievously hit by a drastic fall in the gold prices of their exports, to procure international liquidity by exportation of their gold reserves, by curtailment of imports and by stimulation of exports even at the cost of competitive price-deflation. In order to size up in broad terms the adjustment problem in the thirties we may, following Colin Clark, lump on one side all countries that had a creditor position in the inter-way period (United States, Great-Britain, France, Holland, Belgium, Switzerland, Sweden and Ireland) and on the other all debtor countries. Utilizing the data of the League of Nations on balance of payments, we find that the deficit in the balance of payments of the debtors (excess of interest and amortization dues over receipts on current and capital accounts) amounted to only 146 million dollars in 1927, but jumped to 708 millions in 1929, and 2,645 million in 1932.

This liquidity-gap was wholly covered in 1927 by export surpluses; in 1929,

---

[67] *Cf.* Colin Clark, *The Conditions of Economic Progress*, pp. 462-63.

386 million were paid in gold and the balance by increasing exports and reducing imports. In 1932, gold exports had raised to 1,081 million, the rest being paid by a drastic contraction of imports.[68]

The vicious spiral of deflation had set in; by refusing to lend abroad and exacting repayment at the bottom of depression, the creditor countries rendered in fact impossible the restoration of international equilibrium, the more so because the improvement in their liquidity position, subsequent to debt collection, failed to provoke a compensatory credit expansion.[69]

To be sure, the responsibility for the widening of the deflation cannot be ascribed to any single group; quite independently from the cessation of capital inflow, the resistance to depression and the balance-of-payments position in many capital importing areas had been weakened by misuse of foreign loans and unproductive borrowing during the twenties, by artificial price maintenance schemes and by the continuous financing of artificially high levels of consumption and imports, through foreign borrowing.

But there is little doubt that a large share of responsibility for the spreading and aggravation of the depression is to be attributed to the instability of capital exports by the major industrial countries, which expanded and narrowed erratically the international margin of savings on which the neo- and semi-capitalist areas are dependent. By and large, the fluctuations in raw-material and semi-industrialized countries were of adaptive type. They lacked international "buffer reserves" to withstand the pressure on the balance of payments and had literally to export gold and import deflation.

However, the behavior of capital exports was not unstable but "perverse" in the sense that it tended to expand in times of prosperity and rising prices and to contract precisely countries less liquid internationally. In the course of the deflationary processes, the tightening of the international financial markets and the pressure for debt collection is generally greater than that of the domestic market because, due to institutional resistance, the liquidity preference is greater as regards foreign than domestic loans.

The type or form of foreign investment is also important for the study of cyclical affects. It has been found that direct or equity investment proved much burdensome for debtor countries than portfolio investments. The reasons are both of a technical and of a cyclical nature. Direct investments are general more productive because they are carried mostly on a strict profitability basis, the misman-

---

[68] *Apud* Colin Clark, *ib.*, pp. 462-63.

[69] This result is, incidentally, precisely the opposite of the one visualized in the traditional theory of international trade. Gold flowed from countries with a depressed price-level to countries of higher price-levels.

agement of funds being in many cases reduced by technical assistance and managerial supervision by the investing concerns. Another important factor, of a cyclical nature, is that equity investments do not involve fixed interest or amortization charges since dividend remittances accompany fluctuations in internal business.[70]

It is now widely recognized that the <u>rigidity of loan contracts</u> and the inflexible character of interest and amortization payments creates serious transfer problems, which aggravate the deflationary pressure on debtor countries. Thus, as automatic cyclical adjustment of debt payments either through remission or rebate of payments during bad years, i.e., periods of falling export prices and exchange stringency, would be an important step towards increasing the resistance of debtor countries to imposed deflation.

A word might finally be said concerning the change in the character and function of short-term capital movements, that took place since the First World War and exerted a greatly disturbing influence in the late thirties. Exchange uncertainty and political instability increased the "elements of friction" and decreased the responsiveness of capital flows to variations in exchange and interest rates. Instead of playing a "passive" or "balancing" role in response to changes in the balance of payments position, the short-term flow came to be governed by risk and speculations.

The gravitational force that impels capital to semi- and neo-capitalistic countries ceased to be operative; capital proceeded up-stream, i.e., from countries with a deficit to countries with a surplus in the balance of payments. Conspicuous examples of disequilibrating short-term movements have been the in-flow of capital into France after the devaluation of 1926, the out-flow the Eastern and Central Europe in the early thirties and the invasion of "hot money " after the devaluation of the dollar in the United States.

---

[70] *Cf.* The Department of Commerce publication, *The United States in the World Economy*, p. 104.

# SUMMARY

The preceding sections have indicated, on one hand, the importance of capital movement in the transmission of cyclical shocks, and on the other the difficulty of tracing a clear pattern or measuring their effects. The three basic explanations of the mechanism of real transfer in terms of price changes, demand changes, or income changes, were reviewed. The analysis of the secondary effects of capital movements led to the conclusion the real transfer can be larger, smaller, or equal to the monetary transfer, the outcome being determined by the operation of the marginal propensities, of the multiplier, and also of the institutional datum, namely, the banking organization. The contribution of the over-investment theory to the explanation of cyclical transmission through capital movements was critically assessed, with respect to the international margin of savings. Finally, the question of imperfect sectional and cyclical behavior of capital was briefly examined, the broad conclusion being that capital movements may give rise to parallel and synchronous as well as to divergent international fluctuations, it being impossible to determine a specific pattern.

A brief review of the experience of the thirties revealed that capital movements showed an erratic and "perverse" behavior and played a major role in the spreading of international instability.

The advantage of cyclical flexibility of exchange remittances involved in the direct investment method was contrasted with the rigidity of portfolio loans. Attention was finally brought to the changing character of short-term money flows during the inter-war period.

# SECTION III

# INTERNATIONAL TRADE AND THE CYCLICAL BEHAVIOR
## Setting of the Problem

Trade is unquestionably one of the main carriers of prosperity and of depression. Income fluctuations may be propagated by fluctuations in prices or in volume of goods trades. The dependence of a segment each country's production and income on foreign demand creates a variable degree of international solidarity of economic behavior. An isolated economy would be immune from contagion by foreign cyclical fortunes, although the very absence of international influence would, by the same token, facilitate the spreading of purely autogenous depressions.[71] Conversely, a perfect mobility of goods would bring about a high degree of equality in cyclical behavior. The mixture of uniformity and diversity in the international cycle is, therefore, to a large extent, explained by the relative strength of the factors of localization, and factors of mobility, by which the degree of openness of a country to international influences is partly measured.

It must be noted, however, that trade has a twofold aspect; it can act not only as a conveyor of, but also as a brake to depressions. This latter aspect has been emphasized by some of the business cycle theories, as noted by Svend Laursen. The over-investment theory, for instance, calls attention to the role of trade in preventing stagnation of investment; the imperialist versions of the under-consumption theory emphasize the role trade in preventing the glut of markets, while the monetary theories stress particularly the inter-connection of national price-levels through trade links.

The localization of trade may derive from natural factors, such as the location of productive resources or transportation costs, or from artificial factors, such as tariffs or monetary devices. Before proceeding, however, to the examination of the influence of localization of trade on the international cyclical behavior, we shall consider the relevant aspects of the theory of international trade and its utilization for business cycle analysis.

---

[71] *Cf.* A. Mchlenfels, "Internationale Konjunkturzusammenhänge", in *Jahrbücher für Nationaloekonomie und Statistik*, CXXX, 1929.

# CHAPTER I

# THE THEORY OF INTERNATIONAL TRADE AND BUSINESS CYCLE ANALYSIS

## A. The Mechanism of Equilibrium and Adjustment. The classical and Demand Schools. The Contribution of the Savings-Investment Analysis.

It is possible to distinguish four different approaches to the problem of the mechanism of adjustment or equilibrium in international trade.[72] The traditional theory emphasized the equilibrating role of shifts in price level subsequent to gold flows. This is the familiar price-goods-specie flow mechanism of the Hume-Thornton-Mill model.

A second approach, roots of which can be traced back to Ricardo, Longfield and Bastable, but which found its first precise and most successful formulation in Ohlin's treatise on *Inter-Regional and International Trade*, emphasized shifts in demand and purchasing power, which are supposed to have an equilibrating virtue of their own independently of price movements. Another version developed mainly by Angell, following Coschen, emphasized especially the foreign exchange aspects and the role of the demand and supply of bills of exchange.

A fourth approach has been more recently developed by applying the savings-investment analysis to the field of international trade. The concept of the Keynesian multiplier has been used mainly by Harrod, Colin Clark, and Machlup to the analysis of cumulative income changes brought about by foreign trade. Greater attention has been paid to the cyclical aspects of trade balances and the emphasis has been shifted from the final equilibrium position visualized by the traditional theory to the short-term disequilibrium of the transition.

The shortcomings of the classical theory, as a tool for business cycle analysis, are well known and will only lightly be touched upon. The classical mechanism of price-level changes is linked to the quantity theory and to the full employ-

---

[72] Compare Lloyd Metzler: "One may distinguish three broad groups of trade theories: (1) those which relay mainly upon price-level, interest-rate adjustment, (2) those which emphasize the influence of shifts in monetary purchasing power upon the distribution of resources, the balance of trade and so on, (3) those which consider the dependence of the level of real income upon the international situation." As an example of the first we have the classical economist, of the second, Bertel-Ohlin, and of the third (real income approach) we have R.F. Harrod. *Cf.* "Unemployment Equilibrium in International Trade", in *Econometrica* (vol. 10, 1942), p. 97.

ment assumption, and is only a particular case of an ampler range of adjustment possibilities.[73] The inadequacy of the comparative labor cost postulate (given the existence of variable proportions and different combinations of productive factors), the artificiality of the dual-market analysis, and the assumption of a uniquely determined direction of the change in the terms of trade have already been assailed by Ohlin. More important for our purpose, the time lags in a process of adjustment, which may in themselves start a cumulative process, and move the system further away from equilibrium, are neglected. The traditional theory implies, to use Lundberg's expression, that "the adaptation process itself does not influence the fundamental conditions of equilibrium". In short, the central falacy of the classical theory lies in that it pays attention to individual elements affecting national income (export-import prices, wages and capital movements) and to equilibrating movements between them, but neglects cyclical fluctuations in the income level itself.

In Ohlin's formulation, the over-simplified assumption of internal mobility and international immobility of factors are rendered more realistic through the recognition of different degree of national and international mobility and compensatory movements of both goods and factors. The emphasis laid on the national interdependence of the pricing systems, on the independent effects of shifts in relative demand and on the indeterminateness of the outcome of the terms of trade subsequent thereof, are important contributions to a closer understanding of the problem of transfer. But, again, the formulation is unsatisfactory from the viewpoint of cyclical analysis. While it explains satisfactorily the effects of a <u>horizontal</u> transfer of purchasing power, it does not sufficiently emphasize the fact that the total world purchasing power is not a constant but is in itself fluctuating cyclically.[74]

The total expansional or contractive effects of shifts in purchasing power in paying and receiving countries cannot be adequately expressed only in terms of proportional changes in demand (however refined the analysis of the direction of demand movements may be), because they may be reflected in cumulative fluctuations of the income level itself, an outcome of which Ohlin is aware but whose

---

[73] Under conditions of less than full employment and elastic supply, money flows need not cause an immediate rise in price levels. Moreover, the price changes may affect the home goods industry rather than sectional prices (export-import). In a situation of underemployment equilibrium in the trading countries, the adjustment may come about by output-income variations rather than by price changes.

[74] The neglect of time-lags in the process of adjustment presents also special problems. Ohlin is fully aware of the difficulty (*International and Inter-Regional Trade*, Harvard University, 1933), p. 413, but his theory is not sufficiently dynamic, for the application of period-analysis.

implications he does not elaborate.[75] In fact, the transfer of purchasing power from a country with a high propensity to save or slow velocity of circulation[76] to one with a high propensity to invest is a conspicuous instance of case where there would exist not a simple equilibrium transfer but a net world income expansion, while in the opposite case there would be permanent disequilibrium in the balance of trade through accumulation of savings.

Ohlin's approach can thus be considerably refined for the purpose of cyclical analysis with the theoretical tools provided by the savings-investment theory. Two central notions, one developed in connection with the savings-investment analysis, the other adapted to it, are relevant for the integration of trade effects into the general picture of income-level fluctuations: the foreign trade multiplier and the principle of acceleration.

The usefulness of the two concepts is impaired but not eliminated by the unsatisfactory character of the attempts for their arithmetic mensuration. One may be justly skeptical of the worthiness of the current mania for simplified models,[77] ordinarily constructed under a set of restrictive assumption, and yet admit that they contributes significantly for a better understanding of the relationships involved. As noted by Professor Machlup, they have all an explanatory and pedagogic usefulness even through their predictive value is frequently small.

## B. The Foreign Trade Multiplier

The foreign trade multiplier is an attempt to bring into play in the closed investment multiplier, the influence of foreign factors. It relates "the level of a country's total activity in dealing with foreigners. The level of activity is con-

---

[75] Leontieff has remarked that both the price-level and the demand mechanism are particular cases of a more general theory. He argues that only if the terms of trade remain unchanged will purchasing power necessarily move from lender to borrower. Otherwise there does not exist any single theoretical relationship between variations in the terms of trade and the direction of the transfer of purchasing power. (Leontieff, "The Pure Theory of Capital Transfer", in *Explorations in Economics*, 1936, p. 849.) A Classicist would easily concede that, given changes in purchasing power, changes in relative prices need not occur but could argue conversely that, given changes in prices, the transfer of purchasing power need not occur. The inter-relationship is therefore too complex to be conveniently described in terms either of demand or of prices taken separately.

[76] Vinner's concept of "final purchase velocity" is relevant is this connection. *Op. cit.*, pp. 365-74.

[77] Professor Hayke has already denounced this "fashionable pseudo-quantitative economies of averages".

ceived to be related to income from abroad by a multiplier".[78] Once the self-adjustment mechanism of the classical theory is discarded, the preoccupation with a favorable balance of trade ceases to be a "waste of time", and the mercantilistic position (if purified from its predatory aspects) appears under a new light. A change in the trade balances becomes a ponderable factor in the determination of the level of employment, in two ways, directly, because it affects the level of foreign investment, which just as the domestic investment is linked by a multiple relationship to the income-level; indirectly, because the gold flow or outflow affects also the level of investment through their relation to the quantity of money and the rate of interest. Barring the effect of counteracting changes in the liquidity-preference schedule (and, we may add, in technological data), interest rates will be lowered in the country enjoying a favorable balance and raised in the debtor country. Investment and incomes will be shifted in the same direction.

Keynes" commendation of favorable trade balance does not suffer, however, from the naive unrestraint of the Mercantilistic theories. The attempt to secure a trade surplus through restrictive policies is held to be harmful and self-defeating. A trade balance which is too large is held to have unfavorable effects on employment abroad and also, eventually, on employment at home. The existence of a reversal mechanism—although neither instantaneous nor automatic as in the traditional theory—is also implied in the Keynesian doctrine. The rise in investment and income brought about by favorable trade balances may raise the wage unit and costs at home and stimulate imports (which, from the viewpoint of the national economy are leakages from the income-flow). So, the direct effects of the trade balance are eventually reversed. But the indirect or monetary effects may also be stopped in two ways; the domestic liquidity preference may increase and impede the fall in interest rates; or, conversely, the fall in interest rates may induce a reverse flow of capital to high-interest rate countries.

Keynes himself did not develop the full implications of the multiplier concept, which has given rise to an elaborate algebraic literature and a plethora of models. "Families of multipliers" have been devised, differentiated according to the nature of the originating impulse, e.g., the autonomous foreign trade multiplier, the induced foreign trade multiplier, etc.

International trade causes the net multiplier effects to be different in an open and in a closed system. Besides the internal leakages and seepages,[79] which condition the multiplying effect in a closed system, we must take into account in an open system of two complicating forces at work. On the one hand, "some part

---

[78] G. Harrod, *The Trade Cycle* (Oxford, 1936). Professor Machlup offers some interesting comments on what he terms a "protectionalistic" and "imperialistic interpretation of the multiplier". *Op. cit.*, p. 211.

[79] For a definition of these terms, *cf.* Machlup, *op. cit.*, p. 14.

of the multiplier of the increased investment will accrue to the benefit of employment in foreign countries[80] through increased imports. On the other hand, the favorable repercussion of the imports on the level of foreign activity may again result in induced exports and cause a partial recuperation of the leakage.

There are two alternative ways of taking those international complications into account; either by adjusting the multiplicand (which would be constituted by domestic investment plus foreign balances, as suggested in the original Keynesian formulation), or by adjusting both the multiplicand and the multiplier, as done by Colin Clark and Harrod.

In order to cover the modifications introduced by induced exports and imports, the basic multiplier formula for the closed system has to be changed by the insertion of foreign trade elements in the multiplicand:

$$\Delta Y = \Delta V - \Delta M + \Delta X \ \frac{1}{1 - \frac{\Delta C}{\Delta Y}}$$

or, alternatively, in both the multiplier and the multiplicand:

$$\Delta Y = \Delta V + \Delta X \ \frac{1}{1 - \frac{\Delta C}{\Delta Y} + \frac{\Delta M}{\Delta Y}}$$

Where V stands for home investment, X for exports, M for imports, M/Y for the propensity to import and C/Y for the propensity to consume.

The income generating effect is entirely predicated upon the lag of imports behind exports and the subsequent rise in money incomes. For, as remarked by Colin Clark and Crawford:

> In the short period there is no necessity that an increase of exports should be followed by an increase of imports, and, therefore, an increase in either the volume or price of exports will generate income without increasing the quantity of goods available and thereby start an upward fluctuation.[81]

In the foreign trade multiplier analysis, it is customary to lump under the term "foreign balances" not only the commodity balances but also the service, interest and dividends out-turns, listed as invisible exports and imports. A more precise formulation would actually require the separation of a foreign trade multi-

---

[80] Keynes, *The General Theory*, p. 120.

[81] For a detailed enumeration of hypothetical cases of instantaneous adjustment, in which the multiplier technique would not be applicable, *cf.* Machlup, *op. cit.*, p. 31, note.

plier from a foreign dividend multiplier, the latter being smaller than the former, in view of the higher propensity to save of interest and dividend recipients. At this level of abstraction, however, such a degree of precision is unwarranted.

## 1. Basic Concepts of the Multiplier Analysis.

(a) <u>Autonomous and consequential imports</u>. The relationships above expressed in aggregate terms present no particular difficulty. But once we abandon generalities to deal with specific cases, the theoretical simplicity breaks down. Imports, for instance, cannot be treated as a block. The effect on employment and income or, in other words, the <u>total leakage</u> will vary according to the nature of imports. If only investment goods are imported, no employment will accrue, immediately, to the factors at home. If imports consist of raw materials to be embodied in re-exports part of the leakage is immediately recovered. If finished consumption goods are imported, to the detriment of home made goods, the deflationary effects will again be larger than otherwise. The dynamization of the theory by the time-period analysis changes also relevantly the application of the multiplier. Thus, the important of investment goods (which is a total leakage in the first income period) will be income-generating in the second income period, by providing means of employing local raw materials.[82] Account must also be taken of the fact that income leakages in one period may be subsequently counteracted by favorable foreign repercussions induced exports), the final size of the multiplier depending on the length of the period of adjustment and on differential psychological magnitudes. The possible complications are endless but further refinements of the analysis are likely to yield diminishing returns.

One of the basic concepts of the multiplier analysis is that of the marginal propensity to import, first used by F.W. Paish, but actually implying an old idea.

The marginal propensity to import indicates the proportion of increments of income that will be spent on imports. It can be viewed from two different angles; from the viewpoint of <u>income allocation,</u> it is a subspecies of the marginal propensity to consume, which is thus divided between consumption of domestic and foreign goods. From the viewpoint of <u>income employment</u> effects, the marginal propensity is better considered a "leakage" and as such it is a counterpart of the marginal propensity to save.[83] The foreign trade multiplier would thus be the reciprocal of the marginal propensity to save plus the marginal propensity to import.

---

[82] Imports of capital goods into new countries, while technically a leakage affecting money incomes, must clearly be regarded as an energizing rather than a deflationary force.

[83] For a refutation of the viewpoint that only autonomous and not consequential imports should be regarded as leakages. *Cf.* Haberler, *op. cit.*, p. 470.

Another distinction emphasized by Colin Clark is that between <u>autonomous</u> and <u>consequential</u> changes in imports, the latter being induced by prior income changes, and the former resulting from external factors, such as tariffs, currency depreciation, changes in consumers' tastes, etc. In his view, only the autonomous and not the consequential imports are to be considered as leakages. For the practical multiplier analysis, however, changes in exports are generally regarded as autonomous factors and all changes in imports as consequential or induced.[84] Colin Clark, while finding, in his studies on the Australian foreign trade, that for most of the period 1922 to 1938 the above procedure seemed satisfactory, was able to identify for the years 1927 and 1930 some autonomous changes in imports, which ware accounted for through an adjustment of the multiplicand. This statistical optimism was, however, belied in his studies on the British foreign trade, in which no clear out distinction could be found between autonomous and consequential changes; all imports thus were shoved back into the multiplicand, a procedure which required an upward adjustment of the multiplier formula previously used.[85] In fact, multiplicand was rendered unduly small since not only autonomous but also consequential changes were deducted. In effecting a compensatory adjustment of the multiplier, Colin Clark actually over-adjusted it, and reached, as noted by Professor Robertson a clearly wrong formula.

This difficulty is a very serious flaw in the multiplier analysis, just as the existence of autonomous changes in consumption, such as government expenditures on consumables, or "honorary investments" (Robertson) blurs the neatness of the closed system multiplier theory, which lumps all investment <u>autonomous</u> and all consumption as <u>induced</u> by changes in income. In point of fact, there is not, in the actual world, any unidirectional chain of causality; both exports and imports can change autonomously and consequentially and, except for the case of sudden and conspicuous changes, the statistical separation is well nigh impossible.

The prolonged discussion that took place with regard to Clark's and Harrod's formulas need not be reviewed here.[86] It will suffice to note that, in principle,

---

[84] This is the so-called autonomous foreign trade multiplier. If induced rather than autonomous changes are considered it is possible to construct a foreign-trade-induced multiplier (assuming as starting point autonomous changes in investment in one of the trading countries). Still a third multiplier, the home-investment multiplier, in which induced exports and imports are taken into account, can be devised. So, for each country a "family of multipliers" can be constructed according to the nature of the elements in the multiplicand.

[85] *Cf.* Haberler, *op. cit.*, p. 470, note 3.

[86] A detailed discussion can be found in Haberler, *op. cit.*, p. 464. Villard, *Deficit Spending and National Income* (New York, 1941) pp. 172-85, Shang-Kwei-Fong, *op. cit.*, further elaborated the analysis by the introduction of investment goods.

autonomous changes by increase in exports and decrease in imports should be taken account of by adjustment of the multiplicand rather than of the multiplier, while induced changes belong properly in the multiplier.[87]

Harrod advances the theorem that the income generating force derives from the volume of exports and not, as generally held, from the export surplus (foreign balance):

> An increase of exports may so stimulate internal activity as to entail a greater increase of imports, its consequential passive balance, so far from being a sign that the stability of foreign dealings are exerting a restriction influence, may indicate precisely the opposite.[88]

It appears, however, that Harrod is advancing a determinate conclusion on the basis of indeterminate premises. It is indeed quite conceivable that a not stimulating effect may be obtained even if there is no export surplus, since a parallel upward shift of both exports and imports need not be necessarily self-cancelling (although such a situation may be considered unusual). As an illustration, we may visualize the case of a country whose export increase takes place in the investment-goods sphere, whilst the parallel import expansion taken place in the raw materials sphere. Than, owing to the affect of the acceleration principle, the income expansion in the capital-goods industries is not entirely neutralized by the import expenditures. A similar situation will prevail if exports are matched by imports only after a considerable lag during which the stimulating effect of exports is allowed to percolate freely throughout the economy. There would then be income-creation merely through an increase in the volume of exports independently of as export surplus. Those are, however, particular cases, it being impossible to determine, on general grounds, whether the expansionary increase in exports will or will not be effect by deflationary increase in imports. The outcome is thus, at best, indeterminate, and Harrod's contention, at best, a more probability.

On the other hand, barring those exceptional circumstances, the conventional association of the multiplier effect to the existence of foreign balances seems to hold its own, since, as noted by Professor Haberler:

---

[87] Compare Machlup, *op. cit.*, p. 13: "Foreign trade plays, then, a double role in the foreign trade multiplier theory; one as multiplicand, and secondly as one of the determinants of the multiplier. This double role of foreign trade, I believe, is likely to defend every attempt at statistical verification of foreign trade multiplier theory".

[88] Harrod, *The Trade Cycle* (Oxford, 1936), pp. 155-56.

In the case of an excess of exports (or the opposite) the primary effect is clearly stimulating (or depressing)... whilst a parallel shift of both exports and imports must be assumed to be neutral.[89]

(b) <u>The marginal Propensity to Import</u>. In the calculation of the multiplier, the marginal propensity to import is assumed to be stable, an assumption which is subject to the same qualifications as that of the other psychological propensities. In reality the marginal propensity to import can hardly be expected to remain constant when the average and total propensities to import change with every autonomous increase or decrease in imports. The marginal propensity of one country to import the products of another country is indeed subject to a wide range of ever-changing influences, such as tastes, techniques of production level of prices and wages, exchange rates, income distribution and tariff and commercial policies.

The relationships of the marginal to the average propensity is not, however, an univocal one, notes Professor Machlup:

> An increase in total import demand may result in an increased, decreased or unchanged marginal propensity to import.[90]

The phase of the cycle is also likely to affect the marginal propensity to import which, caeteris paribus, will be higher in full employment (when domestic supply is inelastic) than in a period of underemployment and elastic supply. Again, changes in the distribution of income of the trading groups in each country may significantly alter the marginal propensity to import.

Arithmetical estimates of the marginal propensity to import have been made for a few countries, as follows:[91]

| | | |
|---|---|---|
| Great Britain | 0.17 | (Kahn and Colin Clark) |
| United States | 0.073 | (Imre de Vegh) |
| Canada | 0.36 | (Imre de Vegh) |
| Australia | 0.25 | (Colin Clark) |
| Queensland | 0.39 | (Colin Clark) |
| Denmark | 0.40 | (J. Waring)[92] |

---

[89] Haberler, *op. cit.*, p. 468. A possible conciliation of the two viewpoints, through the distinction between static and dynamic conditions, is suggested by Shang-Kwei-Fong. In static conditions. Harrod's analysis is valid; exports are stimulating, imports being merely consequential. In subsequent periods, however, consequential imports exert an influence of their own on income (in the deflationary sense) so that only the export surplus is actually energizing.

[90] Machlup, *op. cit.*, p. 20.

[91] Machlup, *op. cit.*, p. 200, note.

A question of some theoretical interest is that of the determination of an optimum propensity to import. The problem is akin to that of the optimum marginal propensity to save, a Malthusian concept recently revived by Professor Lange.

The optimum propensity to import would be defined with relation to the attainment of a proper balance between the leakage from the domestic income-flow and the proportion of it that is recovered through the stimulation of foreign income. A too large propensity to import would hinder domestic expansion, whilst an excessively small marginal propensity would eventually reflect back in the loss of exports due to declining foreign incomes.

(c) <u>The Income-Propagation Period</u>. The improvement of the foreign trade multiplier analysis through the introduction of period analysis is mostly due to Professor Machlup, who developed the concept of the <u>income</u>-propagation period.[93] The bearing of the income-propagation period on the multiplier theory obvious; the expansional effect of increased exports (and deflationary effect of an increase in imports or decrease in exports) will be rapid or slow according to the length of the relevant income propagation period. It affects both the cumulative lag of imports behind exports, and the speed at which the leakages from imports are recovered through induced exports. Larger gold flows will be necessary to settle trade balances if the period of propagation is longer than otherwise. The same observations will apply, <u>mutatis mutandis</u>, to the effects of international capital movements.

This concept, as far as its foreign trade applications are concerned, is akin to Viner's "final purchase velocity". Viner had already called attention to the influence of international difference in the final-purchase-velocities on the process of adjustment. To quote:

> The final purchase velocities in the two countries not only determine the amount of specie transfer necessary for adjustment but they also help to determine what affect the remittances shall have on the absolute price-levels in the two countries combined. If in the receiving country money has a higher velocity than in the paying country, the transfer of means of payment will result in a higher, level of prices for the two countries combined, and vice-versa.[94]

---

[92] The relationship of increments of income to increments of imports seems to be invariably positive and fairly constant, although artificial devices, such as import quotas and tariffs may decrease or even eliminate the correlation between the two variables. A negative marginal propensity to import is, however, conceivable, e.g., if a country's imports consist mainly of rougher and cheaper types of goods. Then, a rise in the income level would actually decrease the propensity to import.

[93] See his article "Period Analysis and Multiplier Theory", *Quart. Journal of Economies* (November, 1939).

[94] Viner, *op. cit.*, p. 369.

## 2. Limitations of the Multiplier Approach

Although extremely useful for as understanding of the mechanism of transmission of income changes, the multiplier analysis, at its present stage, is subject to serious limitations. The analysis has to be conducted under very restrictive assumptions, which are nevertheless unavoidable if unmanageable conceptual complications are to be averted.

The restrictive assumptions, usually disguised under the "caeteris paribus" clause, are the following:

i. Stable psychological propensities.

ii. Stable prices. The co-existence of a price-elasticity of-demand for exports and imports together with an income elasticity of demand complicates hopelessly the mathematical formulation and the statistical verification of the multiplier. The multiplier analysis concentrates usually on income-elasticities (the price aspect being sufficiently covered in the classical theory) but the fact cannot be escaped that price changes may alter one of the basis data, namely, the marginal propensity to import. If export prices are constant, at least for a certain period, the export expansion may falter, since marginal costs are apt to rise as a result of the stimulation of collateral domestic industries. The rise in domestic prices, in turn, may increase the marginal propensity to import.[95] At rising export prices, the maintenance of a trade surplus will depend on the interplay of the foreign elasticity of demand for imports and on the domestic elasticity of supply and of demand for exportable goods.[96]
The analytical limitation of stable prices assumption is not very serious if we start from a situation of unemployment and elastic supply, but renders the theory unrealistic for full employment conditions.

iii. Stable wage rates. The bearing of wage rates on export-import costs and investment is obvious. Neglect of their effects reduces the validity of the multiplier models to the situation of a perfectly elastic labor supply.

iv. Stable interest rates. Since interest rates, as it is well known, are closely related to the rate of investment, savings and the price of capital goods, any assumption as to their stability seriously limits the validity of the multiplier analysis. In

---

[95] This is the foreign trade counterpart of the "leakages through price inflation" (Clark) that occurs in the closed system multiplier.

[96] For these observations we are largely indebted to Mr. Svend Laursen, in his unpublished doctoral thesis *International Propagation of Business Cycles*.

fact, changes in foreign balances effect bank reserves and banking policy and may induce changes in interest rates, which in turn may induce investment changes. The problem is further complicated by the existence, in international transactions, of money of different degrees of liquidity (say, gold, or short-term assets) for which there are different schedules of liquidity-preference.

v. Stable exchange rates. Export surpluses are not unfrequently followed by exchange appreciation, in which case they are short-lived and the leakages through increased imports are more likely to neutralize the multiplier effect.

Some attempts have been made, usually at the cost of mathematical precision, to expand the multiplier analysis by dropping one or more of the above restrictive assumptions and by studying the interaction between the multiplier and the principle of acceleration.[97]

Lloyd Metzler constructed some models which take into account also changes in home investment, a desirable step whose practicability is, however, impaired by the somewhat unpalatable assumption of a constant marginal propensity to invest.[98] Another procedure is to reduce all income changes to net investment changes, an increase in the propensity to consume domestic goods (import decrease) being equivalent to net home investment, while a shift from domestic to foreign goods (import increase) would correspond to a net investment in the foreign country and a net dis-investment at home.[99]

## 3. The Principle of Acceleration and the Foreign Trade Multiplier

The application of the acceleration principle together with the multiplier, for the explanation of the international cycle, has been developed chiefly by Harrod, whose unrestrained satisfaction in the rechristening of the old principle of acceleration as "the Relation" has been often commented upon.

---

[97] Professor Angel has called attention to the fact that the failure of the early Keynesian analysis to take into account the possibility of induced investment seriously limits its applicability and determinateness. In the Keynesian assumption, the successive increments of income are divided between consumption and savings or hoardings, no allowance being made for the possibility of new (induced) investment. A generic term, marginal prosperity to spend, which would cover both consumption and investment, is suggested in lieu of the marginal propensity to consume. Cf. *International Business Cycles* (McGraw Hill Book Co., 1941), p. 195.

[98] A similar objection, could of course be raised with regard to Samuelson's induced-investment coefficients for the closed system.

[99] *Cf.* Metzler, "Underemployment Equilibrium in Investment in International Trade", in *Econometrica* (vol. 10, No. 2), p. 112.

According to Harrod, two elements have to be added, in an open system, to the domestic dynamic determinants, namely:

i. the ratio of the increase of active current items to the increase of investment at home, and ii) the proportion of a rising expenditure devoted to foreign made goods.[100]

The stimulation of new domestic investment by foreign balances will increase income and consumption _via_ the multiplier. The increase in the domestic demand for consumables, in turn increases the demand for capital goods, _via_ the "Relation". Thus the effect will be aggrandized first by the multiplier and secondly by the principle of acceleration. The second external factor, namely, the rise in the proportion of expenditures devoted to foreign goods exerts, however, a restrictive influence, since the multiplier "depends on the proportion of income which people choose to spend on home-made goods".[101] Conversely, an increase in the demand for domestic goods will increase the demand for investment goods and foster home investment.

The international propagation of cyclical movements will depend on the relative strength of the domestic internal determinants and of the external ones. In the American depression of 1929, for instance, the slump was brought about mainly by internal factors, while in Great Britain an external factor (the decline of foreign balances subsequent to the overvaluation of the pound) is to be held responsible. While the cyclical process could be explained on purely endogenous grounds, as a normal manifestation of the capitalistic system of production, it can be either aggravated or attempted by international factors which interfere with the operation of the multiplier and of the acceleration principle, and which may even generate "induced depressions", in spite of the favorable conspectus of the internal determinants of the system.

The best formulation of the interactions of the multiplier and of the acceleration principle in a closed system is due to Samuelson, who constructed models showing several patterns of cyclical oscillations in national income, by assuming different specific numerical values for the marginal propensity to consume (mechanism of the multiplier) and for the projection of induced investment (principle of acceleration).

His technique has been applied to the study of international cyclical processes by Shang-Kwei-Fong in an unpublished doctoral thesis, "Business Cycles and the International Balance of Payments". (Harvard University, 1941). He uses

---

[100] Harrod, _op. cit._, p.151.

[101] _Ibid._, p. 149.

four coefficients representing, (a) the marginal propensity to consume home-made goods, (b) the proportion of investment induced by previous consumption, (c) the marginal propensity to import, (d) the proportion of investment goods that is imported—and constructs several models showing the different patterns of income fluctuations that will ensue in the trading countries. A basic distinction is made between <u>independent investment</u>, which is influenced by the rate of interest and the marginal efficiency of capital, and <u>induced investment</u> that is related to the rate of consumption. The model starts with the simplifying assumptions of under-employment in the trading countries, stability of wages, of interest rates and of profit expectations, absence of gold flows and of multiple credit contraction and expansion. Those assumptions are later relaxed to allow for changes in the marginal propensities, in relative prices and wages (reflected in movements of the terms of trade), in interest rates, in the credit structure and also to take account of capital movements. The study offers interesting side-lights and in general bears out many of the postulates of the so-called "modern theory" of international trade and capital transfer, to wit: the course of the terms of trade may turn either in favor of or against the lending country; favorable terms of trade are held to represent a gain only if the level of domestic employment is not impaired; the effect of capital movements on investments in the lending and borrowing countries need not be proportional to the payment transfer, since the deflationary effect in the lending country may be partly, or wholly, neutralized if funds came out of dishoarding or credit inflation, while, conversely, the inflationary affect in the receiving country may be dissipated into hoards; the trade-follow-loan theorem is held to be valid only for the specific case of tied-in-investment or when particular structural relations exist between the lending and borrowing countries.

In spite of an elaborated formalistic apparatus, the gain in realism by the introduction of several variables in the multiplier analysis, does not greatly enhance its value for the formulation of practical policies. As the restrictive assumptions are relaxed, so is the determinateness of the analysis. When all variables are taken into account the earlier attempts at numerical precision look flimsy indeed.

The tragedy of the multiplier technique lies precisely in the fact that its practical value is largely dependent on the establishment of precise numerical relationships, <u>ex ante facto</u>, which in the present status of analysis can only be arrived at in abstracto, when they are not rendered tautological by the use of a <u>ex post facto</u> statistical elaboration.

## 4. The Multiplier and the Balance of Payments

The theoretical schemes which show the operation of the foreign trade multiplier are but ideal and highly simplified pictures of the trade mechanism. In actual business world, the process of multiple expansion and contraction is not allowed to follow its course but is usually obstructed by governmental action to protect the balance of payments. An autonomous expansion of home investment, especially in small countries having a high marginal propensity to import, is likely to bring about immediate pressure on monetary reserves and on the balance of payments, unless the favorable repercussion on foreign incomes is sufficiently rapid to induce increased exports. If other countries fail to expand at the same time, the expanding country may try to protect its balance of payments by tariffs or trade policies aimed at lowering the propensity to import.

In large countries, enjoying ample monetary reserves, the balance of payments problem is much less pressing. The most favorable conditions are realized when its imports are a small part of the national income (low propensity to import) but its exports are a large fraction of world export (high coefficient of foreign repercussion). As noted by W. A. Salant:

> In general, we may say that a country may pursue an independent monetary policy without regard to the balance of payments if foreign trade plays a small part in his economy, but its foreign trade is a sizeable portion of world trade.[102]

The experience of the last recovery for a number of countries may serve as an illustration. The attempts of internal expansion made by Denmark, after the last depression, were thwarted by an abnormally large propensity to import (the stimulus to recovery inciding on the building industry which depends greatly on imported materials), by the weakness of the favorable foreign repercussion (the British and German demand for Danish exports having proved inelastic), and by the lack of an international margin of maneuver in the balance of payments.

Sweden presents the opposite case. In her recovery, the foreign repercussion factor (induced exports) more than neutralized the leakages through imports, the expansion being further facilitated by the favorable position of the balance of payments.

The German case is, in turn, sui generis. Leakages through imports were prevented by bilateral arrangements which, by equilibrating imports and exports, had the effect of practically neutralizing the foreign trade multiplier, thus leaving undisturbed the operation of the internal factors of expansion.[103]

From the viewpoint of the propagations of booms and depressions, it is the marginal and not the total or average propensity to import that counts. Some countries, like the United States, have a low average and total propensity to import but

---

[102] W.A. Salant, "Foreign Trade Policy and the Business Cycle", in *Public Policy* (Harvard University Yearbook), vol. II, p. 220.

[103] *Cf.* Salant

a high marginal propensity to export, while others, like Great Britain, are in precisely the opposite position. This is clearly illustrated by the composition of their import trade. Great Britain imports mostly foodstuffs and basic raw materials of inelastic demand, while the United States, enjoying a high degree of self-sufficiency, imports mostly luxuries and industrial raw materials, the demand for which is comparatively elastic in terms of income. Thus, though only a small fraction of the American national income is devoted to imports, the proportion of each increment of income spent on them is much larger. The volume of imports being extremely sensitive to fluctuations in the domestic income level and representing at the same time a large share of world trade, the American business cycle is likely to exert great influence on cyclical fortunes abroad. In countries with a low marginal propensity to imports, much as Great Britain, imports are less sensitive to changes in the income level so that downward changes are not likely to have as drastic effects on the volume of imports and on foreign incomes. But, by the same token, the spill-over of an internal boom would be a slower and less intensive process.[104]

## 5. The Evaluation of the Contribution of the Multiplier Analysis for the Study of Cyclical Propagation

Granted that the abstractness of the models and the failure of statistical verification seriously hinder the predictive value of the multiplier, as a policy making device, its contribution is nonetheless significant for an understanding of the different mechanism of spreading of prosperity and depression. It tells us how changes in export balances may exert a multiple effect on income, out of proportion to the primary or direct effect of the monetary transfer. Similarly, we find that an import surplus may have secondary income effects more than proportional to the loss of purchasing power. The law of conservation of purchasing power loses thus meaning and the concept of proportional or equilibrating changes in demand gives place to the concept of multiple changes in demand.

The course of the terms of trade and the inflationary and deflationary affect of capital movements do not appear any longer as easily predictable as in the traditional theory, since they are made dependent on the interaction of the marginal propensity to save and to import in the trading countries.

The multiplier technique helps to explain the different patterns of expansion and contraction in the international cycle. An expansion originating in a country with a high marginal propensity to import will quickly spill over to other trading countries, the rate of domestic expansion being accelerated or retarded according to the income propagation period and the marginal propensities of the countries

---

[104] *Cf.* League of Nations, *Economic Stability in the Post-War World*, p. 97

with which it trades. Given an autonomous impulse, the multiplier will be the larger, the smaller the marginal propensities to import and to save of the expanding country. An income increase originating from an export surplus will go on as long as the stimulating affect of autonomous exports in not effect by induced imports, induced savings and induced decrease in exports. The equilibrium in the balance of trade will be achieved when autonomous items are equalized with induced items.

In the actual world, with varying propensities and multi-lateral trading, the complications are infinite. But a few basic generalizations can be made. It has been said that there are two counteracting forces to be accounted for in the multiplier; the leakage through imports, that tends to check the expansion, and the induced exports that further reinforce it. The relative importance of the two factors will be different according to the size of the country and its dependence on foreign trade. In a small country, as noted by Professor Machlup, the brake to internal expansion is likely to come through <u>induced imports</u> (small countries having usually a high marginal propensity to import), while the reduction in exports resulting from the decline in foreign income is not likely to be severe, since the experts of a small country represent only a small part of the imports of other countries.[105]

In large countries, the importance of the two factors is likely to be reversed. For, large countries are apt to have a low marginal propensity to import, so that only a small part of the income increase resulting from autonomous exports or home investment will find its way abroad. But, by the same token, the foreign induced decline in exports is likely to be substantial, since the exports of a large country are apt to constitute a large part of the imports of small countries.

These relationships have been aptly summarized by W.A. Salant, in these words:

The reaction of a change in a country's imports on its exports will be greater:

1. The greater are the marginal propensities to import and the multipliers of the countries from which it imports.
2. The greater its share in world trade.
3. The more heavily are its exports concentrated in the countries from which it imports.[106]

We may say, in conclusion, that after an initial disequilibrium, the size or speed of the adjustment-movements needed to restore equilibrium in the balance of trade and of payment depends primarily on the multiplier effect, as determined by the marginal propensities to save and to import and by the income propagation period.

---

[105] *Cf.* Machlup, *op. cit.*, p. 201.

[106] W.A. Salant, *op. cit.*, vol. II, pp. 214-15.

# CHAPTER II

# EMPIRICAL AND STRUCTURAL FACTORS IN THE SPREAD OF CYCLES

## A. Localization of Trade and the Cycle Behavior

1. <u>The Natural Factors</u>. The internationalization of cyclical behavior is directly related to the degree of international specialization of labor. Trade not only may chock the boom, <u>via</u> import leakages, but may also attenuate depression, <u>via</u> an increase in exports. The higher the degree of specialization, the greater the need for international trade and the more likely is the spreading of cyclical movements through fluctuations in exports and imports. As mentioned before, the propagation may be in the vertical or in the horizontal sense. Conversely, the lesser the degree of international specialization (obstructed by the existence of transportation costs), the wider is the scope for purely local booms and depressions.

Transportation costs and other natural obstacles to the mobility of goods and factors, thus explain the occurrence of purely regional or partial over-production. Due to the lack of mobility of goods and factors—changes in tastes, in income and in technology—may cause regional over-production and depression in certain areas, while an expansionary process and underproduction occur in neighboring areas.[107] This will happen, for instance, if transportation costs raise the price of products of the depressed area by an amount sufficient to prevent their absorption by the expanding areas, at the prevailing elasticity of demand; then that one region will suffer a net contraction and the other will show a net expansion without any equalizing movement between them.

The immobility of labor exerts a localizing influence similar to that of transport costs. This is well expressed in a recent League of Nation's study:

> Immobility of labor is a second factor limiting the international as well as the internal spread of cycles. The areas of localized unemployment which may persist in a country despite boom conditions existing in other parts are due to this immobility. If labor were able to move freely from the depressed to the booming areas, this would help to check both depression and booms and keep conditions in different areas more closely in step.[108]

---

[107] *Cf.* Neisser, *op. cit.*, p. 30.

[108] *Economic Stability in the Post-War World*, p. 90.

2. <u>The Artificial Factors</u>. The transmission of cyclical shocks through the trade mechanism may also be affected by artificial factors which, to the extent that they decrease international specialization, have effects similar to those of transportation costs.

Artificial obstacles to mobility of goods may be created by administrative action (tariff, import quotas) or may result from institutional and organizational influence. The latter are embodied in the so-called "law of continuity of the flow goods" which describes the tendency of trade to be channelled along lines determined by investment affiliations and market or managerial customs and agreements.[109]

The general affect of artificial trade barriers is to break the synchronization of international cycles. They may be directed either at protecting the rate of expansion of a country or at avoiding contamination by depression. The tendency towards economic autarchy is thus an outcome of the drive towards stability.

The arsenal of anti-cyclical devices bearing on international trade is quite diversified, tariffs, import quotas, wage deflation, exchange depreciation, etc.

Using Salant's convenient classification, we may broadly speak of policies affecting the <u>balance of trade</u>, the <u>amount of trade</u>, and the <u>direction of trade</u>, either by monetary measures or by direct administrative controls, as summarized below:

Monetary measures:
  (a) Exchange manipulation (depreciation, Devisen-politik, exchange control)
  (b) Special monetary vincula (sterling block, dollar block, etc.)

Administrative measures affecting:
  (a) The balance and amount of trade:
    1. <u>On the import side</u> (defensive policy)
      i. Tariffs, which in turn may be merely <u>cost-equalizing</u>, to enable local producers to meet international competition, or <u>prohibitive</u>, aimed at shutting off the market of foreign made products.[110]
      ii. Import quotas, either discriminatory or non-discriminatory
    2. <u>On the export side</u> (offensive policy)
      i. Export subsidies.
      ii. Dumping.
  (b) The direction of trade – Compensation agreements, preferential regimes, etc.

---

[109] *Cf.* Mühlenfels, *op. cit.*, p. 822.

[110] *Cf.* Mühlenfels, *op. cit.*, pp. 821-23. The cost-equalizing tariff has only a partial insulting effect, since every fall in the price-level of competing countries would narrow the margin of protection.

It is our purpose to discuss the merit or demerit of the policies involved, or two dwell upon the age-long controversy between free traders and protectionists. It will suffice to note that the argument is frequently blurred by the failure to distinguish between a short and long-run viewpoint on one hand, and between nationalistic and a universalistic point of view on the other.

The obvious theoretical advantage of international specialization along the line of comparative costs cannot be denied. The point is, whether given the inherent instability of the economic system those advantages can be realized. Once free trade is not a synonym of full employment, it is always possible that, because of the instability of international demand, specialization may fail to lead, in the short run, to a maximization of income. The recurrence of business cycles affects both the importance and the extent of the international division of labor and limits therefore the applicability of the comparative costs analysis.[111]

It is clear that specialization, chiefly if concentrated in the production of a few commodities, renders a country defenseless against the vagaries of international business fortunes. Only diversification of production can increase the structural elasticity and shock-absorbing capacity of countries exporting a narrow range of primary products. Thus, the drive of some agricultural countries towards industrialization and diversification of output can be justified as a practical anti-cyclical policy, an aspect neglected by the conventional comparative cost analysis. For, the degree of openness of a country to the spread of international cycles is in inverse relationship to its internal structural elasticity.

This is the grain of truth in the alleged higher resistance of countries with a "continental spread" to cyclical fluctuations. A diversified economy increase the shiftability of factors in response to foreign shocks.[112] But, while the resistance of countries enjoying a continental spread to foreign induced deflations is greater, nothing follows as to their immunity to autonomous depressions. The United States presents an excellent example of a country with a small coefficient of openness to the world cycle and yet a high internal instability. In this case, as in that of other comparatively self-sufficient and well-integrated economies, the international component of the cycle is usually of secondary importance. Sweden may perhaps be taken as an illustration of the opposite case of countries with high internal stability but great vulnerability to foreign induced depressions.

---

[111] The point can also be made that the comparative advantages principle cannot by itself adequately explain international specialization, since the latter depends also on the business cycle. The example of industries that become intra-marginal in depression (due to fall in wages and costs and higher prices of imported manufactures) and sub-marginal in prosperity are fairly in young industrial countries.

[112] The elasticity of the economic structure may be, and often is, neutralized by social rigidities (trade unions, etc.).

This digression has, however, led us far astray from our main objective which is to analysis the influence of artificial factors in the localization of booms and depressions.

(a) <u>Tariff and the Cyclical Behavior</u>. We shall now resume our theme by considering the influence of tariff upon cyclical behavior. Tariffs are perhaps the most widely used device for insulation from trade effects. Contrarily to transportation costs, they are <u>flexible</u> (in the sense that they can be changed by legislation) and their effect is confined to one administrative unit, while transport costs are regional.[113] Contrarily to import quotas, tariffs do not destroy but only modify the relationships between income and imports.

The immediate anti-cyclical purpose is to divert demand from imported to local goods; in this way a deflationary movement at home may be halted and a compensation provided for loss of exports due to falling foreign demand. In spite of the lack of flexibility and administrative cumbersomeness of tariffs as instrument of cyclical policy, there seems to be a constant historical pattern relating the recrudescence of protectionism to periods of depression. We quota Professor Haberler:

> Although the trend of international commercial policy has been steeply in the direction of protectionism ever since the beginning of the last quarter of the nineteenth country, a certain cyclical movements is unmistakable. Every major depression brought a new outburst of protectionism while prosperity periods have usually been marked by short steps in the direction of free trade.[114]

It is sometimes advanced that, on the basic of the multiplier theory, it may be possible through an appropriate anti-cyclical policy for individual countries (barring of course the effects of retaliation by other countries) to maximize the multiple effect on income, either defensively (the "Zoll-politik"), by preventing import leakages through a raise in tariffs or through import quotas, or offensively, by increasing the multiplicand through stimulation of exports by subsidies, bounties, etc., (the "Praemium-politik"). This belief is reinforced by the fact that, theoretically, the foreign trade multiplier is always positive and therefore income-stimulating. This reasoning is at the core of the neo-mercantilistic interpretation of the multiplier, to use an apt expression of Professor Machlup.[115]

---

[113] *Cf.* Haberler, *op. cit.*, p. 414.

[114] Haberler, *op. cit.*, p. 414.

[115] *Cf.* Machlup, *op. cit.*, 2, p. 211.

It has been frequent during the last decade for some countries to try both policies simultaneously, in spite of the fact that the "Praemium-politik" and the "Zoll-politik" are prima facie contradictory and self-cancelling, even if sufficient, care is taken to apply the policies to different groups of countries. For, the basic fact cannot be avoided that, except in special conditions, tariffs and import restrictions are bound to depress foreign incomes and therefore to react back on exports.

Besides the administrative and politico-economic difficulties involved, there are, moreover, other inherent limitations to the policy of the "predatory multiplier". For, insofar as higher tariffs reduce the import leakage and reinforce the multiplying effect on income,[116] they are rendered progressively ineffective since the demand for imports will increase concurrently with the income level, the more rapidity so the larger is the income-elasticity of demand for imports.[117] Thus, unless tariffs are continuously readjustment to make up for changes in the propensity to import, the deflationary effects of import leakages can at best postponed but not eliminated.

This, of course, is not meant to deny that for any individual country, under specific conditions, tariffs may prove a useful and even necessary instrument for stimulation of domestic employment and for prevention of mass unemployment. As a general anti-cyclical device, however, their usefulness is certainly limited. Whatever relief they may bring, it is in the nature of a palliative rather than of a cure and certainly not one that can provide a remedy for a worldwide depression.

When all is said, it becomes clear that while both export balances and autonomous home investment have a stimulating influence on income, the latter mechanism is preferable. For as noted by Mrs. Robinson:

> An increase in home investment brings about a net increase in employment for the world as whole, while as increase in the balance of trade of one country at best leaves the level of employment for the world as a whole unaffected. A decline in the imports of one country is a decline in the exports of other countries and the balance of trade of the world as whole is always equal to zero.[118]

---

[116] On the assumption, of course, that exports do not fall pari passu because of retaliation or induced fall in foreign incomes. The last factor may be very important for countries whose exports constitute a large fraction of income. *Cf.* Mosak, *op. cit.*, pp. 172-173.

[117] Since the marginal propensity to import is ordinarily well below unity, the net effect will still be inflationary. But it is easy to see that the stimulating effect of the tariff is pro tanto diminished and more easily nullified by other unfavorable repercussions.

[118] Juan Robinson, *Studies in the Theory of Employment*, p. 210.

The first part of Mrs. Robinson's statement is unobjectionable. The second proposition calls, however, for some comment, for it reveals some remnants of the static equilibrium concept of the traditional theory of international trade. Now, it is perfectly true that in an accounting sense exports and imports, for the world as a whole, are merely different sides of the same operation and are in equilibrium at any moment of time. But if we recall that trade involves a transfer of purchasing power, the truism that what one country gains the other loses by trade, loses its cogency. For, in the same operation one country may gain more than the other loses, and vice-versa. If, for instance, export balance were, by hypothesis, so arranged as to involve a transfer of funds from countries with chronic over-saving tendencies to countries with a high marginal propensity to spend,[119] the gain of income and employment in the latter would exceed the loss in the former, so that the net world effect would be inflationary. In other words, the primary effects of trade, for the world as a whole, are self-cancelling but the secondary repercussions need not be so. There is, in fact, no other explanation for the economic growth resulting from the trade with young countries.

This is merely the reverse side of the question of whether capital movements entail proportional or non-proportional changes in purchasing power in the paying and receiving countries, a point discussed elsewhere.

Only, if we assume full employment and accept the discredited, but often unconsciously upheld, law of preservation of purchasing power, the zero world balance of trade becomes a truism.

(b) <u>The Regional Insulation Approach</u>. While tariffs may be used, from a national standpoint, to minimize the impact of trade upon national income, the recent depression strengthened the popularity of the <u>block insulation</u>, approach based on locational interdependence, political association, or both.

The regionalization approach combines usually tariff frontiers with special monetary vincula. From the standpoint of cyclical behavior the regionalization of trade acts, <u>mutatis mutandis</u>, in the same way as its localization. It tends to decrease the uniformity and synchronization of cyclical movements for the world as a whole, but it leads usually to an increased parallelism of behavior within the regional group, particularly is view of the fact that the articulation is made between complementary economies or at least between on nuclear and several satellite economies. In either case, we have examples of vertical propagation of fluctuations.

The relative success of some economic blocks in achieving recovery from the last depression has given rises to conflicting interpretations. The outstanding

---

[119] We are using the term in the sense suggested by James Angell, id est, as the sum of the marginal propensity to consume and to invest.

case is the generally speedier rate of recovery of the sterling area, which has been attributed by some to the successful operation of the Ottawa Imperial preference system, by others to the influence of monetary factors (such as the early sterling devaluation or the special financial arrangements to increase the balance of payment liquidity within the area), and by others still to internal factors such as the fall in wages and costs in Great Britain, which facilitated quick recovery, especially in the building industry. The particular circumstance that Britain even after devaluation, was able to continue to import raw materials at cheap prices, due to the severity of the depression suffered by primary producers, must also be taken into account.

Whatever the relative influence of the several factors may be, it is unquestionable that the fight against deflation, often hopeless from the viewpoint of an individual country, may be rendered much easier by the formation of blocks of complementary economies.[120]

The regionalization of trade was one of the outstanding structural changes of the last decade, its extent being clearly indicated in the following table, taken from the League of Nation's Review of World Trade for 1938:

**Table VI**
**Trade of Certain Countries with their Economic Blocks**

| Country | Economic Block | Trade with the Block (Percent of Total Trade) | | | | | |
|---|---|---|---|---|---|---|---|
| | | Imports | | | Exports | | |
| | | 1929 | 1932 | 1938 | 1929 | 1932 | 1938 |
| United Kingdom | British Empire | 30 | 36 | 42 | 44 | 45 | 50 |
| United Kingdom | Other sterling countries | 12 | 13 | 13 | 7 | 10 | 12 |
| France | French Empire | 12 | 21 | 27 | 19 | 32 | 28 |
| Japan | Japanese Empire | 20 | 33 | 41 | 24 | 30 | 58 |
| Germany | Countries of Southeastern Europe | 5 | 6 | 12 | 5 | 4 | 12 |

The main drawback of the regional approach is of course the division of the world into economic and political spheres of influence, within which commer-

---

[120] For two different interpretations of the recovery in the sterling block, *cf.* Neisser, *op. cit.*, pp. 143-60, and Salant, *loc. cit.*

cial and political ties tend to grow stronger, at the cost of multilateral trading and equal economic opportunity on an international basis.

From the purely economic viewpoint, the "block recovery approach" presents, as noted by Professor Neisser, three basic limitations:
- (a) The impossibility of closing the economic circulation in view of the incompleteness of economic resources in any regional group;
- (b) The problem of the "beginning", id est., the need for ample monetary resources in the leading country to finance the initial expansion;
- (c) The danger of interference by deflating competitors.

The resistance to deflation and the chances of recovery are quite uneven as between different countries. In small countries, whose cycles are more often imported than autonomous, the international margin (size of monetary reserves and position of the balance of payments) is likely to be the determined factor of any cyclical policy.

As regards isolated agricultural countries, no amount of internal credit expansion or adjustment one really cure an imposed deflation. For, firstly, their investment activity depends on producers' goods, which have to be obtained from industrial countries on unfavorable terms of trade, and secondly, they are usually debtor countries, whose gold and exchange reserves are drained off in depression, adding to the liquidity of the banking system of creditor countries, but failing often to provoke in the latter any stimulating credit expansion.[121] The initial stimulus to recovery must therefore spring from an industrial and financial center, a fact that cannot but increase the temptation, in every major depression, for the formation of economic blocks.[122]

The problem of the international cycle, is by and large, the problem of the level of employment in the major industrial countries. From the fact that artificial trade barriers have been at times successfully used to protect a country from cyclical shocks it should not be inferred that autarchy is the best road to stability. For one thing, immunity from foreign induced cycles does not imply immunity from endogenous cycles. For another thing, the erection of barriers to trade, if it helps preventing the importation of depressions may, by the same token, prevent the

---

[121] *Cf.* Neisser, *op. cit.*, p. 144: "The difficulties of non-industrial countries are further enhanced by the fact that they are usually debtor countries: the typical gold migration to creditor countries which characterized the pre-war depressions, may be supposed to increase their liquidity without, however, necessarily enforcing a lasting recovery.

[122] An argument for the formation of regional preference or tariff families between small countries (the Scandinavian block for instance), which has recently won popularity, is based on the possibility of better utilization of economies of large scale production by the pooling of several small markets. Industries that would be sub-marginal if producing only for the domestic markets may reach an optimum economic output if guaranteed a regional market.

importation of prosperity. Thirdly, the economic advantages of international specialization are real indeed and to discard them altogether would be tantamount to attain stability at the cost of poverty. The remedy to escape contamination by foreign depressions is not to out off trade ties but to secure a more stable international trade.

## B. The "Law of the Falling Export Quota". The Trade Slump of the Thirties and the Long-Term of International Trade

The slump of world trade during the great depression was so unprecedented that it raised anew the question of whether it was due merely to a particularly virulent form of cyclical disease or whether it reflected permanent structural changes, or an aggravation of a downward long-term trend. While at the beginning of the depression world trade fell by less than world output, it lagged much behind in the recovery. By 1937, primary production had exceeded by 10 per cent the 1929 level, crude foodstuffs by 6 per cent, industrial raw materials by 19 per cent and manufactures by 20 per cent. Stocks of primary products were 6 per cent lower. Yet, by 1937 world trade was still 3 per cent below the 1929 level. A comparison with earlier depressions renders obvious the violence of the disturbances in international trade. Estimates of Professor Wagner indicate that the volume of world trade during the depression of the early nineties and after 1907 declined by 7 per cent below the long-term trend. Estimates of the experts of the League of Nations indicate a reduction of 20 per cent in the first quarter of 1931.[123]

International and regional trade thus gained ground at the expense of international trade. The trend towards autarchy was reinforced by agricultural protectionism in industrial countries (agrarianization of industrial economies) and industrial protectionism in primary producers (industrialization of agrarian economies). We have, thus, seen in the last decade a continuous decline of international specialization of production.

This whole conspectus of structural changes in, and violent decline of, foreign trade prompted the revival of the old German controversy that centered around the "Agraar oder Industriestaat" and the "Gesetz der fallenden Export Quote".

Sombart, making an inductive generalization on a somewhat slim statistical basis, concluded that the share of trade (or of exports at any rate) in the whole of economic activity, has diminished. Eulanburg, on the other hand, held that the constantly decreasing national supply of natural resources for production, should

---

[123] League of Nations, *Course and Phases of the World Economic Depression* (1932), p. 189. Colin Clark, in his *Conditions of Economic Progress* goes as far to suggest that 1929 may have constituted the peak of world trade, not likely to be surpassed in the future by any considerable amount.

eventually lead to an increase of imports and, consequently, of exports.[124]

According to the "law of falling export quota" there is a secular trend which, for both institutional and technical reasons, subjects international trade to a declining rate of growth as compared to the social product. Although trade, as a result of industrialization and spreading of economic development would tend to grow in absolute terms, it will constitute a diminishing share of the social product.

On the whole no consistent relationship between the rate of increase of trade and that of income has been statistically confirmed.[125] We lack so far an adequate empirical basis to classify the principle of the "falling export quota" as an unqualified law of economic growth. Economic development and the spread of industrialization have brought about a vigorous and continuous upsurge of international trade, it being difficult, in view of the lack of income statistics over a

---

[124] *Cf.* E. Wageman, *Struktur und Rhythmus der Weltwirtschaft* (Berlin, 1931), pp. 138-44. According to Wageman, available statistical data for the major trading countries, do not seem to lend support to the "law of falling export quota". The growth of world trade from 1881 to 1913 for 33 countries shows a fairly constant yearly average rate of around 3 per cent, thus, approaching, with minor deviations, the Cassellian 3 per cent yearly quota of economic development. Comparisons of the volume of industrial production with foreign trade per capita in United States and in Great Britain for various years from 1899 to 1928 (for the United States) and from 1907 to 1930 (for Great Britain) do not seem also to confirm the "law of falling export quota". The British export quota increased from 25.1 per cent in 1908 to a maximum of 26.2 per cent in 1913, declining finally to 17.8 in 1930. The United States export quota declined from 12.8 per cent in 1899 to 9.7 per cent in 1914, climbed again to 15.7 in 1919 and declined to 9.6 in 1927. Similar results are reached by a comparison of the evolution of exports measured as percentage of national income in Germany, France, Great Britain and the United State. Between 1892 and 1928 the percentage of exports to national income rose in Germany from 12 to 16 per cent, in France from 17 to 26, while in Great Britain it decreased from 19 to 18, and in the United States from 7 to 6. In view, however, of the heterogeneity and imperfection of national income estimates, we should take the last conclusion "cum grano salis". Wageman advances the further hypothesis, which seems plausible enough although no statistical tests are available, that the export quota per capita tends to be higher in the neo-capitalist than in semi- or in nature capitalist countries, the share of foreign trade being inversely proportional to population density and directly proportional to the degree of capitalization. *Ibid.*, p. 144.

[125] It may be noted, however, that recent statistical research for the determination of the marginal propensity to import has thrown considerable light on the relationship between income and imports. Data for twelve countries, examined in the Department of Commerce publication *The United States in the World Economy*, and in the I.L.O. study *World Economic Development* (Montreal, 1944) by Eugene Staley, show on the whole that "over a long period there is a tendency, exhibited on all the charts which cover enough years, for the ratio between imports and income to decline as income rises". This result is quite consistent with our theoretical expectations. A word of caution, however, must be added. Import statistical cover merely merchandise trade and do not include invisible imports (services) which are precisely the ones for which the demand increase at rising income levels. This factor, nevertheless, is not likely to alter significantly the relation between the two rates of growth.

sufficiently wide range of years and countries, to determine whether the growth has been only in absolute or also in relative terms. Early fears that industrialization would diminish the range of possible international exchange have been disproved. The growth of industry and the rise of income level in new countries has created markets and now wants. International demand is still far from inelastic. It is, moreover, a familiar observation that the inter-industrial trade shows nowadays greater intensity than the industrial-colonial trade.

While the technical difficulties in the way of a statistical demonstration of the law are almost unsurmountable, the general principle can be formulated into a useful working hypothesis, which is moreover rendered plausible by two important structural development: One is the long-run trend of the growth of tertiary industries and the other is the emergence of synthetic industries and their impact on international specialization.

Colin Clark has demonstrated the close historical association between the rise in the income-level and the growth of tertiary (service) industries. As the income level goes up, labor is diverted from primary and secondary to tertiary production. Now, since the bulk of the service industries are by nature non-exportable, the relative share of trade in the national income would tend to decline in the sense foreseen by the "Gesetz der fallenden Export Quote".

Besides this secular trend, a recent structural change which works in the same direction, must be taken into account. The rapid progress of chemical industries and the strides made in the production of synthetic materials (mainly rubber, gasoline and rayon) tend to decrease international specialization and division of labor, thus further reducing the share of trade in the total income.[126]

The prolonged slump of international trade in the thirties might well be explained by the superimposition of cyclical, secular and structural movements.

At this juncture, a possible reformulation of the law of the fallings export quota would suggest itself by the distinction between transitional periods between structural changes and temporary equilibrium positions. Thus, at the initial phase of industrialization, the need for imports and therefore the volume of trade would grow <u>pari passu</u> or even faster than national income. The industrial ripening, on the other hand, would bring about steeper rise of income than of external trade, in view of the expansion of the internal market. Similarly, the initial phase of growth of tertiary industries[127]—usually characterized by large transportation undertak-

---

[126] To the extent, however, that synthetic production accelerates the depletion of local mineral resources, the need for imports would be postponed rather than reduced.

[127] The emergence of tertiary industries is related more directly to the income level than to the level of industrial production as such. In some cases the periods of intensive growth of tertiary industries are associated with industrialization (say the United States railway boom of the seventies). In other cases, it may be more directly associated with the rise in agricultural productivity, as in the case of Australia and Argentina.

ings—is likely to be accompanied by a temporary gain in the rate of increase of trade over that of income.

When industrial maturity or a high level of agricultural productivity are reached and a relatively stable occupation distribution of the population attained, the rate of growth of income would again exceed the rate of growth of trade. The "Gesetz der fallenden Export Quote" would come into its own.

The relationship between trade and income level need not be, in this hypothesis, a linear one. Both would approximately follow the pattern of the Gomprez or logistic curves, with different slopes. In the course of development a maximum point of rapprochement between the two curves will be reached at the transitional phase from either the primary to secondary and tertiary industry, or from secondary to tertiary industries, followed by a continuously growing spread between the two curves until a stationary period is attained.

# CHAPTER III

# THE PARADOXES OF WORLD TRADE

## A. The First Paradox
## Contrasting Price Behavior in Industry and Agriculture

The existence of contrasting economic structures renders international trade at the same time indispensable and paradoxical. The first paradox has its roots in the peculiarities of response of output to price in agriculture as compared to industry.[128]

The response of the industrial system in face of a falling demand is to curtail employment and output. Price-protection is an essential element of industrial psychology. Output is relatively elastic and controlled by entrepreneurial decisions. The structure of production and the length of its period depend on subjective factors as much as on objective ones. In periods of depression, the burden of adjustment in internal as well as in international trade, falls on output rather than on prices.

In agriculture, by contrast, the amount of production is largely determined by natural factors, which govern variations in crop yields. The period of production is an organic datum. Curtailment of output cannot be done, in many cases, without permanent injury to agricultural productivity. The time-lag between changes in prices and actualization of changes input often gives rise to permanent disequilibria, a phenomenon now known as the corn-hog cycle, or more generically, as the cob-web theorem.[129]

A fall in the demand for farm products, bringing a threatened reduction in income of primary producers, will not entail a reduction in output, but within a certain range of prices below the equilibrium position may even increase output,

---

[128] From a broader viewpoint, we may group for the study of differential price-reactions, industrial products on one side, and raw materials on the other, provided allowances are made for wide differences of behavior within the raw materials sphere, as between primary products of agricultural and non-agricultural origin. In mining, for instance, supply is relatively elastic so that both output and prices are likely to contrast in depression, while in agriculture the burden of adjustment will rest almost entirely on prices. In the following pages, the analysis will lay stress on the peculiarities of agricultural production as such, most of the considerations expounded being applicable, therefore, to only part of the raw materials sphere.

[129] *Cf.* Mordecai Ezekiel, "The Cob-Web Theorem", *Quarterly Journal of Economics* (February 1938), pp. 255-80.

thereby further aggravating the weakness of prices.[130] In this case, the response to a fall in demand is, paradoxically, an increase in supply.[131] The burden of adjustment in international trade falls on prices rather than on the volume of exports and is translated into a deterioration of the terms-of-trade of primary products.

It might be argued that the comparative inelasticity of demand for some agricultural products and raw materials (especially food products) should serve as a stabilizing influence in the business cycle. Apart from the structural factor of long-run excess production in agriculture, it may be noted, however, that while the demand for raw materials is fairly inelastic as a whole, it is quite elastic for the production of any individual country, what tends to create severe price competition. The irresponsiveness of consumption to changes in prices of raw materials plays also a de-stabilizing role

Besides the purely economic explanations of the contrasting behavior of industrial and agricultural output, in terms of differential supply and demand elasticities, there are deep-seated institutional and psychological factors to be considered.

Sombart had already called attention to the connection between the rise of entrepreneurial activity and the emergence of the inorganic age. The pursuit of profit in the industrial sphere is not bound by the organic limitations of agrarian production. The former developed a profit psychology, which is extremely sensitive to price fluctuations, while the latter preserves a less sensitive "substance psychology". Over-simplifying a bit, we could say that in industry prices govern the scale of output, while in agriculture it is the scale of output that governs prices.

There is, furthermore, an institutional factor which further restricts the elasticity of agricultural output, namely, the conditions of ownership. The scale of agricultural output depends on decisions of a great number of individual farmers, while in industry, due to interlocking of enterprises and prevalence of cartels and monopolistic arrangements, it is easier to achieve a greater degree of consonance in output controlling measures.

A third factor may be added to explain the cyclical differences in price behavior. Agricultural production, in spite of the recent outgrowth of commodity agreements and price-defense schemes, approaches more closely competitive conditions in world markets than manufactures. The great staples of world trade are

---

[130] This mode of behavior of agricultural production, characterized by strong income effects, is now described by the "regressive supply curve".

[131] The expression "paradox of world trade" has been borrowed from Wageman, who lays stress, for the explanation of agricultural crises, on the shocks created by competition between "profit economies" (Ertragswirtschaften) and "consumption economies" (Bedarfswirtschaften). In the former group price falls would set in motion an "automatic" equilibrium mechanism (increase in demand, contraction of output), while in the latter group the same shock may provoke a disequilibrating export expansion. *Cf.* his *Zwischenbilanz der Krisenpolitik* (Berlin, 1935) p. 84.

fairly well standardized, while differences in brands, trade marks and consumers' tastes make imperfect competition the normal condition of industrial selling. Thus competitive price deflation is much more frequent in the raw materials sphere and constitutes one of the principal vehicles of the horizontal spreading of depression.[132]

In international trade, the price-ratio between industrial and primary products—exchanged between industrial and raw material areas—revels not only a cyclical but a long term movement, often superimposed, the latter being particularly affected by structural changes. Increased agricultural productivity, over-expansion of crop areas in the first World War, low income elasticity of demand for food products, all contribute to explain the unfavorable trend of raw materials prices that persisted throughout most the twenties and thirties.[133]

1. The Price Scissors. The price scissors, namely, the relative stability or smaller decline of industrial as against the violent price deflation in agriculture (and for that matter in the entire raw materials sphere), is a common phenomenon of the depressions. In the last depression however, the disparity was so great as to constitute, to borrow Professor Mills' expression, a veritable "schism" of prices.

The terms of trade had moved in favor of raw materials since the turn of the century reversed their course throughout the twenties and the early thirties. Agricultural prices, in fact, never quite recovered from the commodity crisis of 1921. Structural changes superimposed on trend factors conspired to maintain the gap between raw materials and industrial prices. The years of 1921 and 1932 mark the minima and 1927 and 1937 the maxima points of the terms of trade for primary producers. In 1937 New Zealand had to export 58 per cent in volume than in 1929 to get the same quantity of imports. For Argentina, the figure was 52 per cent and

---

[132] This point is well expressed by Professor Neisser: "While the export of raw materials and certain standardized foodstuffs meets the competition of the whole world and small price differentiations would be sufficient to undersell a competitor, increasing the export of manufactured goods would require a much greater lowering of the price in order to overcome established preferences and relations". *Cf. op. cit.*, p. 114.

[133] Studying long-period terms of trade, as revealed by the price ratio of British exports and imports. Colin Clark concludes that the terms of trade ware comparatively stable during the 1840-ies, moved favorably to primary production between 1850 and 1880, reacted favorably to manufactures from 1880 to 1900, improved again slightly for primary products up to 1925, and moved sharply in favor of manufactures during the thirties. Data for other countries suggest that prices of primary products failed altogether to share in the expansion of the twenties which constituted in fact a period of relatively depressed primary production. Forecasting the course of terms of trade from 1945 to 1960, Colin Clark anticipates rising prices of primary products, due to the probable expansion of international investment (which, he claims, has been historically associated with improvement of terms of primary producers) and to shifts of population from primary to secondary and tertiary industries. *Cf. The Economics of 1960* (London, 1944), chapter VII.

for the Dutch East Indies, 48 per cent. By contrast, England, France, Germany and the United States were giving, respectively, 13, 13, 31 and 16 per cent less exports than in 1929 for a given quantity of imports in raw materials.[134]

The recovery of 1933–1936 narrowed but little, and did not eliminate this unfavorable margin. A new and violent slump or raw material prices occurred in the American depression of 1937 and persisted throughout 1938

The following table, transcribed from Professor Mills' exhaustive work Behavior of Prices, bears out clearly the long run downward trend of terms of trade of agricultural areas and the sharper cleavages that occurred in 1921 and 1932:

### Table VII
### Net Barter Terms of Trade for 4 Industrial and for 4 Agricultural Areas
(Number of export units exchanged for a fixed quantity of imports)

|  | 1913 | 1921 | 1929 | 1932 | 1934 | 1935 |
|---|---|---|---|---|---|---|
| United Kingdom | 100 | 82 | 88 | 76 | 74 | 76 |
| France | 100 | 95 | 105 | 91 | 89 | 88 |
| Germany | 100 | - | 95 | 65 | 70 | 76 |
| United States | 100 | 78 | 95 | 81 | 75 | 73 |
| Hungary | 100 | 156 | 116 | 127 | 113 | 104 |
| New Zealand | 100 | 135 | 92 | 145 | 119 | - |
| Argentina | 100 | 159 | 107 | 162 | 156 | - |
| Dutch East Indies | 100 | 153 | 126 | 183 | 172 | 171 |

The disparity in international behavior of prices and output, already commented upon, is clearly brought out in international trade by a comparison of gold values and quantum of trade in:

|  | Foodstuffs | | Raw Materials | | Manufactures | |
|---|---|---|---|---|---|---|
|  | Quantum | Unit Prices in gold | Quantum | Unit Prices in gold | Quantum | Unit Prices in gold |
| 1929 | 100 | 100 | 100 | 100 | 100 | 100 |
| 1932 | 90 | 52 | 81 | 45 | 98 | 64 |

---

[134] Data from Professor F.C. Mills, *Behavior of Prices* (New York, NBER, 1927), pp. 183-84, who offers an exhaustive discussion of the matter.

2. <u>Price Instability and the Cyclical Behavior</u>. The cyclical instability of raw material prices renders colonial areas an easy prey for the virus of depression. Because of the large share of exports in their national income and of the dependence on a narrow range of products, a fall in exports prices is the normal vehicles for the importation of depressions originating in industrial countries. The effect of fluctuations in export prices upon the income level is somewhat different for agricultural and mineral products, what accounts for substantial differences in the cyclical behavior within the raw materials sphere:

> In the case of agriculture, where aggregate production is not immediately affected by changes in demand, price movements involve roughly proportionate changes in income. The effects of any changes in the prices of mineral products on income tends to be greater because conditions leading to a fall in prices are likely to lead also to a fall in output, and hence a more than proportionate fall in both individual and national income.[135]

The price-inelasticity of the demand for imports of industrial countries, especially in the case of the United States, is another serious disequilibrating factor. The American demand for raw materials, which is a major determinant of their world terms of trade, is highly sensitive to fluctuations in the level of national income, but comparatively insensitive to price fluctuations. In other words, while the income-elasticity-of-demand for imports is high, the price-elasticity-of-demand is low. Thus even a drastic fall in prices of primary products in depression falls to elicit a corrective increase in demand.

As noted in a recent Department of Commerce study:

> The difference between the behavior of receipts and payments on current account may also be attributed in substantial part to the lack of responsiveness of United States imports to changes in prices. This factor, indeed, constituted a self-aggravating element of disturbance in the balance of payments. A decline in the supply of dollars, for any reason, tends to exert a deflationary pressure on foreign prices, which under other circumstances, might be expected to produce a relatively larger volume of imports into the United

---

[135] *Cf.* League of Nations, *Economic Stability in the Post-War World,* p. 310. The structural inelasticity of certain agricultural areas is clearly brought out by the percentage share of certain crops in total exports. In 1929, wheat and maize made up 47 per cent of Argentine exports, wool 41 per cent of Australia, coffee 71 per cent of Brazil, sugar 75 per cent of Cuba, cotton 81 per cent of Egypt, and tobacco 57 per cent of Greece. The situation changed considerably in the thirties, owing to industrialization and crop diversification policies of several governments.

States and thus to compensate the initial decline in the outflow of dollars. Because of the nature of United States import demands, however, a fall in foreign prices only tends to reduce the supply of dollars further and to intensify the disturbance. This perverse tendency toward aggravation rather than correction of international imbalance was particularly serious factor during the great depression, when its effects were superimposed upon those produced by the falling off in economic activity in the United States.[136]

3. <u>Capital Movements and the Terms of Trade</u>. Aside from the deflationary pressure to which primary products are subject in depression, due to supply and demand elasticities, the perverse behavior of capital movements is an added element of instability for raw material areas. For capital in-flows tend to coincide with periods of high export prices (optimistic investor's psychology) while the deflationary effect of a price fall is intensified by withdrawal of capital and debt collection. Under the pressure to meet debt payments and interest charges, raw material countries are obliged to curtail imports and push exports, thus starting the mechanism of competitive price deflation.[137] The experience of the last depression is particularly significant. Short and long-term loans to primary producers which amounted in 1929 to 300 million dollars dropped to zero in 1931 and were followed by net debt repayment. It is easy to see that this stoppage of capital flow at a time of falling export prices and worsening of trade terms placed an intolerable burden on the balance of payments of those countries. This growing disequilibrium was met partly by gold shipments, partly by exchange depreciation and the imposition of exchange and import controls, and partly by structural adjustments aimed at reducing the dependence on foreign manufactures and at diversifying the national output.

A widely discussed question is that of whether the shifts in the terms of trade are themselves an effect or fluctuations in capital flows, or whether they are both governed by deeper cyclical movements. The causational influence of capital movements—a theory which has a distinctly classical flavor—has been recently upheld by Roland Wilson and Colin Clark. The latter writer, who is primarily concerned with long-term trends, finds a close association between periods of intense capital exports by creditor countries, and of improvements in the terms of trade of

---

[136] *Cf. The United States in the World Economy*, p. 88.

[137] Timoshenko has remarked that the behavior of exports and imports of depressed countries in the last crisis was governed more by creditor-debtor relationships than by structural divergences. Germany, the only large industrial debtor country, reacted much in the same way as the agricultural areas.

primary producers and vice-versa.[138] Available material for individual countries (White's study on the *French International Accounts* and Silverman's study on Britain's terms of trade) do not cover sufficiently long periods for the determination of a long term trend and, on the whole, do not show a sufficient degree of co-variations to permit an international generalization.[139]

It is doubtful that a uni-directional chain of causation—from capital movements to terms of trade—can be either theoretically or statistically established. We have seen that the instability of prices of agricultural production is tooted in particular modes of behavior derived from psychological and institutional reasons, quite apart from capital movements. Thus the co-variation often observed between the two movements cannot be taken as a proof of causation, even though it is undeniable that the instability of capital movements is in itself a major element in the explanation of the characteristic price slump of primary products.

While the greater elasticity of their economic structure renders the resistance to imposed deflation and the recovery easier for industrial and creditor countries, their plight is only slightly better. For the amelioration of the terms of trade and the increased liquidity resulting from debt collection, in periods of depression, weakens the purchasing power of primary producers and hits grievously the import demand for industrial products.

---

[138] Colin Clark suggests the existence of long alternating cycles of foreign investment divided between "capital- hungry" and "capital-sated" periods (1850-1875, 1900-1930 and by forecast 1945-1960) are characterized by heavy capital imports into agricultural to secondary and tertiary industries; price of primary products and terms of trade of raw materials countries show a relative improvement. On the other hand, during the "capital-sated" periods (1875-1900, 1900-1930 and by forecast from 1960 on) the terms of trade and price of primary products tend to decline, due to slower absorption of population into secondary industries, this price fall being aggravated by the relative inelasticity of world demand for those products. Two other hypotheses have been advanced to explain the long cycles of terms of trade; one runs in terms of "productivity cycles" and the other in terms of "purchasing power or reciprocal supply and demand cycles" (A . Kahn). The productivity theory explains the alternation of price trends by variations in the rate of technological advance in industry as compared to agriculture. The unfavorable trend of the British terms of trade from 1790 to 1860 is thus traced to the extremely rapid advance in industrial productivity during the industrial revolution. From 1860 onward the great improvements that took place in agricultural production resulted in more favorable terms of trade for manufactures. Finally, according to the purchasing power hypothesis, in the first phase of the development of new countries the influx of capital, the high rate of investment and the bidding up of factor prices cause a raise in their export prices as compared to exports of industrial countries; this situation gradually reverses itself after economic maturation is reached by the debtor country. *Cf.* A . Kahn, *Great Britain in the World Economy* (New York, Columbia University Press, 1946), pp. 144-48. A forerunner of all these hypotheses is Cairne's "three stage loan theorem" which, however, refers to movements in the balance rather than in the terms of trade.

[139] *Cf.* Harry White, The *French International Accounts, 1880–1913* (Harvard University Press, 1933) and A.G. Silverman, "Some International Trade Factors for Great Britain, 1880–1913", in *Review of Economic Statistical*, XIII (1913), pp. 114-24.

# B. The Second Paradox of World Trade

The second paradox of world trade stems directly from the capitalistic modes of production and affects mainly the industrial nations. The spreading of industrialization and economic progress is accompanied by structural modifications in the composition of internal and international trade. Changes in the composition of population as a result of a declining rate of growth and the rise of income level in nature capitalistic societies are forces operating to increase the demand for durable consumers' goods as compared to basic food consumption, while at the same time demands of newly industrialized areas for their exports is increasingly concentrated on investment goods. The proportion of capital and durable goods in the total exports of major industrial countries and in the total imports of major agricultural areas has shown a steadily upward trend, as indicated in the following table taken from the League of Nations study *International Currency Experience in the Inter-War Period*:

### Table VIII
### Composition of exports from the United Kingdom, Germany and the United States
(In percentages)

|  | 1880 | 1900 | 1913 | 1920 |
|---|---|---|---|---|
| Capital goods | 26 | 39 | 45 | 55 |
| Consumption goods | 74 | 61 | 54 | 45 |

### Percentage share of machinery, vehicles, metals and metal manufactures in total imports

|  | 1929 | 1938 |  | 1929 | 1938 |
|---|---|---|---|---|---|
| Brazil | 33 | 40 | New Zealand | 32 | 40 |
| Bulgaria | 32 | 49 | Peru | 31 | 37 |
| Finland | 24 | 36 | Poland | 22 | 37 |

The implications of these structural changes are obvious. For, the demand for capital and durable goods is subject to particularly violent cyclical fluctuations due to familiar technical reasons that need no further review. Instability is the penalty for roundaboutedness of production. Thus, the exports of the major industrial countries are increasingly constituted by deferrable goods, particularly vulnerable to the vagaries of international demand. Another disquieting feature is that, due to the tendency of synchronization of business cycles, the fluctuations in foreign demand for durable goods, far from compensating for, are likely to coincide with, the slack of domestic demand.[140] An industrial country like England, which imports foodstuffs of inelastic demand and exports durable goods of elastic demand, is likely to face serious adjustment problem in a world trade deflation.

The problem is of course closely intertwined with the previous one of fluctuations in purchasing power of agricultural countries, which are the principal purchasers of capital equipment. The impact of fluctuations of purchasing power of primary producers on the demand for industrial products has of course been long recognized, or even exaggerated (by the agricultural theory of cycles). Sir Willian Beveridge has, however, recently called attention to an important empirical finding having a bearing on the theory of cycle generation, namely the coincidence of the turning points of British cycles with harvest periods in the Northern and Southern Hemispheres. This fact, plus the observation that export industries in Britain have shown a constant lead over the general cycles, both in recession and in recovery, would tend to indicate a strong link of industrial production to variations in agricultural purchasing power.

It is unquestionable that a higher degree of stability of prices of primary products—either via the formation of international buffer stocks (a proposal that is gaining growing support[141]) or via the conclusion of long-term purchase contrasts (as suggested by Sir Willian Beveridge for Great Britain) would do much to even out sharp fluctuations in the international component of the demand for durable goods and to decrease the conductivity of trade to depressions.[142] To the extent, however that the instability of demand for durable goods is radicated in particular modes of capitalistic behavior, even complete stabilization of trade and prices would not be a cure. Instability may be the unavoidable penalty to pay for economic progress and technological development, as society widens its margin of choice and moves further away from the subsistence-level.

---

[140] "The industrialization of countries hitherto predominantly agricultural has probably tended to increase instability in the older industrial countries. The new countries have generally concentrated at first on simpler manufactures (clothing, food, paper, etc.) while the older ones have had to change over from the export of those products to capital goods, for which demand is much less stable." *Int. Currency Exp.*, p. 201.

[141] See *Economic Stability in the Post-War World*, chapter XIX.

[142] The device of long-term contracts has been widely used in wartime by United States and Great Britain either to stimulate production of critical materials, or to preclude buying by the enemy. Valuable experience has been gained which may facilitate its utilization for price stabilization purpose.

# Summary to Section III

After pointing out, at the outset, the importance of international trade as a conductor of cyclical effects, we proceeded to the discussion of the theory of international trade, from the viewpoint of the cyclical analysis. The shortcomings of the classical and demand schools, derived from their static approach, were briefly reviewed and the contribution of the savings-investment analysis, via the foreign-trade-multiplier and the principle of acceleration, critically assessed. The conclusion reached was that is spite of difficulties of statistical verification, the foreign-trade-multiplier brought a significant contribution to the understanding of the mechanism of propagation of booms and depressions.

In a second section, the natural and artificial factors tending to localize business fluctuations were briefly reviewed. The advantages and limitations of tariffs and regional trade arrangements, as anti-cyclical devices, were appraised. The long-run relationship of trade to income, and the interaction of structural, cyclical and trend factors were discussed in connection with the law of the falling export quota.

In a third section, the actual experience in the propagation of fluctuations through trade effects upon contrasting economic structures was examined. A divergent price behavior was found to exist between the raw materials and the industrial sphere, the burden of adjustment falling in one case upon volume, and in the other upon prices of exports. Finally, the paradox of the spreading of economic progress being associated with growing cyclical vulnerability of trade was discussed.

# PART THREE

# PARALLELISM AND DIVERGENCIES OF CYCLICAL BEHAVIOR

The whole process of cyclical fluctuations can be described, to use Schumpeter's expression, as an "irregular regularity".

A detailed analysis of cyclical behavior on an international scale, such as that presented for instance in Thorp's Business Annals, presents us with a bewildering maze of uniformities and diversities which seem at first sight despairing and unmanageable:

> Business cycles differ in their duration as wholes and in relative duration of their component phases; they differ in industrial and geographical scope; they differ in intensity, they differ in the features that attain prominence; they differ in the quickness and in the uniformity with which they sweep from one country to another.[1]

Despite the fact the areas of disagreement in international cyclical behavior are almost as wide as the areas of agreement, one way discern throughout the economic sphere some general contours of cyclical behavior characterized by consonance in the fluctuations of certain economic magnitudes. We may, thus, following Aftalion distinguish between regular and irregular international cyclical variations.[2] The word regular is here employed in a very strict sense, and refers only to consilience in the direction of the variations in the phases of the cycle, but does not imply regularity in the amplitude and timing of the movement, both of which will differ internationally according to the originating influence and to the structure of the receiving mechanism. In this sense, upward and downward fluctuations in prices, employment and output may be broadly identified as regular features of the international cycle.

By contrast, the concept of irregular cyclical variations will apply to those magnitudes whose movements differ internationally in timing, amplitude as well as in direction. As examples, we may take the behavior of the balance of trade, of capital movements, of gold flows, exchange rates, and of the balance of payments as a whole.

The purpose of this section is double: to verify, on one band, similarities and dissimilarities in the international behavior of certain economic magnitudes, and on the other hand, to determine the impact of difference in economic structure upon the cyclical behavior.

---

[1] *Cf.* Mitchell, Introduction to the N.B.E.R. volume of *Business Annals*, p. 37.

[2] The concept, as used here, bears no relationship to Mitchell's "irregular" fluctuations, which in his definition, result from the action of random factors which fail to cancel out. Our concept implies merely a lack of parallelism of the cyclical behavior viewed from the international aspect, without reference to the regularity or randomness from the viewpoint of a closed economy. *Cf.* Mitchell, *Business Cycles*, p. 282.

# SECTION I
# REGULAR CYCLICAL VARIATIONS

# CHAPTER I

# THE INTERNATIONAL BEHAVIOR OF PRICES

## A. The Kondratieff Wave and the Movement of Wholesale Prices

The international parallelism of price behavior in prosperity and depression is one the oldest and most widely accepted generalizations. The data available for significant periods of time refer mainly to the western industrial countries and show a wide measure of agreement. The co-variation stands more clearly for the long wave (Kondratieff cycle) but there is also a fairly satisfactory synchronization for the Juglar cycle. The solidarity of international prices conforms moreover to what one would expect on a priori grounds, since prices are, as pertinently noted by Schumpeter, "among the most important conductors of cyclical affects".

This parallelism of behavior is much more clearly noticeable for the pre-war than for the post-war period. Price movements were greatly distorted by the war inflation and the after-war depression, their behavior being directly influenced by monetary and exchange policies. "Inflation" countries and stabilization countries showed a quite different price behavior during the twenties. The solidarity of price behavior later regained ground with the internationalization of the depression.

For long-period analysis, wholesale price series are still the only that are available in satisfactory form, notwithstanding the fact that they are liable to overstate the cyclical phenomenon, owing to the well-known wider amplitudes of fluctuations in wholesale as compared to retail prices.

It is obvious that the material used for international price comparisons must be handled with a great deal of caution because of (a) different techniques of price level construction in different countries and periods, and (b) different significance and changing weight (from the viewpoint of an individual country's cyclical behavior) of the prices that compose the indices.

Even when all these limitations are taken into account, the fact remains that there exists over the long wave a high degree of consonance in price variations, to such an extent that international trade cycles are in many cases identified as price cycles. The interpretation to be given to this phenomenon calls for some comments:

1. The co-variations of international wholesale prices is to a certain extent as noted by Schumpeter, purely tautological, since the price indices are dominated by

the great staples of world trade, which are subject to the prices equalizing influence of international trade.[3]

2. There is no necessary causal meaning attached to the co-variation of world prices. To a large extent price movements are more symptoms of more fundamental cyclical disequilibria, the emphasis placed on prices by the monetary theories as a factor of cyclical generations being certainly exaggerated. Even the very plausible contention that the fall in raw material prices plays a causal role in the depression of agricultural economies cannot be dogmatically upheld. One may, for instance, ascribe to prices merely a symptomatic value, the causal role being played by over-production, inelasticity of demand, stickiness of supply, etc.

3. There is a high degree of correlation but not a necessary connection between prosperity and rising prices and between depression and falling prices. A boom characterized by technological developments, for instance, is quite compatible with stable or even falling prices (at least group prices), the most conspicuous example being the American prosperity of the twenties.

4. From the international as well as the national viewpoint, group or sectional prices reveal pronounced disparities of behavior, a notion which is of the utmost importance in the structural approach to cycle theory.

So much for the general aspects of prices. We must now trace the historical evidence on international price movements during the cycle. The general consilience of wholesale price movements in the countries for which longer series are available,[4] namely, England (since 1780), United States (since 1891) and France (since 1858) was already clearly illustrated by Kondratieff and formed the original basis for his hypothesis on the long-waves of economic life.[5] The turning points of the long price waves were thus summarized by Kondratieff:[6]

---

[3] *Cf.* Schumpeter, *op. cit.*, vol. II, p. 461.

[4] Complications of wholesale price levels on a fairly wide basis are of comparatively recent development; the technique of index number constructions was developed mostly by Jevons.

[5] Chart I of Kondratieff's article "The long Waves of Economic Life" (translated into English and printed in "Readings in Business Cycle Theory" Philadelphia, 1944), on page 23 should be inspected.

[6] The long wave of prices is one of the most widely accepted generalizations (Wolf, Van Gelderen, Kondratieff) although some authors like Leon Dupriez are inclined to deny the existence of any such movement, insofar as agricultural prices in Europe are concerned. At least three different explanations have been suggested for the long wave of prices: Cassell formulated the well-known theorem linking fluctuations in price level to fluctuations in the rate of gold production; Cyril Wantrup linked the phases of the prices cycle to war-time expansion and subsequent depressions; a third explanation connected with the names of Spiethoff and Schumpeter, would link the three identifiable historical Kondratieffs to successive waves of innovation.

|  | FIRST CYCLE | | SECOND CYCLE | | THIRD CYCLE | |
|---|---|---|---|---|---|---|
|  | Beginning of the rise | Beginning of the decline | Beginning of the rise | Beginning of the decline | Beginning of the rise | Beginning of the decline |
| England | 1789 | 1814 | 1849 | 1873 | 1896 | 1920 |
| United States | 1890 | 1814 | 1849 | 1866 | 1896 | 1920 |
| France | - | - | - | 1873 | 1896 | 1920 |

A detailed analysis of the parallelism of price behavior in Great Britain (1843–1914), United States (1849–1914) and Germany (1879–1914) is offered by Schumpeter in his great work on business cycles (Cf. vol. II, pages 461, 475). Chart IV on page 464, which expresses the degree of percentage changes in the price level of the three countries, is particularly interesting because it illustrates at the same time general consilience in the direction and timing of the movement and the disparity in their amplitude. Schumpeter finds that the international comparison of price levels shows quite already the Kondratieff wave, even though the association is far from perfect, owing to the disturbing influence of wars and monetary disorders. The Juglar price cycles are in turn much more clearly discernible than the Kitchins.

A specific analysis of the short price cycles, (average length of about 39 months) has been made by Dr. Gehard Tintner for the Austrian Institute of Trade Cycle Research. He finds substantial international co-variation of groups of prices in five countries, the percentage of prices sharing in the international cyclical movements amounting to as high as 70 per cent of all prices for England, 75 per cent for Germany, and 79 per cent for the United States. The failure of individual prices to correspond to the general cyclical movements (i.e., in the European mining and metal industries) is explained by the co-existence of a <u>second rhythm</u> or special cycle intertwined with the world cycle.[7]

A comparative analysis of price movements and cyclical fluctuations in the last country seems to indicate clearly the influence of the long-term price trend on the shorter superimposed cyclical fluctuation. The ratio and average length of periods of prosperity as compared to periods of depression are found to be different in the upswing and in the downswing of Kondratieff, depressions being longer and more severe in the downswing, and prosperity periods predominating in the upswing.

---

[7] *Cf.* Gerhard Tintner, *Prices in the Trade Cycle* (Vienna, Julius Springer, 1935), pp. 58-61.

## B. Monetary Policies and Recent Price Developments

More abundant material and much less regularity in international price behavior are to be found as regards the period 1918–1930. Structural changes and disequilibria brought about by the First World war interrupted, as noted before, the growing tendency toward synchronization of cyclical fortunes. The cleavage of monetary policies as between the <u>deflationist</u> and the <u>inflationist</u> countries was directly reflected in divergent price trends. The following table, taken from the League of Nations study *Course and Phases of the World Economic Depression* (p. 92) illustrates the dispersions of wholesale price levels in various countries:

### Table IX
### Movements of Wholesale Prices (1913=100)

|  | 1922 1st half | 1923 2nd half | 1928 | 1929 1st half |
|---|---|---|---|---|
| Australia | 156 | 169 | 165 | 164 |
| Austria | - | 128 | 130 | 132 |
| Canada | 149 | 152 | 151 | 146 |
| Czechoslovakia | 160 | 148 | 143 | 138 |
| Egypt | 134 | 133 | 123 | 121 |
| Estonia | 114 | 116 | 121 | 120 |
| Finland | 138 | 145 | 145 | 138 |
| Germany | - | 137 | 140 | 137 |
| Netherlands | 155 | 147 | 149 | 143 |
| New Zealand | 148 | 154 | 147 | 147 |
| Sweden | 167 | 164 | 148 | 143 |
| Switzerland | 165 | 172 | 143 | 141 |
| United Kingdom | 144 | 150 | 140 | 138 |
| United States | 144 | 146 | 140 | 139 |

The spreading of the depression in 1930 re-established the solidarity of international price movements, which again become less marked during the recovery.[8] The recovery of the thirties is, however, of particularly difficult analysis. The trend towards autarchy an economic self-sufficiency, trade restrictions and exchange manipulations distorted the whole price structural and further narrowed the area of

---

[8] This would tend to lend support to Professor Mills' tentative conclusion (based on the analysis of several American cycles), according to which the decline of wholesale prices at a time of recession tends to be a more concentrated and uniform movement than the rise of prices in revival. *Cf.* Mills, *The Behavior of Prices*, p. 158. *Cf.* also *Prices in Recession and Recovery* (N.B.E.R., 1936).

solidarity of prices which had already been shattered by the breakdown of the gold standard.

The price behavior was, of course, quite different for countries on and off the gold standard but for all of them the co-variation was greater in the depression. The decline of wholesale prices in terms of gold was in general larger in gold standard countries than in non-gold standard countries. In terms of national currencies the opposite occurred. Data gathered by Professor Mills in *Price in Recession and Recovery* permit a rough comparison of wholesale price level variations both in terms of gold and of national currencies for 32 countries. The fluctuation in gold values was wide, ranging from 36 in Germany to 71 per cent in Japan, with a median decline of 52 per cent as compared to a median decline of 36 per cent in terms of national currency. The chart on page 168 of the above cited study is of striking interest for demonstrating the broadness and sweeping character of the downward price changes for the period 1929 to 1935, as measured by deviations from the 1929 level.

On the basis of Professor Mills' study, the following patterns of behavior can be distinguished:

1. The consonance in the downward direction of price movements was more marked for the recession period 1929–1931 than in later phases of the depression and recovery. There existed, however, wide differences in the amplitude of the movement, which to the extent that they affected the terms of international trade, created a serious disequilibrium of difficult correction.

2. In the period 1931 to 1933, characterized by the progressive disintegration of the gold standard after Great Britain's defection, there was a general consilience in the direction of price movements but the parallelism was not unbroken and very wide divergences in amplitude persisted.

3. In the third phase (1933–1936), already a recovery stage, the pattern of price movements lacked the previous degree of synchronization, reflecting the difference in the degree and timing of recovery but also the influence of external factors (trade restrictions, quotas, exchange controls) which aggravated the disalignment of national price levels. The lag in price recovery was particularly marked in the gold standard countries, subject to heavy deflationary pressure.

## C. Sectional Prices

For the understanding of cyclical behavior, as affected by the type of economic structures, the analysis of sectional prices is much more enlightening than the cursory view of the wholesale price level. The latter reflects more or less tautologically the cyclical process but does not throw light on the mechanism of cycle transmissions.[9] In the preceding section we were interested primarily in detecting the consonance in the direction of price movements, variations in amplitude and timing being a secondary consideration. For the analysis of relative price and their cyclical repercussions, however, the analysis of the amplitude or degree of dispersion and of leads and lags become a fundamental consideration.

1. <u>Amplitude.</u> We shall now proceed to consider the international implications of the two principal generalizations on price behavior which seem well established both on theoretical and empirical grounds:

   a) Wider amplitude of fluctuations in raw material as compared to industrial prices.
   b) Wide amplitude of fluctuations in producer goods as compared to consumer goods prices.

a) For purposes of broad comparison we may first attempt to study the international group-behavior of raw materials as compared to industrial prices, although in both cases there are important sub-group differences.

It is a familiar fact that every depression is characterized by comparatively wider price swings of raw materials. In the depression of 1907–1908 raw material prices dropped by 11 per cent in the United States, and those of manufactures by 8 per cent. In 1921, the price index for finished products in Sweden and in United States stood at 27 and 33 per cent, respectively, above that of raw materials. The severity of the price fall of raw materials has also been one of the outstanding features of the last depression. Measured in sterling prices, raw materials prices fell from 1929 to 1933 by 41 per cent, foodstuffs by 33 per cent and manufactures by only 18 per cent.

Important sub-group differences should, however, be taken into account. In the last depression, for instance animal food products suffered less than vegetable food products; as regards raw materials of non-agricultural origin, mineral products were grievously hit while fuel prices remained comparatively unscathed. A clear idea of the instability of price of primary products can be gathered from the following tabulation showing price changes in the comparatively mild depression of 1937:

---

[9] Compare Schumpeter: "From our analysis of the cyclical process of evolution it follows, indeed, that cycles are not satisfactorily described as aggregative movements that leave structural relations within the system untouched. It is of the very essence of the process that it remodels the structure of the system. But it does not follow that comparisons of the cyclical behavior of group prices since output and prices are mutually interdependent.

## Table X
### Variability of Prices of Primary Products
### (1936–1938)

| Commodity (and Market) | Dates of High and Low Prices | | | Percentage Changes | |
|---|---|---|---|---|---|
| | 1st Minimum 1936 | Maximum 1937 | 2nd Minimum 1938 | 1st Minimum to maximum | Maximum to 2nd minimum |
| Wheat (Liverpool) | June | Apr. | Dec. | 75 | –60 |
| Maize (Chicago) | Mar. | Apr. | Oct. | 133 | –77 |
| Rice (London) | Mar. | Oct. | Apr. | 33 | –14 |
| Sugar (London) | Sept. | July | Apr. | 48 | –24 |
| Tea (London) | June | Sept. | Nov. | 35 | –24 |
| Coffee (New York) | Apr. | June | Apr. | 49 | –49 |
| Cocoa (New York) | Apr. | Jan. | Dec. | 129 | –62 |
| Beef, chilled (London) | Mar. | May | Mar. | 45 | –17 |
| Butter, Danish (London) | Apr. | Oct. | Mar. | 46 | –23 |
| Wool, Merino (London) | Sept. | July | Nov. | 45 | –42 |
| Cotton (New York) | Mar. | Mar. | Nov. '37 | 27 | –45 |
| Rubber (London) | Jan. | Mar. | Mar. | 91 | –50 |
| Timber (Sweden) | Jan. | Apr. | Oct. | 57 | –33 |
| Copper (London) | Jan. | Mar. | June | 100 | –48 |
| Tin (London) | June | Mar. | Apr. | 66 | –45 |
| Lead (London) | June | Feb. | May | 99 | –53 |

(Source: League of Nations: *Economic Stability in the Post-War World*, p. 83)

The reasons for differential price behavior as between the industrial and raw material spheres have already been touched upon, and may be attributed to the following general factors:

i. <u>Psychological</u>. Manufacturing industry is more closely related to profitability, agriculture to subsistence (Bedarfsdeckungprinzip); mining occupies an intermediate position which accounts for a different price repercussion

ii. <u>Institutional</u>. Smaller product differentiation and sharper competition in the raw materials area as against product differentiation and prevalence of cartelistic prices in industry.

iii. <u>Technical</u>. Supply of and demand for agricultural products, especially foodstuffs are relatively inelastic, what makes output and consumption irresponsive to price changes. Low income elasticity of demand for food products, as compared to a growing demand for manufactures at high income levels. In the case of mining products, by contrast both supply and demand are relatively elastic. The factor making for price instability is then the instability of industrial demand and the prevalence of speculative stock policies.

iv. <u>Historical</u>. Long-run trend towards overproduction in agriculture.

b) The wider amplitude of fluctuations in the output of <u>durable</u> producers' and consumers' goods is a well-established inductive generalization that will occupy us later. The behavior of their relative prices follows approximately the same pattern although with somewhat less constancy. The first systematic comparison between producers' and consumers' goods' wholesale prices was due to Professor Mitchell in the early work on index numbers (Bulletin No.173 of the Bureau of Labor Statistic). Substantial evidence of greater cyclical vulnerability of producers' goods' prices was found for the period between 1890 and 1913.

Somewhat disconcerting, however, and worth noting is the experience of the last depression. Professor Mills calls attention to the fact that in the early thirties, contrarily to what happened in pre-war business cycles, prices of producers' goods remained relatively high. We quote:

> Is most industrial countries for which we have appropriate records, depression prices of capital equipment were relatively higher than the prices of goods intended for ultimate human consumption. In Germany industrial finished goods for use of producers were only 17 per cent lower in price in January 1933 than in 1929; industrial finished goods for sale to final consumers were 35 per cent lower. In Canada producers' equipment in February 1933 was 8 per cent lower in price than in 1929; consumers' goods were 27 per cent lower. In the United States in February 1933, producers' goods intended for use as capital equipment were 27 per cent lower than in 1929; consumers' goods were 35 per cent lower.[10]

In Japan, however, the opposite took place. In June 1932 the prices of producers' goods were 48 per cent and those of consumers' goods only 30 per cent lower than in 1929.

---

[10] Mills, *Prices in Recession and Recovery*, pp. 184-85.

The relatively high degree of resistance of producers' goods in the United States to price deflation is the more interesting because of the high rate of capital expansion in the decade of the twenties.

Durable consumers' goods showed substantially the same characteristics of behavior and in general displayed the same reaction as producers' goods. The recovery period from 1935 to 1937 was characterized by greater fluctuations and larger gains in producers' rather than in consumers' goods prices.

**Table XI**
**Price Movements of Producers' and Consumers' Goods**

| Country | Index Number of | Net Percentage of Changes (Jan. to Jan.) | | | Price Index January 1938 |
|---------|-----------------|------|------|------|------|
|         |                 | 1935 | 1936 | 1937 | (1929=100) |
| Canada  | Producers' equip. | 0.3 | 1.9 | 3.1 | 99.9 |
|         | Consumers' goods | 1.1 | 4.5 | 1.3 | 83.7 |
| Germany | Producers' equip. | –0.6 | 0.1 | –0.1 | 81.6 |
|         | Consumers' goods | 0.9 | 4.9 | 3.7 | 89.0 |
| Japan   | Producers' equip. | 1.3 | 3.9 | 1.0 | 105.9 |
|         | Consumers' goods | 3.1 | 7.1 | 7.1 | 106.3 |
| Poland  | Producers' equip. | –6.2 | –2.5 | 2.5 | 73.4 |
|         | Consumers' goods | –0.9 | 2.5 | –0.9 | 57.2 |
| Sweden  | Producers' equip. | 5.5 | 15.8 | 8.3 | 107.5 |
|         | Consumers' goods | 4.0 | 2.3 | 6.0 | 95.3 |

(Source: League of Nations, *World Production and Prices* (1938), p. 94.

On the whole, throughout the cycle of the thirties, prices of equipment goods were maintained on a favorable level relatively to prices of consumers' good. This is partly explained by a much larger contraction in output and also by the fact that the price indexes of consumers' goods are heavily weighted with food products, which were severely hit during the depression. The frequent occurrence of monopolistic and cartelized prices in the industrial sphere supplies also part of the explanation. No conclusive indication can be obtained to justify theoretical inference but, on the whole, the experience of the last depression lends little support to the Hayneckian model of crisis through changes in relative prices.

2. <u>Procession of Prices</u>. The leads or lags of groups of prices between themselves or as related to other economic magnitudes is a critical unsettled problem in busi-

ness cycle theory. Actual experience has often disproved the leads and lags postulated by the various theories and forecasting techniques. An early, somewhat unqualified, and today largely abandoned statement of causal precession was made by Professor Fisher, who attributed to variations in the rate of changes of price-level a causal influence upon the volume of trade (as measured by W. Pearson's index), the latter being linked to the former by lagged correlation, whose coefficient would as high as + .721 for a seven month lag and + .941 for a 9 ½ month lag. The Harvard barometer is also based on the assumption of a definite procession of stock market prices over commodity prices and market rates, described by movements of the three curves A (speculation), B (business), and C (money rates).[11]

It seems now that early inference on procession of prices or on sequence of market reaction were based on an over-estimation of the inductive possibilities offered by the correlation calculus. Leads and lags may very from cycle, and the "strategic factors in the business cycles" themselves may shift in weight and importance according to the economic structures of the country concerned.

A regards the behavior of group prices, great emphasis both statistical and theoretical has been placed upon the precession of prices of capital and durable consumers' goods over those consumers' goods, as an explanation of the turning points in the cycle. Some historic-empirical evidence is available which, however, is far from conclusive.

Kuznetz's study on *Secular Movements of Production and Prices* seems to lend supports to the contention that, at least in the major cycles, prices of equipment goods lead over those of consumers' goods. Schumpeter finds also that the producers' goods price composite for the United States (during the period 1840–1913) "shows greater amplitude and also some precession" as compared to the price composite of consumers' goods. He disavows, however, any theoretical significance in this finding.[12]

It has also been advanced by some authors that prices of raw materials lead in the early stages of the boom and taper off more quickly in recession. Others hold, however, that there is an inverse relationship between industrial recovery and the level of agricultural prices, industrial recovery being generally preceded by periods of low agricultural prices, and vice-versa.

No clear pattern of procession or timing of changes in group prices was detected by Dr. Tintner in his study on *Prices in the Trade Cycle*, in which international comparisons of the behavior of German, Britain and American prices are made. He finds that in general the prices of goods produced chiefly with labor

---

[11] For discussion and criticism of business indexes and forecasting techniques *cf.* Mitchell, *op. cit.*, chapter III, IV. Also Wageman, *Economic Rhythm*.

[12] *Cf.* Schumpeter, *op. cit.*, vol. II, p. 480.

(agrarian products, minerals) show a slight lead over goods produced chiefly with capital. This lead is clear in the case of foodstuffs (except cattle and meat), while machines, chemicals and textiles lag noticeably. International differences are apparent: Consumable producers' goods and raw materials lag in the United States (pre-war cycles) and move in Europe ahead of the general cyclical movement. Other products behave differently in boom and slump. The majority of foodstuffs participate earlier in the slump than in the boom, while metal products and textiles, as well as interest rates, participate relatively late in boom and depression, but earlier in the boom than in depression. All of these conclusion are, however, purely tentative and must be accepted with caution.[13]

The problem of precession of prices remains beclouded by a great deal of uncertainly, in spite of its importance for cycle forecasting and for cycle control policies. In the present status of investigations all that can be advanced, to quote Professor Clark, is that:

> No one factor behaves with sufficient regularity in relation to the general business cycle to serve as an infallible index of prediction. And no group of factors can be used with absolutely reliable results.[14]

---

[13] This upward flexibility and downward stickiness of interest rates would, in Dr. Tintner's view, lend some measure of support to the monetary theories of the cycle. *Cf. op. cit.*, pp. 63-7.

[14] J.M. Clark, *Strategic Factors in the Business Cycle* (New York, N.B.E.R., 1934), p. 161

# SUMMARY

The existence of a high degree of international co-variation in wholesale prices seems supported by considerable historical evidence especially as regards the long or Kondratieff wave. The heavy weight of internationally traded goods in wholesale prices indexes renders, however, this result somewhat tautological and in any event more symptomatic than of causal value. Recent experience confirms the view that the solidarity of price movements is greater in recession than in recovery. The analysis of the behavior of group prices on an international scale reveals that raw material prices fluctuate more widely than industrial prices, while at the same time the prices of durable (producers' and consumers') goods show greater cyclical sensitiveness than prices of non-durable goods. The question of lends and lags of group prices is object of conflicting interpretations, and the empirical base available insufficient for theoretical inferences.

# CHAPTER II

## OUTPUT AND EMPLOYMENT

The lack of a single parameter such as the price-level for the mensuration of total output or employment renders international comparisons extremely difficult. For the analysis of cyclical variations resort has been made to empirical evidence on representative products or groups of products of key importance in economic activity. Indexes of pig iron production and consumption, for instance, constitute a classical criterium for international comparisons and form the backbone of Spiethoff's scheme. Reconstructed indexes of industrial activity (on the base of heterogeneous series in production, consumption and transportation) have recently been used by Schumpeter for comparison of cyclical fluctuations in output in United States, Great Britain and Germany. On agricultural and mineral production, representative individual series (wheat, goal, etc.) are available for fairly long periods.[15] Statistic on unemployment are available in reliable form only since the First World War, except in the case of Great Britain, where wide use has been made of Trade Union records for earlier periods.

In any event, whatever statistical material is available, it clearly indicates a substantial international consilience in the direction of employment and output changes in the business cycle. Prosperity is generally characterized by rising output and employment, the reverse occurs in depression, although this association is not invariant or univocal. In exceptional cases depression is compatible with expanding output (e.g. the regressive supply curve in agriculture or the case of heavy technological displacement in industry), while prosperity is not incompatible with "vicarious" or "disturbance" unemployment. Moreover, there is no simple relation between total employment and total output since, due to technological progress, human labor is continuously becoming a less efficient factor of production.

Important international cyclical differences in employment-output behavior exist, however, for several branches of production. These differences are of course reflected in the general cyclical behavior of countries heavily concentrated in those productive activities.

According to output-employment behavior we may broadly distinguish the following spheres of production.

---

[15] *Cf.* Schumpeter, *op. cit.*, vol. II, p. 493. For Great Britain we have now available Beveridge's new index of industrial activity, which goes as far back as 1786 (*Cf. Full Employment in a Free Society*, pp. 277-289). For agricultural and mining series cf. Kuznetz, *op. cit.*

## A. The Sphere of Raw Materials of Agricultural Origin

This sphere comprises semi-capitalist countries (India, Malaya) with high population density and low income per capital, and neo-capitalist countries (Australia, Argentina) with relatively high income level and active foreign trade. In the semi-capitalist countries, depression is generally semi-chronic; their cyclical reactions are comparatively weak; the impact of world crises is manifested in an aggravation of the burden of indebtedness of the farming population producing for export, and in an increase of disguised unemployment or surplus labor in farm areas. Neo-capitalist countries, on the other hand, are usually very sensitive to fluctuations in foreign trade. Depression is imposed on them by a decline in price of their export products due to shrinkage of industrial demand, while the volume of their output is relatively insensitive to the cycle. In both cases, price instability and inflation, rather than unemployment, are the central problems of the business cycle. Due to the inelasticity of the productive structure, income variations are roughly proportional to price changes.

## B. The Sphere of Raw Materials of Non-Agricultural Origin

For countries engaged predominantly in mineral production (Venezuela, Bolivia) the business cycle imposes adjustments both in output and in prices. A fall in foreign their products entails a reduction in prices and a contraction in output, so that the impact of the world depression on their income level is more than proportional to the deterioration of their terms of trade.

## C. The Industrial Sphere

Within the industrial sphere proper, there is a substantial difference in behavior between durable (producers' and consumers') goods on one side, and non-durable goods on the other, the type of cyclical reaction of individual countries being determined by the relative predominance of one or the other branch of production.[16]

The wider amplitude of fluctuations in the output of durable goods is an accepted generalization on both theoretical and statistical grounds. Thus, industrial cycles have often been described as cycles in the production of fixed capital. A graphic comparison of the wider swings of output and employment in producers' goods industries in five countries (United States, United Kingdom, Germany,

---

[16] As noted by Sir William Beveridge, the peculiarities of cyclical behavior are determined more by the durability of the goods than by their place in the productive process. Durable consumers' goods are subject to the same magnified fluctuations in demand as fixed capital, while non-durable producers' and consumers' goods show approximately the same cyclical reaction.

Sweden and Australia) can be found in Professor Haberler's treatise on *Prosperity and Depression* (pp. 280-281).

The observation of this phenomenon gave rise to a prolonged controversy on the principle of acceleration (Aftalion, Bickerdike, Clark), later rechristened as "The Relation" by Harrod.[17] Although today, after the studies of Kuznetz and Tinberghen, much less reliance in placed on the principle of acceleration as an explanation of the turning points (its applicability being qualified to take into account the existence of excess capacity, variations in the serviceability of investment goods or in expectation of entrepreneurs, etc.), the principle of acceleration remains a powerful tool the analysis and description of the inherent instability of capitalist modes of production.

The experience of the last depression confirmed theoretical expectation regarding the greater instability and cyclical sensitiveness of producers' goods as compared to industries of consumers' goods.[18] The former showed much ampler fluctuations in employment and output; the behavior of prices, however, differed somewhat from the expected norm, as pointed out in the preceding section.

If we take industrial production as whole, it contrasts with raw material production in that the burden of adjustment in the business cycle is divided between output, employment and prices, while in the raw material sphere price deflation assumes larger proportions than output contraction. We may thus say that the typical capitalist crisis is primarily an employment output phenomenon while the business cycles of the peripheral areas of capitalism are predominantly a price phenomenon.[19]

---

[17] In its original formulation the principle of acceleration postulated merely an aggrandizing or magnifying effect of changes in the demand for consumption goods over the demand for producers' goods. The theory was later refined by Professor Clark to take into account the influence of changes in the rate of demand. Ragner Frisch gave the principle its final formulation by distinguishing between the replacement-demand for durable goods (which depends on variations in the size of consumer-taking) and the expansion-demand (which depends on the rate of changes of consumer-taking).

[18] Wageman notes that during depression periods in semi-and non- capitalist areas local manufacturing production also falls less than that of industrial areas; the reason lies in the fact that those industries are ordinarily in the phase of development and expansion and thus enjoy greater resistance; in addition to that they mostly consumers' goods whose behavior in the cycle is stable than of producers' goods. *Cf. Struktur and Rhythmus der Weltwirtschaft*, p. 62.

[19] In agrarian societies periodical labor surpluses are concealed under the form of disguised unemployment, i.e., excess supply of labor on farms. The problem is, however, less dramatic and conspicuous than the problem of cyclical unemployment or technological displacement in industrial countries. It may be noted that there is a growing tendency to blur the traditional distinction between cyclical and technological unemployment. In Schumpeter's scheme, for instance, displacements of labor through shifts in technology are the very essence of the cyclical process.

# SUMMARY

International fluctuations in output and employment during the business cycle be considered as <u>regular variations</u> since they show a wide measure of agreement as to the direction of the movement. Substantial differences in the amplitude of the changes and in the magnitudes affected exist between predominantly industrial countries, on one side, and predominantly industrial countries on the other. Price instability and inflation rather than unemployment or over-saving are the main cyclical problems of non-industrial countries, whose fluctuations are usually of an induced or secondary nature. Within the industrial sphere, the elasticity of the productive structure, and its responsiveness to changes in the monetary stream, result in wide cyclical swings of output and employment, while at the same time, for technical and institutional reasons, industrial prices show a greater degree of stability than prices of primary products.

# SECTION II
# IRREGULAR CYCLICAL VARIATIONS

Despite divergence in amplitude and timing, which are determined by the peculiar reactions of structural systems, we have seen that fluctuations in prices, employment and output follow closely the ebbs and flows of international cyclical movements.

The behavior of other important economic magnitude is far less predictable. They may move in different directions in the course of the cycle, and they may show an entirely different trend from cycle to cycle. We shall subsequently analysis the behavior of exports and imports (balance of trade), capital movements, gold movements, exchange rates, and the balance of payments as a whole.

# CHAPTER I

# THE BALANCE OF TRADE

We are not here concerned with fluctuations in the aggregate value or volume of world trade. To the extent that they are concomitant to price and output fluctuations they show, as examined above, a clear cyclical pattern. Owing to the predominance of raw materials in total world trade and their particular characteristics of behavior, fluctuations in the value of world trade during prosperity and depression have usually a much wider amplitude than fluctuations in volume.

To get an insight into mechanism of cycle propagation, it is not the "aggregative movement" of trade but the relative behavior of exports and imports that is relevant. Throughout the study, special attention will be paid to the influence of structural and functional relationships.

## A. Direction of Fluctuations

If we start with the convenient and restrictive assumption of a cycle confined to a single country, or if there is considerable lead over the international cycle, the developments are fairly easy to trace. In prosperity, the balance of trade will tend to become unfavorable or less favorable. Prices and income will rise. Imports will be encouraged. Exports are more likely to decrease or remain stationary since as the boom progresses, a larger share of productive factors will be shifted to industries the home market. Export industries will suffer to the benefit of domestic industry. In depression the opposite occurs.[20] According to Aftalion, this was generally the course of events in France and Germany in the local cycles of 1927 and 1928. The French recession of 1927, following the stabilization of the franc, was accompanied by an improvement is the balance of trade, while the recovery of 1938 was followed by an adverse balance. Germany, on the other hand, had a prosperous year in 1927, with a surplus of imports, while the recession in 1929 and the depression in 1930 were followed by an improvement in the balance of trade.[21]

---

[20] *Cf.* Wagemann, *Economic Rhythm*, p. 297, who makes the following generalization concerning the behavior of the German balance of trade: "As far Germany is concerned, an increasingly unfavorable balance of trade has for the decades past been an indication of a cyclical trade revival, while an increasingly favorable balance has spelled crises and depression."

[21] *Cf.* Aftalion, "Les Variations Cyclique Irrégulières dans les Relations Internationales", in *Révue d'Economie Politique* ( vol. XLVII, 1933), pp. 273-91.

This pattern of cyclical reactions, as described by Aftalion, is primarily applicable to industrial countries whose imports are closely tied up with the level of domestic activity and which enjoy greater elasticity of substitution of factors of production as between home and export industries. Raw material countries, on the other hand, are usually heavily dependent on exports for which there is no alternative domestic use. The shiftability of factors is also smaller. Thus, the movements of balance of trade in the earlier phase of recovery and depression are likely to be precisely the reverse of that of industrial countries.[22] Prosperity is likely to be initiated by an improvement of the balance of trade due to both better terms of trade and greater volume of exports. Imports will follow suit after a time lag and in view of the usually high income elasticity of demand for imports in raw material countries the balance of trade will worsen in the latter phase of the upswing. The downswing of the cycle will usually be attended by a deterioration of the terms, contraction of volume of trade and accumulation of unsold stocks due to inelasticity of output. Whether the contraction will be felt mostly in the value or in the volume will depend on the nature of the exports. Industrial raw materials are more likely to decline both in value and volume, while in the case of food products of inelastic supply and demand, prices will bear the burden of adjustment. Imports are likely to be severely curtailed in an effort to maintain an export surplus to meet fixed charges in the balance of payments. Such a process of adjustment is the more severe because the deterioration of terms of trade will cause imports to fall more in volume than in value.

This comfortable symmetry of movement—deterioration of the trade balance in prosperity and improvement in depression for industrial countries and the reverse for raw material countries—is, however, grossly over-simplified.

Once we introduce more realistic assumption, the cyclical pattern is blurred and the regularity of fluctuations disappears, owing to the complications introduced by the following factors:

1. International interdependence of cyclical movements.
2. Capital exports.
3. Different composition of exports and imports.
4. Different marginal propensities to imports.
5. Anti-cyclical governmental policies.

---

[22] Compare Wagemann: "Wir esehen dann, dass Nei Industrieländern die Handelsbilanz in derPerioden der Hochkonjunktur passiver wird, in denender Tiefkonjunktur aktiver. Umgekehrtist es bei den Agrar-und Rohstoffländern, deren Handelsbilanz am aktivsten bei der Hochkonjunktur und am passivsten bei der Tiefkonjunktur ist". *Struktur und Rhythmus der Weltwirtschaft*, p. 178.

1. If we drop the assumption of a local or a national cycle, the behavior of the balance of trade will be affected by the relative intensity and processions of the cyclical phases in trading countries. Countries in which the recovery starts earlier, which enjoy a higher degree of prosperity, or suffer from relatively milder depressions, will incur a deficit or decrease their surplus in merchandise movements, owing to the combined effect of a higher level of prices and costs (which tends to decrease exports) and a higher income level (which tends to increase imports). Theoretically, the movements of the balance of trade would in this assumption an equilibrating influence by hindering the boom (through import leakages) and attenuating the depression (through induced exports).

2. The introduction of capital movements further complicates the picture; if the revival in a capital-exporting country, which has an elastic supply of loanable funds goes parallel with an export of capital,[23] its balance of trade may continue to improve with the upswing of the cycle.[24] This, of course, provided that there is a fringe of unemployed resources so that the increased level of internal activity will not necessitate diversion of resources from export to home industries. The effects on the balance of trade may then be indeterminate. At a later phase of the boom, the tightening of the capital market is likely to curtail capital exports, while at the same time, as the supply of domestic factors becomes inelastic, imports are likely to increase and exports to decrease. The balance of trade will then tend to become unfavorable.

3. The composition of exports and imports is also relevant for the determination of the cyclical behavior of the balance, is view of the different elasticities of supply and demand. Thus, the exports of a country trading in finished manufactures and durable consumers' goods—the demand for which is elastic—are likely

---

[23] The variable patterns of capital movements during prosperity and depression will be discussed later. We are not concerned here with the question of whether capital movements play an active or passive role in the process of adjustment. The classical theory generally attributed the causal function to capital movements, the balance of trade being the adjustable item. Keynes and most of the moderns claim, on the other hand, that trade is the insensitive and capital movement the sensitive factor in the mechanism of adjustment. *Cf.* Iversen, *op. cit.*, pp. 67-73. Also Machlup *op. cit.*, p. 136. Our problem here is merely to determine to what extent capital movements may affect the cyclical behavior of the balance of trade.

[24] This seems to have been the usual cyclical behavior of the British balance of trade throughout most of the 19th century. Capital exports during the expansion phase of the cycle permitted heavy expansion of exports and narrowing down of the usually unfavorable balance. The reverse occurred in the downswing. *Cf.* A. Kahn, *Great Britain in the World Economy* (Columbia University Press, 1946), pp. 127-30.

to suffer violent cyclical fluctuations because of the large amplitude of fluctuations in international demand for durable goods in the several phases of the cycle. The balance of trade will be particularly affected upward and downward if the country at the same time takes the bulk of imports in products of inelastic demand, such as foodstuffs.

Trading in non-durable consumption goods is more likely to be stable. Imports of raw materials fluctuate much more than those of basic foodstuffs, but there again it must be noted that fluctuations in the physical volume of exports and imports will show an entirely cyclical pattern from fluctuations in prices, according to whether the adaptation to changed demand schedules is made mainly through changes in prices or in output. A striking example of this is found in the experience of United States during the last depression. Exports of food and raw materials fall by only five per cent in quantity from 1929 to 1931, while the volume of exports of finished manufactures fell by 75 per cent. The behavior of prices was, however, decidedly the reverse. For the world trade as a whole, the quantum of between 1929 and 1933 fell by 40 per cent in manufactures, 18 per cent in foodstuffs, and 13 per cent in raw materials. The sterling prices of manufactures, however, fell by only 18 per cent, while that of foodstuffs dropped 33 per cent, and that of raw materials 41 per cent. We must recall, moreover, that exports and imports show different degrees of sensitiveness to internal fluctuations.

Summarizing the results of a study of fluctuations of the German balance of trade, made by the German Institute for Business Cycle Research, Wageman distinguishes two groups of export industries: (a) exports largely independent from international trade fluctuations (products of inelastic demand such as basic foodstuffs and textiles), and (b) exports that show a close relationship either positive or negative to the trade cycles:

    i. Positive relationship – engineering industry (the level of exports is positively correlated with the domestic cycle).
    ii. Negative relationship – bar iron, wood pulp (depression will favor exports by diminishing internal consumption).

4. Some of the above processes can be conveniently described through the use of the concept of the marginal propensity to import, highly popular in the foreign trade multiplier analysis. The marginal propensity of imports expresses as noted before, the proportion of increment of income that will be spent on im-

ports.²⁵ F.W. Paish distinguishes two broad types of countries; those with low marginal propensity to import, and those with high marginal propensity to import. The former can be broadly identified as industrial and creditor countries, and the latter as raw material or debtor countries.

The process of adjustment of the balance of trade to fluctuations in the balance of payments will in each case show a different pattern which, of course, will affect the general cyclical behavior. The high MPI countries import chiefly durable producers' goods and finished consumers' goods "for which the demand changes more than in proportion to changes in expenditures". Thus, a cyclical fall in income and expenditures would be reflected in a sharp decline in imports and may also entail a diversion of demand from expensive foreign goods to cheaper and rougher types of domestic goods.

The low MPI countries, on the other hand, buy mostly basic foodstuffs and raw materials "perhaps together with the cheaper types of finished goods". In this case "the first impact of reduced expenditures is felt mainly upon the demand for local products, while the demand for certain cheap import goods, other than raw materials, may even increase."²⁶

While the cyclical pattern in depression in fairly definite for the first group of countries, namely, adjustment through contraction in imports, the situation is much less definite for creditor countries with a low marginal propensity to import. Expansion of exports may take place in the countries with high marginal propensity to import, whose incomes have been swollen. If, however, the process of adjustment is not sufficiently rapid restriction of bank credit will usually ensue, with a fall in prices and income and eventual stimulation of export. Foreign lending may also be curtailed, if there is a drain on bank reserves.

The extent and speed of the adjustment of balance of trade to fluctuations in the balance of payments will also depend on the number of intermediate income and price changes necessary to bring about a decrease in imports or an increase in exports. Let us consider, for instance, the repercussions of fall in exports off an imaginary country. If the proceeds from exports are normally used to buy imports, the latter would fall quickly, the equilibrium of balance of payments being restored in fairly short order. If, however, exporters employ their receipts to buy local goods

---

[25] The concept has so been used by Colin Clark, Schumpeter, Salant and others. Strictly speaking, as noted by Shang-Kwei-Fong, it should refer only to "increment in the imports of consumer goods in relation to increments in income earned in the last period". The marginal propensity to import would thus be the marginal propensity to consume foreign goods. Its quite legitimate, however, for the income-investment analysis to consider imports both of consumption and of investment goods as leakages from total investment, just as one speaks of leakages through the marginal propensity to save.

[26] *Cf.* F.W. Paish, "Banking Policy and the Balance of International Payments", in *Economica* (vol. III, Nov. 1936).

and services, the adjustment process will be longer. Local incomes will fall in the first place and only subsequently will imports decline. The whole chain of reactions depends also on anticipations, different patterns of behavior occurring according to whether the fall in exports is expected to be temporary or prolonged.

5. The typical behavior of the balance of trade is also distorted by the impact of governmental policies aimed at avoiding import leakages or maximizing the trade surplus. Some trade restrictions, such as import quotas, render imports completely irresponsive to income changes, while others, such as tariffs, merely modify the marginal propensity to import.

## B. Amplitude of Fluctuations

Speaking in absolute terms, one should expect imports to show a closer correlation to the swing of domestic cycles than exports, since the former are a fairly constant function of national income while the latter depend on the international cycle. This is particularly true for industrial countries whose imports consist of raw materials, the demand for which fluctuates closely according to the level of home activity.[27]

This conclusion is borne out in Soltan's studies of foreign trade fluctuations in Germany, France and England from 1881 to 1913. The cyclical fluctuations of imports were found to much greater than those of exports.

In raw material countries the picture may be somewhat different, since their cycle are much likely to be autonomous and are frequently more repercussions of foreign cycles. While in industrial and creditor countries exports are an important but seldom a predominant component of cyclical behavior, in agricultural and raw material countries (barring the autonomous effects of changes in crop yields) exports are the umbilical cord through which international booms and depressions are transmitted. The correlation of exports to domestic cyclical is thus not merely a <u>close</u> one but it has also a <u>causal</u> significance.

Thus, the degree of dependence on foreign trade and the composition of exports are the main determinants of the cyclical sensitiveness in the exports trade. It has been remarked, for instance, that while the correlation of imports to the level

---

[27] This smaller amplitude of fluctuations in exports is not in contradiction to the fact already pointed out that the demand for manufactured products (exports of industrial countries) is subject to wider fluctuations than that for raw materials and food products. In fact, this instability of demand is to a large extent counteracted by the fact that the exports of manufactures are usually much more evenly spread among groups of countries (with divergent demand movements) than imports., which are usually purchased in a few raw material countries. *Cf.* League of Nations, *The Network of World Trade*.

of national income is quite high for both Great Britain and the United States, fluctuations in British exports, on the whole, are much more closely related to the national income than in the American case.[28] This different behavior has been thus expounded by Mitchell and Burns in an article on "The National Bureau's Measures of Cyclical Behavior's":

> While the exports of the United Kingdom have conformed closely to British business cycles and the imports of the United States to American business cycles, the exports of the United States show only faint traces of conformity to American business cycle. The cyclical variations in American imports have reflected the power of the country to purchase foreign goods and have therefore conformed with considerably regularity to the cyclical alternations in general business. On the other hand, exports have been governed mainly by business conditions in America's foreign market, which in considerable measure have been independent of business conditions in this country. In Great Britain, exports form a much larger proportion of domestic production than in United States; they are also dominated by finished manufacture rather than by raw materials or semi-manufactures; hence the state of British exports, is a sensitive barometer of domestic business conditions.[28]

## C. Timing of Fluctuations

No generalization can be advanced on a priori grounds regarding the precession of exports or imports in the cyclical turning point. If the domestic cycle leads over the international cycle, one would expect a procession of imports both in the upswing and in the downswing. The reverse would occur if the domestic cycle is induced rather than autonomous. Empirical substantiation is however lacking.

The experience of the United States is inconclusive. Imports preceded both in downswing and upswing of the depressions of 1920 and 1922, which were relatively more severs in foreign countries. In the great depression, there was an almost synchronous downward movement of exports and imports, with a slight procession of export. In 1937, imports again preceded exports in the depression, but lagged behind in the recovery.

For Great Britain, Sir William Beveridge claims to have established a defi-

---

[28] *Cf.* Mitchell and Burns, "The National Bureau's Measures of Cyclical Behavior" (Bulletin No. 57, 1935), pp. 13-4.

nite law of precession of exports both in depressions and in recovery. From 1795 to 1849, the precession of exports is evidenced by comparison between export statistic and the index of industrial activity, while from 1870 to 1938 a more accurate picture can be drawn on the basic of unemployment fluctuations in export industries. In both cases, the statistics "tell the one and the same story about cyclical fluctuations in Britain, that exports lead into depression and out of it. "

The lead of exports in time is prevalent even for industries with dissimilar cyclical reactions, such as textiles and instrumental industries. Another factor mentioned by Beveridge is the apparent seasonality in the turning point of the cycles, which would suggest a connection of the cycle with the fluctuations in the purchasing power of primary producers that form the bulk of customers of British manufactures.[29]

---

[29] *Cf.* Sir William Beveridge, *Full Employment in a Free Society* (New York: W.W. Norton & Co., 1945), pp. 303-05: "It is difficult to avoid the conclusion that an important and hitherto almost wholly neglected element in the causation of the trade cycle is the relation between primary producers and the industrial users of their products, that a fundamental cause of the trouble has been the conditions under which the primary production has been carried on, making its volume singularly irresponsible to changes in price, and therefore unmanageable in an unplanned market economy.

# SUMMARY

The analysis of fluctuations in the balance of trade reveals the existence of a cyclical but irregular pattern. Amelioration of the balance of trade in depression and deterioration in prosperity as regards industrial countries (and the reverse movement as regards raw material countries) is a frequent pattern of behavior that occurs almost regularly when the cycle is purely national or when it leads over the world cycle. Once complicating factors, such as the interaction of cyclical movements, capital exports, changes in composition of foreign trade, governmental policies, et., are taken into account, the symmetry of the movements is blurred and the cyclical fluctuations of the balance of trade show irregularity both as to timing and to direction.

With regard to the amplitude of fluctuations, it is generally observed that imports show greater sensitivity to domestic cycles than exports. The latter, however, are closely related to the domestic cycles of raw material countries, showing at the same time a close correlation to the business cycle of those industrial countries which are heavily dependent on foreign trade. No definite conclusions can be drawn as to leads or lags of exports and imports in the cycle. The American experience is inconclusive in this respect while for Great Britain a definite procession and seasonality in the turning point of exports has been empirically established.

# CHAPTER II

# THE CYCLICAL PATTERN OF CAPITAL MOVEMENTS

It has long been observed that capital movements tend to fluctuate in the same direction as business conditions. Prosperity is frequently associated with an outburst of investment in foreign countries and depression with debt collection and shrinkage of lending. It is also said that the mobility of capital tends to increase in prosperity (expansionist psychology) and decrease in depression, when elements of friction grow in importance. Capital movements have thus justly been considered one of the main carriers of the seeds of prosperity and of the germs of depressions. In a classical and vivid passage, Taussig thus describes the British experience;

> The fluctuations (of capital movements) are closely associated with the alterations and repressions of industrial activity. During the recurrent upward stage of buoyancy and speculation, large loans are made; after each crisis there is a sharp reduction, perhaps complete cessation. Each of the successive cycles in British economic history during the last hundred years has been characterized by a great wave of foreign investment followed by recession and quiescence.[30]

But the derivations from this cyclical pattern are again almost as important as the conformities. Neither on theoretical nor on empirical grounds can any definite regularity be established. The little that can be said is that capital movements react to differences in interest rates and general profitability prospects, which in turn are related to the supply and demand of funds, and to prevailing and expected market conditions.

Although there is clearly a cyclical fluctuation in the demand and supply of funds, no invariant relationship can be predicted between capital movements and the business cycle of an individual country. The cyclical pattern will depend on the importance of the capital market involved, procession or lag in relation to the international cycle, demand and supply of funds in inter-related capital markets, etc. For, the psychology of the foreign investor, who has to face the extra complications of institutional elements of friction (risk and supervision), is no more re-

---

[30] T.W. Taussig, *International Trade* (New York, 1927), p. 238.

sponsive to differential inter-country interest rates than the domestic investor is to changes in domestic rates of interest.[31]

The economic conspectus and the phase of the cycle in the borrowing country is, of course, of primary importance,[32] although it should be noted that capital movements may play by themselves an active role in initiating upward or downward fluctuations in debtor countries. A typical cycle of capital movements can thus be described, starting from a cyclical trough in a lending country. During the depression the liquidity of the capital market increase as a result of liquidation, debt payment, and slackening of investment activity. As the supply of loanable funds becomes more elastic, the domestic rate of interest falls relative to that of borrowing countries (which during the downswing are rendered increasingly illiquid and suffer heavy drains of funds to meet fixed charges in the balance of payments, until the differential margin is sufficient to effect what Ragnar Nurske calls the "elements of friction". Foreign lending becomes again profitable. The process will go on cumulatively during the upswing, the domestic recovery of creditor countries being further stimulated by favorable foreign repercussions, as capital exports strengthen the demand and purchasing power of borrowing countries. In modern terminology, we could say that the initial autonomous investment (from the viewpoint of the lending country) will, in subsequent periods, give rise to for-

---

[31] The responsiveness of international capital movements to interest rate fluctuations should not be exaggerated. Wide difference of interest rates may persist between money markets without calling forth say equalizing movement of capital. Long-term capital movements are notoriously more affected than short term. The response of capital is governed not only by differential rates and marginal efficiencies but also by institutional elements of friction and psychological barriers. Political considerations may also affect the direction and size of capital flows, quite independently from interest rates, as evidenced by the French experience. In the late 30-ies the flight of capital to the United States, where rates of interest were at low levels, rendered the interest-rate-differentials theory obviously inadequate as a full-fledged theory of causation of capital movements.

[32] *Cf.* Aftalion, *loc. cit.*, "Le facteur determinat semble donc être la situation plus ou moins prospère du pays emprunteur ou la conjuncture favorable attire les capitaux par láppât dúne forte rémunération et ou la conjuncture dafavorable decourage au contraire ce même mouvement par la moindre réemunération du capital".

eign induced investment (stimulation of export industries). The drain on loanable funds will be attenuated by increased savings out of higher income levels.[33]

If the revival in the lending countries proceeds more slowly than in the borrowing countries, or in related capital markets, the process can continue for a prolonged period, without encroachment upon the rate of domestic expansion. If, however, the recovery is more rapid at home, the domestic demand for loanable funds (and the rate of interest) will go up quicker than in other money markets, causing contraction of foreign lending, and even, during the boom, net capital imports. The downswing unchains a wave of liquidations, and the depression is transmitted to borrowing countries, whose balance of payments is subject to the double pressure of worsening terms of trade and fixed interest-amortization payments. The contraction of capital exports seems to precede the depression, the tightening of the capital market being likely to begin at an early phase of the boom.

The few attempts made determine empirically the relationship between capital movements and the business cycle yielded inconclusive, if not directly contradictory results. The most careful investigation was conducted by Harry White in his study of the *French International Accounts from 1880 to 1913*. On the whole, he could not find any degree of correlation significant enough to establish a regular cyclical patterns; from 1882 to 1885 depression coincided with low capital exports; from 1886 to 1889 revival marched pari-passu with rising capital exports; from 1903 to 1906 prosperity and capital exports followed also a parallel course, while no correlation was found the remaining years.

Contrasting this apparent lack of sensitivity of French capital movements to the business cycle with closer relationship noticeable in the United States and Great Britain. White suggests that an explanation might be found in the relative sluggishness of the French pre-war industrial life:

> In a country such as the United States or England where there is a highly sensitive industrial life, we should expect capital exports to decline during periods of prosperity; whereas in a country such as

---

[33] The assumption that capital exports will be reflected in increased demand for the exports of the lending country is a prerequisite for the realization of the real transfer contemplated in the traditional two-way market analysis. That in the real conditions of multilateral transfer, the link between capital exports and commodity trade is by no means a direct or necessary one, is abundantly evidenced by the modern discussion of the problem. If the proceeds of the loan are not spent in the lending country but in third countries, the beneficial repercussions above suggested may be only slow and indirect. These repercussions will be larger the higher is the marginal propensity to import of the borrowing country. Even with a low marginal propensity to import, the favorable repercussion may still be strong if the propensity to invest is higher in the receiving countries. Incomes will rise by more than the transfer and this will eventually raise the average and possibly the marginal propensity to import.

pre-war France, with her rather sluggish industrial life, we should expect the country to be true.

His conclusion seems to be that capital movements are governed by the relative intensity of prosperity and depression in creditor and debtor countries.

The inverse correlation suggested by White between business cycles and capital exports in the United States and Great Britain seems to hold truer the United States (at least in the period 1920–1930) than for Great Britain, if we are to believe the results of a study by Professor Beach,[34] who concludes as follows:

> The timing of the movements (in England) is not parallel in all cases, but there is a high positive correlation between the conditions of business and the volume of capital exports. Capital exports declined during the period from 1881 to 1883, although business conditions were improving, and there was very little expansion in foreign loans in the years from 1895 to 1900. In the other phases of business prosperity; 1886–1890, 1904–1907, and 1909–1911, exports of capital increased greatly. In the period of declining business from 1890–1895, 1900–1904, and 1907–1908, capital exports fall off.

For the United States, the correlation, if any, seems to be negative for the decade 1920–1930. The years of 1923, 1926 and 1929 were years of prosperity with low capital exports, while 1924, 1927 and 1930 were relatively depressed years and coincided with high capital exports. The slackening of capital outflows in 1928–1929 is directly traceable to the speculative boom in the stock market.

The explanation of this inverse correlation seems to lie in the fact in the expansion phase of the short business cycle of the twenties, the long-term rates of interest rose faster than in foreign countries, as the prosperity was felt more intensely in the United States than in England and in most agricultural states which remained relatively depressed. The recession years were accompanied by falling interest rates which encouraged flotation of foreign issues. This interpretation is the one formulated in the excellent study *The United States in World Economy*, published by the Department of Commerce:

> The apparent relationships (between capital exports and the business cycle) was of an inverse character; foreign issues tended to increase in times of domestic business recession and to fall or to increase less rapidly under more prosperous conditions in this coun-

---

[34] Beach, *British International Gold Movements and Banking Policy 1881–1913* (Harvard University Press, 1935), pp. 178-79

try. The explanation seems to lie in the behavior of long term interest rates which generally tend to harden in the expansion phase of the business cycle and to decline in times of business contraction, and thus to discourage or encourage respectively borrowing by foreign countries. Such behavior was particularly true on the occasions mentioned, in view of the fast that rising interest rates in the United States were not accompanied by equivalent increase in foreign countries, with the result that the comparative advantage of borrowing in the American market was decreased. By contrast, domestic bond issues are not influenced to a similar extent by rising long-term interest rates, because such increases are usually accompanied by an accentuated internal demand for capital, resulting from prosperous business conditions that tends to effect its depressive influences of higher interest rates.[35]

For the decade of the thirties the analysis is particularly difficult because of the disturbing behavior of short-term capital movements. In the first half of 1930 there was a sharp upturn of long term lending followed by a slump. The depression years of 1931, 1932 and 1933 were attended by low capital exports, while the revival brought about a slow upsurge of foreign lending. The latter was, however, more than neutralized by the simultaneous influx of repatriated capital and of "hot money", so that from 1934 onwards the United States become a net capital importer. Far from playing their supposedly equilibrating role, short-term capital movements (less conspicuously during the twenties but with explosive force in the late thirties) became one of the major disequilibrating factors in international transactions. Here again the analysis is anything but conclusive owing to the interference of external factors such as the dollar devaluation and the flight of capital from Europe, which both of a non-cyclical character.

A bold attempt to study the cycle of capital movements from the viewpoint of a borrowing country has boom made by Gordon Wood.[36] Wood claims that the Australian experience indicated that domestic business cycles were induced cycles, the dominant factor being the varying rate of capital imports. The indigenous fluctuations would then be, by-and-large, borrowing cycles. His contention finds its best illustration in the boom of 1893, which seems to be directly provoked by an exceptionally heavy capital inflow. It does not seem possible, however, to establish any such simple causal connection. It is true that the fluctuations in capital inflow are one of the main elements in the transmission of cycles to debtor coun-

---

[35] *The United States in World Economy*, p. 93

[36] Gordon Wood, *Borrowing and Business in Australia*.

## Table XII
## Capital Movements and the Business Cycle

| | France | | | Great Britain | | United States | | |
|---|---|---|---|---|---|---|---|---|
| Year | Business[1] Activity | Capital Export (mil.frcs.) | | Business Activity | Capital Export mil. £ | Year | Business Activity | Capital Export mil. dol. |
| 1880 | 3  | 120  | −181 | 0  | 4   | 1920 | −3 | -     |
| 1881 | 2  | 720  | 28   | 2  | 33  | 1921 | −3 | -     |
| 1882 | 0  | 350  | 51   | 2  | 24  | 1922 | 0  | 379   |
| 1883 | −3 | 235  | −89  | 0  | 16  | 1923 | 2  | −33   |
| 1884 | −3 | 235  | 90   | −3 | 41  | 1924 | −2 | 517   |
| 1885 | −3 | 420  | 133  | −3 | 34  | 1925 | 3  | 621   |
| 1886 | −3 | 500  | 100  | −2 | 62  | 1926 | 3  | 181   |
| 1887 | 0  | 700  | −135 | 0  | 67  | 1927 | 1  | 695   |
| 1888 | 2  | 805  | −43  | 2  | 74  | 1928 | 3  | 944   |
| 1889 | 2  | 685  | 210  | 3  | 69  | 1929 | 3  | 306   |
| 1890 | 0  | 590  | −111 | 2  | 55  | 1930 | −3 | 733   |
| 1891 | −2 | 390  | 146  | −3 | 48  | 1931 | −3 | 443   |
| 1892 | −3 | 490  | 296  | −3 | 34  | 1932 | −3 | 221   |
| 1893 | −3 | 695  | 214  | −4 | 40  | 1933 | −2 | 342   |
| 1894 | −3 | 485  | 316  | −3 | 21  | 1934 | 1  | −422[2] |
| 1895 | −2 | 680  | 33   | −3 | 23  | 1935 | 2  | −1508 |
| 1896 | 0  | 865  | 78   | 0  | 39  | 1936 | 2  | −1208 |
| 1897 | 2  | 545  | 87   | 3  | 27  | 1937 | −2 | −877  |
| 1898 | 3  | 930  | −132 | 3  | 17  | 1938 | 1  | −441  |
| 1899 | 3  | 810  | 88   | 3  | 28  | 1939 | 2  | −1497 |
| 1900 | 2  | 1000 | 223  | 2  | 31  | -    | -  | -     |
| 1901 | −2 | 1280 | 213  | −2 | 14  | -    | -  | -     |
| 1902 | −3 | 1080 | 269  | −1 | 11  | -    | -  | -     |
| 1903 | 0  | 1295 | 182  | −2 | 23  | -    | -  | -     |
| 1904 | 2  | 1440 | 481  | 0  | 27  | -    | -  | -     |
| 1905 | 3  | 1620 | 620  | 2  | 63  | -    | -  | -     |
| 1906 | 3  | 1790 | 216  | 3  | 104 | -    | -  | -     |
| 1907 | −2 | 1220 | 245  | 2  | 140 | -    | -  | -     |
| 1908 | −3 | 1490 | 920  | −3 | 130 | -    | -  | -     |
| 1909 | 0  | 1460 | 165  | 0  | 110 | -    | -  | -     |
| 1910 | 3  | 1830 | −30  | 3  | 151 | -    | -  | -     |
| 1911 | 3  | 1030 | 126  | 2  | 292 | -    | -  | -     |
| 1912 | 3  | 1340 | 165  | 3  | 226 | -    | -  | -     |
| 1913 | 2  | 1115 | 610  | 3  | -   | -    | -  | -     |

[1]Symbols for Business Activity are those used in the *Annals* of the National Business Economic Research.

[2]Net capital imports (Source: *U.S. in World Economy.* Table III, Appendix X).

Source: Iversen, *Aspects of the Theory of International Capital Movements.*

tries. But the fall in prices of primary products, which is one of the most widely observed phenomena attending world-wide depressions, exert as important as influence as fluctuations in capital flows.[37] In the last depression the two factors exerted a combined pressure and it is not easy to determine the allocation of responsibility.

---

[37] The point might be advanced that the typical fall in prices is in itself due to changes foreign lending. (*Cf.* Colin Clark, *op. cit.*, pp. 456-58) It cannot be doubted that capital movements certainly exerted a very heavy influence, affecting the intensity of the price deflation. There are, however, intrinsic (technical and institutional) factors which render raw material prices particularly vulnerable to violent fluctuations, so that we cannot speak of one-way causation of cycles by capital movements.

# SUMMARY

Any analysis of the behavior of capital movements is rendered extremely difficult by the peculiar responsiveness of the capital market to political considerations, which affect in an uncertain manner the cyclical behavior of economic factors. The broad conclusions seen to be that capital movements exhibit cyclical fluctuations, which however do not follow any regular or predictable pattern. Movements of capital take place when the profitability prospects resulting from interest rate differentials are sufficient to overcome the "elements of friction" which tend to localize capital. The cyclical fluctuations of the rates of interest depend on the other hand on the elasticity of the monetary market and on the relative intensity and timing of prosperity and depression in lending and borrowing markets. Although a positive correlation between prosperity and capital exports has often been historically observed, the relationship is by no means an invariant one, wide differences prevailing as between countries and between cycles. Even for the name country shifts in the direction of capital movements have been observed in the same phase of the cycle, e.g., capital outflow during the early recovery and capital inflow during the boom. While the transmission of economic fluctuations through borrowing cycles on theoretical and empirical grounds, the allocation of responsibility for cycle generation in agricultural and debtor countries has to be shared between fluctuations in international investment and instability of raw material prices in world trade.

# CHAPTER III

# GOLD MOVEMENTS

The declining role of gold in the settlement if international balances render gold movements proportionately less significant from the viewpoint of cyclical behavior. Short-term capital movements have, to a large extent, replaced gold as an international medium of payment so that credit now looms larger than gold flows in the mechanism of transfer.[38] In depression periods, however, owing to the pressure of debt liquidation and credit contraction, gold flows tend to increase in magnitude. This was particularly true of the last depression which, as noted by Professor Neisser, was characterized by a heavy absorption of gold by creditor countries.

There is no a priori reason to export a regular behavior of gold movements, any more than of the balance of trade or of capital movements, to both of which gold movements are directly related. Again, available empirical investigations do not lend themselves to any other conclusion than the establishment of an irregular cyclical pattern. In creditor countries, gold out-flows predominate in prosperity while gold imports increase in depression. In debtor countries, of course, the reverse process takes place.

Reviewing the cyclical movements of the French balance of payments, Aftalion indicates that, in his country, years of depression are frequently marked by heavy gold in-flows, which many times begin even before the down-turning points. Prosperity, on the other hand, is usually accompanied by low gold imports and net gold exports:

> Trés fréquenment, en France, les importations de métaux precieux ont été considerables pendant les années de crise et de depression, ces fortes importations commençant déjà parfois dans les tout derniers temps de prospérité. Au contraire, les importations restaient faibles pendant la grande partie des périodes de prospérité.

In support of his contention Aftalion quotes the data given in the table on the page which follows.

The explanation given by Aftalion of this rhythm of behavior runs in familiar terms. Prosperity in a creditor country is associated with an optimistic invest-

---

[38] *Cf.* Iversen, *op. cit.*, p. 513. *Cf.* also Angell, "Equilibrium in International Payments 1919–1935", in *Explorations in Economics*, economic essays in honor of W. C. Mitchell (New York, 1936) p. 23.

ment psychology, which elicits a rise in foreign lending; in depression, the domestic propensity to hoard gold increases, while credit contraction and the fear of instability leads to a retraction of foreign lending and to repatriation of gold and capital.

### Table XIII
### Gold Movements in the French Balance of Payments

| Depression[39] years | Important surplus of precious metals (million gold francs) | Yearly Averages |
|---|---|---|
| 1858–1859 | 811 | 420 |
| 1865–1869 | 2038 | 410 |
| 1874–1878 | 2988 | 747 |
| 1891–1894 | 1005 | 251 |
| 1900–1904 | 1531 | 306 |
| 1907–1908 | 1425 | 711 |
| 1913–1914 | 1293 | 646 |
| **Prosperity years** | **Important surplus** | |
| 1860–1864 | 174 | 35 |
| 1871–1872 | –50 | –25 |
| 1879–1882 | –142 | –35 |
| 1888–1890 | 76 | 25 |
| 1890–1899 | 16 | 8 |

Aftalion recognizes that besides those regular manifestations, there have been also irregular movements in the course of several historical cycles. As inspection of yearly figures rather than averages for an entire cyclical phase would, in fact, reveal still less regularity than Aftalion's figures would indicate. For instance, 1904 and 1905 were prosperity years marked by exceptionally heavy specie imports, while in the depression year of 1893 net gold exports took place; in the depression years of 1902–1903 gold imports were considerably smaller than in the upswing of 1904 and 1905.

A more cautious attitude is taken by Harry White who, in his study on the

---

[39] Marked by the crises of 1857, 1864, 1873, 1890, 1900, 1907 and 1913. *Cf.* Aftalion, *op. cit.*, pp. 280-83

*French International Accounts*, was not able to detect any appreciable degree of correlation between gold movements and general business conditions. The relationship seemed to be closer between gold flows and the balance of trade than between the former and capital exports, but in neither case it proved conclusive.

The French experience indicates that two methods were used to counteract the effects of gold out-flows on gold reverses; the discount rate and the gold premium. The discount rate mechanism, contrarily to the British experience, was very sparingly used and seemed largely insensitive to business fluctuations. This can perhaps be explained by the fact that the Banque de France maintained usually larger operating reverses than the Bank of England and controlled a much less elastic credit system.

Great Britain presents the interesting case (highly disconcerting for the classical school) of a positive correlation between gold imports and the expansion phase of the business cycle. Contrarily to what one should expect under the traditional price-specie-flow mechanism, gold tended to flow-in during periods of expansion and rising prices, and to flow out during periods of business contraction. The same was generally the case for the United States from 1896 to 1913.[40]

A possible reconciliation of this phenomenon with the traditional theory of international gold movements, as expounded by Hawtrey, has been suggested by W. Beach, through the observation that British cycles tended to be of smaller amplitude than the world cycles and her price-level less flexible, upwards, than that of "newer" countries. Under these circumstances, it is quite conceivable that, due to a slower rise of British price-level in the expansion phase, her exports would increase, the net in-flow of gold being simply the result of a favorable balance of trade. This explanation is not, however, altogether satisfactory since we must take into account the fact that the parallel increase in international lending would exert a counteracting influence and provoke an out-flow of gold. Beach himself is quite skeptical about the applicability of the classical explanation, in terms of price-level changes, and lays more emphasis on the effects of short-term capital movements. Due to the peculiar conditions of the British (and also of the early American) banking system, namely, an extremely operational reserve margin, the pressure on reserves during prosperity led quickly to a rise in the discount rate, which in turn provoked an in-flow of short-term capital usually more than sufficient to neutralize the out-flow of gold:

> The pressure upon bank reserves led to increased discount rates in the money markets, and the flow of short-term capital, induced as a

---

[40] A detailed analysis of British gold movements can be found in W. Beach, *British International Gold Movements and Banking Policy, 1881–1913* (Harvard University, 1935), p. 173.

consequence, may well have been the dominating factor determining the gold flows over cyclical periods. So long as rates remained above the world levels, the funds would remain in the two centers.[41]

Owing to its thin operational margin, the cyclical control of gold flows was always a more pressing problem for the Bank of England than for the Banque de France. To avoid dangerous expansions and contractions of credit, the discount rate technique[42]—which was supposed to have the double stabilizing effect of controlling internal business conditions and preventing abnormal gold flows—was resorted to, with varying degree of success. In general, the use of the discount-rate mechanism as an anti-cyclical device aimed at preventing gold flows from attaining dangerous proportions rather than at interfering directly with the supposedly self-regulating mechanism of the gold standard. Thus, while the size of the gold flows was kept down to a minimum level, their general cyclical feature—in-flow in prosperity and out-flow in depression—continued clearly perceptible.

The American experience regarding the behavior of gold movements is still less conclusive. On the whole, no significant degree of correlation with the business cycle can be detected. The data assembled by Professor Young and Mr. Beach indicate, for the period preceding the first World War, a behavior substantially similar to that obtaining in Great Britain. For the twenties and the thirties, no regular cyclical pattern is discernible. Gold out-flows took place in the depression years of 1920, 1930 and 1931, as well as in the prosperity years of 1925, 1927 and 1928.[43] During most of the period the United States was a net gold importer, up to the point of suffering from a "gold glut". After the devaluation of the dollar, the gold in-flow assumed unprecedented proportions, partly for the balancing of an increasingly favorable balance of trade, partly as a result of capital flight from Europe. By and large, the in-flow of gold after 1934 was determined primarily by

---

[41] *Cf.* Beach, *op. cit.*, p. 173.

[42] We do not propose to discuss here the effectiveness of the discount rate policy which, as an anti-cyclical device, has now largely yielded primacy to fiscal policies. It suffices to note that, even under pre-war gold standard conditions, its efficacy was greatly over-rated and certainly never amounted to anything such as suggested, for instance, in the Conliffe report. In many cases, the discount rate manipulations defeated themselves; a rise in the rate has often failed to control the boom by provoking capital imports and gold in-flows. Conversely, the lowering of the rate failed many times to stem the depression, owing to the lack of positive reaction on the part of domestic investment and capital movements. In general, the boom-controlling effect proved stronger than the stimulating effect in depression.

[43] The gold out-flow in 1928 is in part traceable to the drain of gold to France following the stabilization of the franc and the repatriation of French capital.

capital movements rather than by the surplus in current accounts, excepts perhaps in the latter part of 1937 and 1958, during which imports fell drastically, as a result of the business recession, while exports were maintained at approximately the same level.

The evidence of the thirties confirms again that gold movements played a disequilibrating rather than a "balancing" role.[44]

---

[44] Cf. *The United States in the World Economy*, pp. 189-90.

# SUMMARY

The "balancing" role of gold movements has gradually diminished in importance, losing ground to short-term capital movements. The empirical studies available are divergently interpreted and on the whole do not show a regular or consistent cyclical pattern of gold movements. Out-flow in prosperity and in-flow in depression appear to have been the normal experience in the French balance of payments, the reverse however occurring in Great Britain, this difference in behavior being largely traceable to the special position of the London financial market. The American experience in the period preceding the first World War followed closely the British pattern, while for the twenties and thirties gold flows show no consistent relationship to internal business conditions. The heavy gold inflow of the thirties was not "balancing", in the sense of the price-specie-flow mechanism, but exerted a major disequilibrating effect.

# CHAPTER IV

# EXCHANGE RATES

The lack of regularity in the cyclical reactions of capital movements and of the balance of trade is to a large extent reflected in the absence of a regular cyclical pattern of exchange rates fluctuations.[45]

On the basis of our observations on the usual pattern of capital movements of creditor countries—out-flow in prosperity and in-flow in depression—we should expect exchange rates of creditor countries to improve in depression and to deteriorate in prosperity, the opposite rhythm prevailing in debtor countries.[46]

Since, however, capital movements are but one of the factors affecting exchange rates, this typical pattern is far from regular. Exchange depression has been such an usual outcome of depression in debtor and raw material countries that it has been regarded as their normal reaction to the cyclical decline in export prices and in the rate of capital imports. As noted by Aftalion, their exchange stability is then impaired both by quantitative (decline in foreign investment) and by qualitative (price instability, insolvency) factors. Much less uniformity of behavior exists in the case of creditor countries. Strangely enough, the devaluation cycle of the thirties may be said to have been opened and finished by creditor countries. It began with the stabilization of the franc at an undervalued level in 1928, it gained momentum with the devaluation of the pound—another creditor currency—in 1931, and ended with the second devaluation of the franc in 1936. The initial depreciation wave spread quickly to debtor countries, whose balance of payments was under heavy pressure, forcing them to liquidate gold stocks (Brazil) or to abandon immediately the gold standard (Argentina).

In the first phase of the devaluation cycle, as noted by Seymour Harris, the devaluation of the debtor countries was, as it might be expected, larger in percentage terms than that of industrial and creditor countries. Surprisingly enough, however, by 1934, with the depreciation of the dollar, the creditors had the lead in the devaluation race.

Thus, the previously suggested pattern of behavior lacks regularity; the downswing of the cycle may bring exchange depreciation all around regardless of debtor-creditor relationships. It appears, nevertheless, that for debtor and capital importing countries the fall in exchange is an almost automatic consequence of the

---

[45] We are disregarding at this stage, the effect of exchange-controls, which are "external" factors from our viewpoint.

[46] *Cf.* Aftalion, *op. cit.*, pp. 283-85.

pressure on the balance of payments, while in the case of creditor or capital exporting countries it is often a matter of deliberate policy to attenuate internal deflation or to improve the competitive foreign trade position.

# CHAPTER V

# THE BALANCE OF PAYMENTS

The cyclical behavior of the balance of payments as a whole is also difficult to trace due to the irregularity of movements and to the different cyclical sensitiveness shown by individual items. The behavior of the balances of merchandise trade, of gold and of capital movements has already been discussed. The balance of services is of particularly difficult analysis because of the heterogeneous nature of the component elements, some of which are highly sensitive and some quite insensitive to the business cycle. Tourist and travel expenditures, for instance, fluctuate widely following the general business cycle, while interest and amortization payments are characterized by contractual rigidity. Income on shipping services is of course closely related to the volume of world trade, it being noted, however, that freight rates, usually determined by international contractual agreements, are relatively <u>sticky prices</u>, much less sensitive to the cycle than commodity prices.

In general, the balance of current accounts and the balance of payments as a whole describe inverse cycles, two broad patterns of behavior being distinguishable as between creditor and debtor countries.[47] Following Professor Aftalion, we shall now summarize the main characteristic of this movement:

<u>Debtor countries</u> – Although prosperity in debtor countries (largely raw material exporters) is usually started by a stimulation of their export trade, this favorable margin of the balance of trade in likely to be quickly narrowed as the demand for imports and for goods and services is stimulated by capital imports and by the general economic expansion. Owing, however, to the in-flux of capital that usually accompanies the upswing of the international cycle, the balance of payments can be easily equilibrated.

In depression the reverse situation prevails. The stoppage or decline of capital imports leads to restriction in imports while the need for exchange to meet interest and amortization payments brings about increased efforts to ameliorate the export position by the sale of surplus production. These efforts to ameliorate the balance of trade usually result in a certain degree of improvement in the balance of current accounts. But, at the same time, the paralyzation of capital in-flows may render necessary net remittances by the debtor which exceed the favorable margin obtained in the balance of current accounts. The balance of payments will then move in an unfavorable direction.

---

[47] The historical or long-run relationship between capital movements and the balance of trade is an already familiar problem since Cairne's hypothesis on the "three stage loan".

This inverse cyclical behavior as between the balance of current accounts and the balance of payments is not, however, a regular one. In the last depression, for instance, the crash of raw material prices created a situation of indeterminate equilibrium for debtor countries; the stimulation of exports proved ineffective due to the irresponsiveness of foreign demand to price changes, while at the same time the reduction in imports was insufficient to offset the decline in receipts on capital account. No amelioration was obtained in the current account position and the balance of payments showed signs of increasing strain, until a collapse ensued by loan default, exchange devaluation, etc.

<u>Creditor countries</u> – For creditor countries, the cyclical behavior, although far from regular, describe generally an inverse movement to that of debtor (raw material) countries.

The behavior of the balance of trade cannot be predicted accurately, all depending on the behavior of capital movements, which in turn is affected by the elasticity of the loan market and of supply in export industries. During the up-swing of the cycle, the internal expansion stimulates the demand for imports, but at the same time the expansion in foreign lending stimulates the export trade. Which of the two forces predominates cannot be predicated <u>a priori</u>.[48] Other items in the balance of current accounts, such as dividends and interest payments, will move generally in a favorable direction. A surplus on current account is likely to ensue.

In depression, the stoppage of capital exports is likely to be accompanied by a drastic reduction of the export trade. The degree of curtailment of imports will

---

[48] Compare Wagemann, *Struktur und Rhythmus der Weltswirtschaft*, p. 168. When analysing the different patterns of behavior of the balance of trade and of capital movements for groups of countries of varying structural composition, Professor Wagemann distinguishes four economic types, with different cyclical behavior:

(1) <u>Germany and European agrarian countries</u>. The trade balance is usually passive. Capital imports decrease in depression, the adjustment being made by decline of imports rather than by increase of exports.

(2) <u>Great Britain and other European creditor countries</u>. In the upswing the balance of trade becomes passive. Imports are usually maintained in depression, while exports tend to shrink. The adjustment is made through a decline in capital exports.

(3) <u>United States</u>. The United States is in the somewhat unusual position of having an active trade balance in spite of its creditor role. The capital account is normally passive.

(4) <u>Neo and semi-capitalistic countries</u>. In the upswing the balance of trade becomes active and the capital account passive.

As regards the question of precedence of trade or of capital movements in determining the conditions of equilibrium of the balance of international payments, Wagemann holds the opinion that the balance of trade is the governing element for countries of the type (3) and (4), while capital movements hold precedence in the case of countries of types (1) and (2).

depend on whether they are products of elastic or inelastic demand. The usual fall in dividend payments and interest receipts is a factor making for deterioration of the balance of current accounts. Capital repatriation and debt collection are likely, on the other hand, to improve the capital account position and redress the equilibrium of the balance payments.[49]

---

[49] For some creditor countries (United States, Great Britain) tourist and travel expenditures become a heavy unfavorable item in prosperity, while for others (France, Switzerland) it becomes a major favorable item. The same observation can be made concerning shipping services.

# SOME GENERAL INFERENCES

We can now look back, with more fatigue than satisfaction, to the proceeds of our inquiry.

The study started out with a bold complaint against excessive atomization of business cycle analysis and with the plea for broader view of international cyclical changes in space and time, in their relation to national productive structures as well as to stages of development. That our introduction ended by a confession of inability to advance significantly either of the desiderata proves that it is easier to curse the villain than to imitate the saint: "Video meliora proboque, deteriora sequor".

It is hoped, nevertheless, that our swift promenade through the continental literature on the broad theme of cyclical and economic evolution, our review of some inductive generalizations concerning the international character of fluctuations and their changing impact upon the institutional conspectus, and finally our glimpse over the closed-system theories, have proved that no self-generating model or tidy cycle-causation mechanism can do justice to the complex phenomenon of the international spread of fluctuations.

While a convenient arrangement of variables and a careful selection of "key economic magnitudes may frequently yield a great deal of logical satisfaction, it must be kept in mind that even the most satisfactory explanations of individual national cycles have limited international applicability and, what is worse, they can seldom be understood by the process of skipping untidy international complications.

After concluding that international cycles can better be explained by the diffusion of disturbance originating in an epicenter, rather than by the existence of international "Konjunkturfaktoren", we proceeded to the study of the process of propagation of cycles. We met, at the outset, the logically clear but statistically difficult distinction between autonomous and induced fluctuations. The autonomous fluctuations that may occur in raw material (semi- or neo-capitalist) countries are, by and large, determined by physico-objective factors, such as variations in crop yields or depletion of natural resources. More often than not, however, owing to the decreasing share of agriculture in total economic activity and to the derived nature of the demand for mining products, their business cycles are induced by fluctuations in the level of economic activity of industrial countries. In the latter countries, I have concluded, autonomous fluctuations are in general initiated by disproportionalities between the structures of production and of demand inherent in the working of the capitalist system.

While in the raw material areas the business cycle is predominantly determined by fluctuations in the exogenous demand, in industrial societies primary responsibility is to be ascribed to the vagaries of <u>endogenous</u> demand. In one case the international, and in the other, the national component of the cycle is likely to play a leading role.

The changing character and weight of the <u>strategic</u> factors in the business cycles of different countries at different stages of development render necessary the establishment of an economic typology for the classification of general patterns of cyclical economic behavior. The establishment of a "Sukzession der Ursachen" rather than the construction of simplified models should be the aim of an international cycle theory.

In the study of the international aspects of fluctuations, attention was also paid to the "shock" factor and the "response" factor.

The complementarity or substitutability of output and exports in relation to the center of the cyclical disturbance determine both the conditions of propagation and the receptiveness to cyclical shocks. In the case of countries related by complementarity, an autonomous fall in endogenous demand or a credit contraction in one of them is likely to generate excess supply and financial illiquidity in the other country. Among countries whose output is mutually substitutable, the horizontal spreading of fluctuations takes place through competitive price deflation (inflation). A distinction was finally established between the "degree of openness" to the world cycle measured by the size of the international margin, and the resistance to autonomous fluctuations, which is determined by the degree of internal elasticity of the system.

The second part of the paper addressed itself to the study of the three main (possible) conductors of cyclical effects, namely, the money systems, capital movements, and international trade.

The quarrel between the advocates of exchange stability and of exchange flexibility was reviewed in connection with the controversy on the cyclical conductivity of the gold standard. It was found that the stability approach stems directly from the classical long-run equilibrium analysis, while the flexibility approach is more deeply concerned with protection from short-term disequilibria. The stability approach seems to underestimate the difficulties of adjustment of internal price systems and productive structures to rapid shifts in international demand or to technological changes, which may present either inflationary or deflationary dangers. The flexibility approach, on the other hand, seems to overestimate both the effectiveness of monetary palliatives in curing mal-adjustments in the distribution of real productive power, and the "insulation value" of exchange adjustments affecting general rather than relative prices.

As an illustration of mixtures of current theory put into practice, one may mention the "International Monetary Fund", which represents a compromise solution aiming at creating an international monetary order sufficiently stable to permit the development of trade and the expansion of international investment, but sufficiently flexible to avoid painful deflationary adjustments in the business cycle.

Closer analysis of recent monetary experience indicates that the so-called "anti-cyclical exchange policies" were usually vitiated by a depression bias, exchange depreciation being much more liberally used than exchange appreciation. The difficulty in policy-making derives in part from the fact that there is no single satisfactory criterion for the definition of an "equilibrium rate or exchange", that would permit the mensurations, in each direction, of the equilibrating or disequilibrating character of exchange adjustment. A combined <u>balance of payments-employment</u> criterion is in current favor, in substitution for simpler criteria based on gold movements or purchasing power parities. The experience of the last depression confirms the view that exchange depreciation is an often inevitable process of cyclical adjustment for countries depending on a narrow range of export products of inelastic supply-demand. On the other hand the fact that trade among depreciated-currency countries increased at the expense of trade with high-priced currencies seems to indicate that the "internal stimulation effect" of exchange depreciation was more strongly operative than the "competitive-position aspect" emphasized in older discussions of the mechanism of equilibrium.

A long discussion was subsequently devoted to the "theory of international values", under both the capital-transfer and the international trade aspects. Our analysis, if anything, brought out clearly the need for bridging the gap between the traditional treatment of capital movements and international trade, and the theory of economic fluctuations. The need of a reformulation of the theory of international values, to do justice to the conceptual modifications rendered necessary by recent developments the theory of employment and of the business cycle, has of course long been felt. In there significant ways, the new Approach departs from the traditional treatment:

(a) Emphasis has been shifted from the study of initial and final equilibrium positions to the transitional sequences and disequilibria relevant for the business cycle.

(b) The study of the <u>primary changes</u> (compensatory movements in prices, exchange or interest rates), which engaged classical attention is now being supplemented by a consideration of <u>total</u> (original and induced) income effects, which may neutralize, aggravate or reverse the original changes.

(c) The problem of gain or loss from foreign investment or of the benefit from trade, heretofore discussed in terms of import-export price ratios or differential yields, is held to be incapable of determinate solution outside the "konjunktural" a conspectus or cyclical phase of the transaction.

An attempt at a revision of the theory of capital movements would greatly exceed the scope of the work and the possibilities of the author and must await for more skilled hands. It is hoped, however, that this inquiry has indicated some of the main avenues of approach.

In the theory of capital transfer account must be taken of new findings on both sides of the investment function, namely, the interest rate and the marginal efficiency of capital. As to the interest rate side, it may be noted that the direction of capital. As to the interest rate side, it may be noted that the direction and intensity of its change in the borrowing and lending countries, and its influence on investment, seem much less simple than when postulated in the traditional treatment. Instead of a single determinate solution (investment in the borrowing and die-investment in the lending country), we have an ampler range of possible outcomes, depending on; (a) relative liquidity preference schedules in the capital exporting and importing countries, (b) organization and operational conditions of the banking system, (c) phase of the cycle during which the transfer is made.

On the "marginal-efficiency of capital" side of the investment function, account must be taken of dynamic variables such as the marginal propensities to save and to spend in the borrowing and lending countries, which determine; (a) the deflationary or inflationary character of the transfer and (b) the amount of adjustment needed in the balance of trade and services to effect the real transfer, and (c) the cyclical reactions provoked by the transaction.

No less important inferences can be derived from recent discussions on the mechanism of trade adjustment proper. Instead of a simple consideration of equilibrating movements between individual determinants of the income level, we must take into account trade fluctuations in the national income level itself. The central question now asked is not how equilibrium is restored in the balance of payments but rather how trade transactions affect the total income level of trading countries. A significant, though far from decisive, contribution towards a more comprehensive understanding of the transmission of fluctuations through trade has been made by the development of the theory of the foreign trade multiplier, in its pure form or in combination with the principle of acceleration (which permits the introduction of the induced investment variable). The mechanism of restoration of equilibrium through income-output changes postulated in the theory of the foreign trade multiplier constitutes, in fact, a more appropriate description of trade adjustments under conditions of under-employment equilibrium than the classical version, with its emphasis on changes in relative prices.

In the foreign-trade multiplier approach, an export surplus can be regarded as net investment and an import balance as a net dis-investment. The factors modifying the rate and extent of the domestic expansion or contraction, and the amount of equilibrium changes needed in the balance of trade or payments, are the marginal propensities to consume, to save, and to import and the income propagation period. In sizing up the effects of the marginal propensity to import, two conflicting factors must be taken into account; the "leakage factor" and the foreign repercussion factor". The lower the marginal propensity to import, the higher the foreign-trade multiplier, but also the greater the money-flows or adjustment needed in the balance of payments. Conversely, the higher the marginal propensity to import the lower the multiplier and also the smaller the adjustment needed in the balance of payments.

Glancing back, in a bird's eye view, at the main developments in the theory of international trade, we may distinguish the following steps:

1. The classical price-specie-flow mechanism (equilibration via changes in relative prices), successively expanded and modified by:
   a. Mills' equation of international demand.
   b. Taussig's adaptation of the theory to modern money and banking conditions (including conditions of incontrovertibility).
   c. Haberler's formulation in terms of opportunity costs rather than of comparative labor costs.
2. The Goschen-Angell approach (equilibrium via the exchange market).
3. The Ohlin approach (equilibrium via shifts in purchasing power and reallocation of productive factors).
4. The income-employment approach (equilibration via changes in output and income).

From this new vantage point, it should prove possible for better equipped investigators to create the final synthesis between the theory of international trade and the recent theory of employment; within this synthesis the successive reformulations of the classical theory of international trade would rank as particular cases of a more general theory, embracing, on the one extreme, the pure price-specie flow theorem appropriate for the Ricardian full-employment world and, on the other, the pure foreign trade multiplier mechanism, more descriptive of the Keynesian world of under-employment equilibrium.

The possibility of insulation against the spreading of cyclical affects through tariffs or regional arrangements was briefly discussed. We pointed out the self-defeating character of the "predatory-multiplier" approach, which aims at the same time at a maximization of the export surplus and at a minimization of the import leakages. An analysis of the tariff and regional trade schemes led to the conclusion that the anti-cyclical insulation effect of trade restrictions, while useful in individual cases for short-run adjustment, cannot provide a constructive solution for the problem of trade fluctuations.

A reformulation was also attempted of the "law of the falling export quota", through the distinction between periods of rapid structural changes and periods of temporary equilibrium in the economic evolution of each after industrial maturity is reached.

The empirical evidence on cyclical fluctuations in international trade was summarized in the two paradoxes of world trade. The first, which explains the characteristic slump of raw material prices in depressions, is the contrasting behavior between the "Erwerbswirtschaften", within which automatic equilibrating mechanism (fall in prices, increase in demand and curtailment of output) is at least imperfectly operative, and the "Bedarfdeckungswirtschaften", in which a price decline often elicits a disequilibrating expansion in output and exports. The second paradox derives from the fact that the increasing accumulation of real capital inherent in the industrialization process, and changes in the structure of demand at rising income levels, tend to increase the share of goods of unstable and deferrable demand in total world trade.

Our third part was devoted to an examination of the parallelism and divergencies of international cyclical behavior. We distinguished between regular variations, such as those in price, employment and output, which show a certain degree of international consilience, and irregular variations whose cyclical behavior is less predictable. The co-variation of wholesale prices and of certain group-prices, both in the long and short-run, seems to be supported by a great deal of historical evidence, it being noted, however, that (a) this co-variation is more symptomatic than causal or explanatory, and (b) it stands out more clearly in depression than in recovery.

An analysis of price-output interactions in the business cycle reveals that raw materials, as a group, show a greater swing in prices than in output, while for manufactures the dispersion is greater in output than in prices. Within the industrial sphere, durable goods are found to be subject to greater cyclical oscillations than non-durable goods, in output as well as in prices, a fact which, despite important qualifications, lends support to the "principle of acceleration" hypothesis. Differences in price-employment-output reactions, due to varying structural composition of the countries involved, are basic factors for the explanation of divergencies in international cyclical behavior. Unemployment crises are typical of "high capitalist" societies, in which the technological horizon is ampler, the substitutability of factors greater, and greater also the sensitiveness to changes in the monetary supply or in the rate of interest. For neo- and semi-capitalist societies, whose productive horizon is limited, inflation, price instability (and disguised unemployment in depression) are the main modes of cyclical reactions.

Among the magnitude subject to irregular cyclical variations, we considered cyclical changes in the balance of trade, in capital and gold movements, in change rates and in the balance of payments as a whole. The balance of trade of industrial (often creditor) and agrarian (often debtor) countries seems to describe inverse cyclical movements, the first being negatively and the second positively correlated to the business cycle. However, complications introduced by capital movements, interdependence of cyclical reactions, etc., blur the neatness of the cyclical pattern. As regards capital flows, the association of prosperity in creditor countries with an increasing rate of capital exports seems to be the typical case, although the historical evidence is far from conclusive. Variously interpreted is also the behavior of gold flows and exchange rates, whose movements in the cycle seem at times at variance with theoretical expectations. The balance of current accounts and of capital account, as a whole, seems also to display an inverse cyclical motion as between creditor (mature capitalist) and debtor (neo- or semi-capitalist) areas. Prosperity in the former group of countries is, more often than not, characterized by a favorable capital account balance and an unfavorable current account balance reverse movement prevailing for the latter group of countries.

This brings us to the end of a long and possible arid journey. Lest the reader be disappointed by the conspicuous absence of "conclusions on policy" we hasten to advance the comfortable postulate that the theorist is neither a preacher nor a prophet. If, however, we have to be one or the other, the fact that along our path we have ascribed responsibility for various international disequilibria to the perverse behavior of certain economic magnitudes (capital movements, prices of primary products, etc.)—this fact, we believe, should render a sermon easier than a prophecy. A counter-cyclical coordination of international investment activity and a scheme for stabilization of prices of primary products, by concerted international action, would go a long way, if not to eliminate altogether the "jerkiness" of world capitalist evolution, at least to minimize the waste and painfulness of the shocks. The initiative for business cycle control, in any event, rests with the major industrial countries, since the international spreading of cycles is by and large a response to fluctuations in employment and output in the areas of concentration of economic power. Smaller countries are often unable even to enjoy business cycles of their own making.

The last war has wrought profound changes in world economic structure that are likely to affect profoundly the international cyclical behavior. The shrinkage of the areas of free economy and the expansion of areas of controlled economy will introduce wholly new factors in the analysis. It may well be that some years from now we shall look back upon business cycles merely as "magnificent episodes of the nineteenth century" which will gradually disappear as the economic instinct loses ground to political and social motivations.

# APPENDIX

## 1. A "Barter-Terms-of-Trade" Theory of the Business Cycle

The preceding discussion yields us an interesting by-product, namely, the question of whether there is a cyclical pattern in the terms of trade, or, what is still more important, whether fluctuations in the terms of trade play an active role in cycle generation. Are we justified in talking of a "barter terms-of trade theory of the business cycle"?[50]

It has often been noted that prosperity in raw material countries usually takes the form of an improvement in the terms of trade, the reverse occurring in depression. Granted the validity of the phenomenon, its explanation and possible effects have led to different views.

One hypothesis, formulated by Folke Hilgerdt, would imply an inverse cyclical movements of raw material as compared to industrial countries. Hildegerdt finds a simultaneity of expansion and contraction in capital movements of the three leading creditor nations, the United States, Great Britain and France, from 1922 to 1929. Those capital movements were likewise positively correlated to the rise and fall of prices of primary products in the United States and other countries, as measured by the ratio between export and import prices of several industrial and agricultural countries, and also by the movements of wholesale prices of raw materials and manufactures in the United States.[51]

The argument runs as follows: In prosperity capital moves from industrial to agricultural countries, generating an upward movement of prices of primary products and a favorable change in the terms of trade of the latter.[52] This would exert a deflationary influence in industrial countries by narrowing the margin of profit in manufacture. Capital exports would subsequently decline, entailing a fall in raw material prices, an improvement of the terms of trade of industrial countries and a stimulation of industrial activity.

---

[50] We are much indebted throughout this discussion to an already mentioned doctoral dissertation by Shang-Kwei-Fong (*Business Cycles and the International Balance of Payments*, Harvard University, 1941).

[51] *Cf.* "Foreign Trade and Short Business Cycle", Essays in honor of Gustave Cassel, pp. 273-91.

[52] That capital exports should turn the terms of trade against the lending country is a basic theorem of the classical school which, however, can be questioned on both theoretical and empirical grounds. Silverman's figures for Great Britain show that for the largest part of the period examined (1800-1913) increased capital exports coincided with favorable terms of trade. Ohlin made a similar observation for the last half of the eighties. *Cf.* Iversen, *op. cit.*, pp. 368-69.

Hilgerdt's a argument raises the very interesting hypothesis, so far unconfirmed by empirical investigations, of an inverse correlation between cycles of industrial and agricultural countries, at least as far as the "short business cycle" is concerned. This suggestion is not in conflict with the well-known phenomenon of international parallelism of fluctuations, since the latter refers mostly to the major Juglar cycle.

Hilgerdt's analysis is, however, open to serious question on several counts. At best, it may be considered a plausible explanation of the turning point but certainly not a theory of the cycle. In fact, the assumption that a rise in raw material import prices leads always to a narrowing of the profit margin and to a decrease in the inducement to invest in industrial countries needs a few qualifications. In the first place, the share of imported materials in total cost is variable among the industries. Other elements of the cost structure may react differently. Anticipation of rising industrial prices may counteract the deflationary influence of increased raw material costs. In the second place, the higher money incomes of primary producers resulting from capital imports and from favorable shifts in the terms of their trade tend to strengthen the demand for industrial products, especially because the income elasticity of demand for imports, is usually high in raw material countries. This would offset the unfavorable influence of increased raw material costs on the marginal efficiency of capital. The often observed empirical fact that raw material prices rises sharply in the early stages of recovery, pari passu with the industrial expansion, and lose ground to industrial prices only at a later stage of the upswing, seems to run counter to the barter-terms-of-trade theory of the cycle.

Hilgerdt's hypothesis would then be plausible only if the prices of manufactured goods were fairly rigid throughout the cycle, or if the marginal propensity to import of primary producers were low. Neither of those conditions is likely occur.[53]

In fact it may be contended that the causational influence of terms of trade is precisely the opposite of that visualized by Hilgerdt. For, the stimulating effect on industrial countries of a fall in raw material prices (unfavorable terms of trade for primary producers) may be entirely neutralized by the actual or anticipated fall in the import demand for industrial products. Conversely, if capital exports from industrial countries increase incomes and prices in the borrowing country, they may by the same token increase the propensity to import. This will react favorably on the activity in the lending country and on the prices of their exports.

On this showing, there would not be any inverse correlation between industrial and agricultural fluctuations. Prosperity in both spheres would show a

---

[53] Compare Iversen, *op. cit.*, p. 75. Also Shang-Kwei Fong, *op. cit.*, pp. 170-73.

positive, if lagged, correlation and would be attended by a rise of both raw material prices and industrial profits.[54]

There is a great deal of plausibility in the contention that the great depression was partly due to the fact that the terms of trade, because of the relatively inelastic demand of industrial countries for raw materials and foodstuffs, because too favorable for those countries, rather than the other way around. It may be advanced in this sense that the agricultural depression began nearly a decade before the industrial depression,[55] partly by inheritance from the first World War of structural maladjustment of a non-cyclical character (expansion of crop areas, technical progress, agricultural protectionism) and partly because of inherent cyclical instability in agriculture (inelasticity of supply and irresponsiveness of demand to price changes).

No empirical investigation has so far been made of the terms-of-trade hypothesis proper, although the attempt to link fluctuations in agricultural prices with the initiation of industrial cycles is an old one. V. Timoshenko and L.H. Bean, for instance, contend on the basis of factual studies of the American experience, that periods of revival have been almost always preceded by a low, and recession very often by a high, ratio of agricultural to industrial prices.

The terms of international trade involve, of course, a much wider variety of factors and possible repercussions than the relative prices of inter-group trade. Even if cycle generation through the latter mechanism could be proved, this would not automatically demonstrate a term-of trade theory as such.[56]

The empirical evidence so far gathered is inconclusive. Reviewing the course of the British terms of trade from the last century to date, Colin Clark makes the interesting observation that:

> The peak (maximum employment and commodity prices) of the trade cycle is always associated with a turning point in the terms of trade, but that this turning point is sometimes a maximum and some-

---

[54] The marginal revenue is likely to, but need not necessarily be, narrowed by rising raw material costs since the prices of finished products may rise pari passu. Other components of the total outlay (e.g., wages) may lag behind in the early recovery or even decrease (e.g. over-head costs). It is clear that the relative movements of factor prices will change in the phase of the cycle. A full analysis of the several possibilities involved cannot be undertaken here. For a careful and detailed discussion compare Shang-Kwei-Fong, *op. cit.*

[55] *Cf.* Eugen Altschull and Frederic Strauss, "Technical Progress and the Agricultural Depression", *Bulletin 67 of the National Bureau of Economic Research.*

[56] It should also be pointed out that the terms-of-trade theory would have to account also for the behavior of prices of raw materials of non-agricultural origin.

times a minimum. Maximum (most in favor of manufacture) terms of trade were found in 1866, 1873, 1890 and 1900 and minimum in 1824, 1839, 1847, 1857, 1882, 1929 and 1937. The trade cycle peaks of 1907 and 1920 preceded in each case by year maximum in the terms of trade.[57]

Those results, though bearing on the major rather than on the shorter cycle studied by Hilgerdt, would tend to disprove the validity of a causal connection between the business cycle and changes in terms of trade, the observation being especially significant in view of the importance of the raw materials trade for the level of British industrial activity

The question thus remains an open one. An ampler range of observation is needed before changes in the terms of trade can be ascribed to the none too enviable responsibility of cycle generation.

## 2. Are Favorable Terms of Trade an Unmixed Blessing?

The abandonment of the full employment assumption and the development of the savings-investment analysis have prompted a reconsideration of the traditional position regarding the terms of trade and the division of gains.

In full employment equilibrium, the net terms of trade are unquestionably a fairly accurate measure of the relative gains from trade. A favorable export-import price ratio would mean a rise in real income of the country concerned, or a rise in the "efficiency "reward of the its factors of production, to use Harrod's expression. The productive factors released by the export industries would be absorbed by other industries to which the demand has been diverted.

But if we abandon the assumption of internal mobility of factors and full employment, the analysis of the possible effect of changes in the terms of trade upon the income-level may yield paradoxical results. Starting from the assumption that the country which enjoys favorable terms of trade has an elasticity smaller than unity for the other country's products, Professor Robertson has pointed out that the immobility of factors between occupations may render a country unable to utilize the productive factors released by the industry enjoying favorable terms of trade. The surplus of productive power no longer required to buy imports would represent only potential wealth, the actualization of which would be hampered by factoral rigidities and lags in the adjustment process.

The favorable terms of trade may then, if domestic employment is unfavorably affected, carry the virus of depression rather of expansion.

---

[57] Colin Clark, *Conditions of Economic Progress*, p. 454.

This argument may further be expanded by considering the possible effects of an improvement in the terms of trade upon the marginal propensities to save, to consume and to import.[58] If the favorable shift in the terms of trade takes the form of a rise in exporter's profits and is not passed on through a rise in money wages, it may have the effect of lowering the marginal propensity to consume without any compensatory increase in the propensity to invest. This rise in the propensity to save may have different effects according not only to the economic structure of the country concerned but also according to the phase of the cycle. It will exert a deflationary influence if it comes during the process of recovery. At a later stage of the upswing, when a shortage of productive factors occurs, it may help to prolong the boom.

In the country against which the terms of trade have turned, the effects may be paradoxically, favorable. The propensity to import will decline, bringing about a diversion of demand to home-made goods and a stimulation of employment of previously idle or under-employment resources. The marginal propensity to consume may rise, what again tend to redress the income level. Whether the final result will, on the whole, be favorable or unfavorable, depend on whether the fall in the efficiency reward of the productive factors (resulting from unfavorable terms of trade) will be compensated by increased investment in home-goods industries competing with imports and by a stimulation of the export trades.[59] The changes for the deflationary effect of bad terms of trade to be minimized or even reversed will, caeteris paribus, be the greater the larger is the foreign elasticity of demand for imports, and the larger the home elasticity of the supply of exports and of the demand for imports.[60]

Again it behooves to note that short and long-run gains from trade may not always coincide. In some cases, the deterioration of terms of trade has served to

---

[58] A careful discussion of the problem is offered by Shang-Kwei-Fong, *loc. cit.*

[59] Several qualifications must be taken into account. No favorable effects will occur if the deterioration of the terms of trade brings about a considerable out-flow of gold or depletion of exchange reserves. For in this case the rate of interest may rise, undermining the propensity to invest. This situation is most likely to obtain for debtor countries which have fixed charges on the balance of payments (interest and amortization dues, et,) that have to be met out of export balances.

[60] This is one of the grounds on which a deliberate deterioration of the terms of trade (e.g., via currency depreciation) may be advocated. A fall in the rate of exchange may have then two effects; one negative by switching demand from imports to homemade goods, and the other positive by stimulating exports. The success of such a policy will of course depend on a complex set of conditions, such as non-retaliation, preservation of a margin between external and internal depreciation, shiftability of resources as between home and export industries, elasticity of foreign demand, etc. For a careful appraisal of the factors involved, cf. John Donaldson, *The Dollar* (New York: Oxford University Press, 1937), chapter VI.

spur industrialization and diversification of production. This experience was common to a number of primary producer countries during the last depression. The shift of factors from primary to secondary production was encouraged by low wages and low raw material prices, contrasting with high prices of imported manufactures. In this way, the downturn of the terms of trade, intensified by currency depreciation and accompanied by a rise in tariff rates, led to structural changes which, while implying a loss of efficiency and a temporary reduction of real income (if viewed from the static standpoint of the comparative advantages theorem[61]) have tended in the long-run to increase the elasticity and shock-absorbing capacity of their economies.

Even, however, if we restrict our analysis to the short-run cyclical effects, a complex host of factors would have to be considered for a correct appraisal of the benefits of favorable terms of trade. The results may be different according to whether the rising export prices are accompanied by a rise in money wages or in capitalist profits, since the marginal propensity to save and to consume will be differently affected. It will also matter whether the benefited export industries produce primarily consumers' or investment goods. Again, the rise in export prices may be caused by increased foreign demand without any shift in the domestic cost function or, conversely, the fall in prices of foreign goods may result from improvement in the productive efficiency (without change in demand), or from a fall in import demand; in each case the repercussions will be different.[62]

The effects of the course of the terms of trade will have to be analyzed in each individual case, according to the underlying cause of the shifts in export-import price ratio.

It is beyond our scope to trace all the intricate possible consequences of a change in the terms of trade. All we need to say, at this point, is that the traditionally held and unqualified belief that favorable terms of trade are an unmixed blessing is valid only in the simplifying assumption of full employment equilibrium.

---

[61] Even this seemingly obvious implication of the comparative cost analysis is now under fire. Manoilescu, in particular, has called attention to the fact that, from the viewpoint of the national economy approach, the specialization according to comparative costs does not lead to maximization of income of agricultural countries, in view of the diminishing productivity of agriculture as compared to industry. He argues that even if the infant industries are relatively inefficient and output more expensive than that of foreign imported goods, the absorption of surplus agricultural labor in more productive industrial occupations would increase aggregate productivity of labor and the income level, thus representing a net income gain.

[62] Taussing has already pointed out that an unfavorable turn of the terms of trade, when derived from an increase in the demand for imports, can actually be considered a gain for the importing country, from the viewpoint of psychological satisfaction and economic choice. But this would lead us into the philosophical problem of the relationships between monetary gain and psychological satisfaction, which is clearly beyond the scope of the present discussion.

# BIBLIOGRAPHY

Aftalion, A. "Les Variations Cyclique Irregulieres dans les Relations Internationales", article in *Revue d'Economic Politique*, XLVII (1933).

Angell, James W. "Equilibrium in International Trade," in *Exploration in Economic*, Economic Essays in honor of Wesley C. Mitchell, New York, 1935.
*Investment and Business Cycles*, New York: Mc Graw Hill Book Co., 1941.
*Theory of International Prices*, Cambridge: Harvard University Press, 1926.

Balogh, Th. "Some Theoretical Aspects of the Central European Credit and Transfer Crisis", article in *International Affairs*, (Journal of the Royal Institute of International Affairs), vol. II, May 1932.

Beach, W.E. *British International Gold Movement and Banking Policy, 1881–1913*, Harvard University Press, 1933.

Bernstein, E.M. "War and the Pattern of Business Cycle", article in *American Economic Review*, XXX, (1940).

Beveridge, Sir William. *Full Employment in a Free Society*, New York: W.W. Norton & Co., 1945.

Bouniatian, Mentor. Les Crises Economiques, Paris: 1922.

Brown, William J. *The International Gold Standard Reinterpreted, 1914–1934*, 2 vols., New York: N.B.E.R., 1940.

Buchanan, Norman S. International Investment and Domestic Welfare, New York: Henry Holt & Co., 1945.

Clark, Colin. *The Conditions of Economic Progress*, London: Macmillan, 1940.
*The Economic of 1960*, London: Macmillan, 1940.
*National Income and Outlay*, London: Macmillan, 1937.

Clark John M. *Business Acceleration and the Law of Demand*, J.P.E. vol. XXV, 1917.
    *Strategic Factors in the Business Cycle*, New York: N.B.E.R. 1934.

Donaldson, John L. *International Economic Relations*, 1928
    *The Dollar*, Oxford University Press, 1937.
    "War, a Social Problem", in *Annals of the American Academy of Social Science*, no, 130.

Fong, Shang-Kwei. *Business Cycles and the International Balance of Payments*, unpublished doctoral dissertation, Harvard University, 1941.

Fisher, Irving. "Are Booms and Depressions Transmitted Internationally Through Monetary Standards", in *Bulletin de l'Institut International de Statistique*, XXVIII, 1935, pp. 1-29.

Frisch, Ragnar "Propagation and Impulse Problems", in *Economic Essays in honor of Gustav Cassel*, London: 1933.

Haberler, Gottfried von. *Theory of International Trade*, London: Hodge, 1936.
    *Prosperity and Depression*, in League of Nations, Geneva, 1941.

Hansen, Alvin. *Business-Cycles Theory*, Grim and Co., 1927
    *Fiscal Policies and Business Cycles*, W. W. Norton & Co., 1941.
    *Full Recovery or Stagnation*, W.W. Norton & Co., 1938.

Harris, S. *Exchange Depreciation*, Harvard University Press, 1936.

Harrod, R.F. *International Economics*, London, 1933.
    *The Trade Cycle*, Oxford, 1936.

Hawtrey, R.G. *Currency and Credit*, London: Longmans Green, 1928.

Hayek, F.A. *Monetary Nationalism and International Stability*, London, 1937.

Heinrich, Walther. *Grundlagen einer universalistischen Krisenlehre*, Jena: Gustav Fischer 1928.

Hilgerdt, Folke. "Foreign Trade and the Short Business Cycle", in *Economic Essays in honor of Gustav Cassel*, London 1935.

Iversen, Carl. *Aspect of the Theory of International Capital Movements*, London: Oxford University Press, 1935.

Juglar, Clement. *Les Crises Commerciales et leur Retour Periodique en France, Angleterre et aux Etats Unis*, Paris: 2nd ed., 1889.

Kahn, Alfred. *Great Britain in the World Economy*, Columbia University Press, 1946.

Keynes, J. Maynard. *A Treatise on Money*, 2 vols., New York, Harcourt Brace, 1930.
*The General Theory of Employment, Interest and Money*, New York: Harcourt Brace, 1936.

Kuznetz, S. *Secular Movements of Production and Prices*, New York: Houghton Mifflin, 1930.

Laursen, Svend. *International Propagation of Business Cycles*, unpublished doctoral dissertation, Harvard University, 1941.

League of Nations. *Economic Stability in the Post-War World*, Geneva, 1945.

Macaulay, Frederic. *Some Theoretical Problems Suggested by the Movement of Interest Rates, Bond Yields, and Stock Prices in the United States since 1856*, New York: N.B.E.R., 1938.

Machlup, Fritz. "Period Analysis and Multiplier Theory", in *Quarterly Journal of Economics,* vol., LIV, (November 1939).
*International Trade and the National Income Multiplier*. Philadelphia: Blakiston, 1943.

Metzler, Lloyd. "Underemployment Equilibrium in International Trade, "in *Econometrica*, X, 1942.
"The Transfer Problem Reconsidered", in *Journal of Political Economy*, L, 1942.

Mills, F.C. *Behavior of Prices*, New York: N.B.E.R., 1927.
 *Prices in Recession and Recovery*, New York: N.B.E.R, 1936.
 "An Hypothesis Concerning the Duration of Business Cycles", in *Journal of the American Statistical Association* (December 1926).

Mitchell, W.C. *Business Cycles: The Problem and Its Setting*, New York: N.B.E.R, 1927.

Norgenstern, O. İnternational vorgleichende Konjunkturforschung", in *Zeitschrift für die gesamte Staatswissenschaft*, 1927.

Mühlenfels, A. "Internationale Konjunkturzusammenhänge", in *Jahrbücher fúr Nationaloekonomic und Statistik*, LXXV, 1929.
 "On the International Spread of Business Cycles", in *Journal of Political Economy*, LI, 1943.

Neisser, Hans. *Some International Aspects of Business Cycles*. Philadelphia: 1936.
 "General Overproduction", in *Journal of Political Economy*, XLII, 1934.

Nurske, Ragnar. *Internationale Kapitalbewegungen*, Vienna, 1935.
 *International Currency Experience in the Inter-War Period*, League of Nations, 1944.

Ohlin, Bertil. *The Course and Phases of the World Economic Depression*, League of Nations, Geneva, 1931.
 *Inter-Regional and International Trade*, Harvard University Press, 1935.
 "Some Notes on the Stockholm Theory of Savings and Investment", *Economic Journal*, vol. XLVII (march 1937).

Paish, F.W. "Banking Policy and the Balance of International Payments", *Economica*, vol. III (November 1936)

Robbin, L. *The Great Depression*, London, 1934.

Robertson, D.H. *Banking Policy and the Price Level*, 3rd ed., London, 1932.
 *A study of Industrial Fluctuation*, London, 1915.

Robinson, Joan. *Essays in the Theory of Employment*, London: Macmillan, 1937.

Röepke, Wilhelm. *International Economic Disintegration*, Macmillan, 1942.

Schumpeter, J.A. *Theory of Economic Development*, Harvard University, 1934.
    *Business Cycles*, New York: McGraw Hill, 1940.
    *Capitalism, Socialism and Democracy*, New York: Harper & Brothers, 1942.

Spiethoff, A. "Krisen", article in *Handwörterbuch der Staatswissenchaften*, 1925.

Taussing, Frank W. "The Change in Great Britain's Foreign Trade Terms after 1900", in *Economic Journal* (XXXV 91925).
    *International Trade*, New York: Macmillan, 1927.

Thorp, Wilhard. *Business Annals*, New York: N.B.E.R., 1927.

Tintner, Garhard. *Prices in the Trade Cycle*. Vienna, Julius Springer, 1935.

Viner, Jacob. *Studies in the Theory of International Trade*, New York: Harper & Brothers, 1937.

Wagemann, Ernst. *Economic Rhythm*, English translation, McGraw Hill, 1930.
    *Struktur und Rhythmus der Weltwirtschaft*, Berlin, 1932.
    *Zwischonbilanz der Krisenpolitik*, Berlin, 1935.

Williams, J.H. *Post-War Monetary Plans*, Alfred A. Knopf, 1944.

Whale, P.B. "The Theory of International Trade in the Absence of an International Standard", in *Economica* (February, 1936).

White, Harry D. *The French International Accounts, 1800–1913*, Harvard University Press, 1933.

Printed by
Sermograf Artes Gráficas e Editora Ltda.
on offset Alto Alvura paper for Editora FGV
April 2004